Walk Softly and Carry a Big Book

(official and unofficial sloganeering
from the 12 Step programs)

from Day By Day

HC 13 Box 4251
Fairview, UT 84629
888 447 1683

www.WalkSoftlyandCarryaBigBook.com

First Edition 2008
Volume I

Copyright © 2008 by Shelly Marshall

Editorial contributions from Vicki Eagle

Many thanks to Penny Pennington and Recovery Emporium, for their personal collection(s) of recovery and self-help slogans, quotes, and anecdotes. The collection of this work drew heavily upon their foundation. In addition there were numerous folks who put together small collections of slogans that we want to thank:

A Collection of Trash, Truth, & Trivia by Scully
Daily Reprieve, designed for Earl Husband
Denial is not a River in Egypt by Sandi Bachom
Keep Coming Back by Meiji Stewart
Meeting Wisdom by Brian L.
Recovery Wisdom from Turning Leaf Press
Simple Sayings by David P.

Most of all we appreciate the many thousands of those attending and sharing in 12 Step meetings, without whom this work could never have been complied.

ISBN 978-1-934569-01-6

Library of Congress Control Number: 2008928483

CONTENTS

INTRODUCTION: DAILY DOSES

Our inherited wisdom in the 12 Step programs has been pithily summarized in adages and aphorisms, wise sayings and proverbs, one-liners and slogans, notes, quotes, and anecdotes. Here is one of the most complete collections of what we tell each other around the tables, in our literature, when we give a pitch, and when the newcomer walks through the doors. Some of it is wise, some simple and some seemingly dim. But remember that our ability to understand and assimilate insight changes both with knowledge, time in recovery, and service to others. What seemed very wise at 30 days may seem silly at three years.

In Section One, *Slogans, Sayings, and Super One-liners* , we list the slogans, sayings, and one-liners that we have all come to know and love in the various 12 Step fellowships. They are organized alphabetically by topic.

We not only put the words that have been handed down to us through the group vine in this lexicon of sayings, but we often put the quotes from the people who inspired us. In Section Two, *I heard it through the Groupvine*, we have attempted to use only those proverbs, one-liners, quotes that are used in the 12 Step fellowships. There are, of course many references to widely used pithy sayings that are in general publics use. But if we use them a lot in the fellowships, they are included here also. In this sense we have tried to focus on our program quotes—those phrases that mean something to us in recovery. Naturally, there are many more worthy sayings in general use, but if they don't contain meanings and wisdom that the fellowships adhere to—things we repeat to each other and here in the rooms and from our sponsors, they probably aren't listed here

Acronymity is the foundation of all our traditions as well as the title of Section Three of our book. This chapter explores the acronyms we've made up and chuckled over since Bob and Bill met in 1935 in Akron (Acronym), Ohio. In Section Four we deal with those innocuous slips of the tongue that sometimes have us rolling on the floor---we call it *Freudian Sips*, oops, we mean "slips"! And finally our book on sloganeering winds up with a look at how we look at prayer. This is Section Five, the *Higher Powered Pages*.

This collection was not done by one person or even a handful. These are your words and this is your book. It is what we say to each around the tables, what our speakers delight us with, what our newcomers shock us with. Most of all it comes from you, your heart and soul and your recovery. Suffice it to say that you too are an author, one of the many thousands of "authors" who have oft repeated these sayings, slogans, proverbs and prayers.

So sit back, thumb through the collection, chuckle and reminisce—for this is our collection of wisdom in shorthand, 12 Step sloganeering.

FORWARD

At one of my first meetings a fellow named Don H. talked about the Big Book being a text with stories in the back. He explained that the front part of the book is the "meat of the program" and the stories are the "hamburger helper."

I am a student of our literature, among my weekly committed meetings are a Big Book Study and a Step Study --- it's where I know I will hear the solution discussed. But I also go to at least one discussion meeting. The folks that chair those meetings share their experience, strength, and hope that help me identify with what I've read and how the solution of the program works in their life and my life today. The "hamburger helper" is like that --- mini meetings in print.

Walk Softly is that kind of a book. Shelly has pulled together little tidbits about recovery that get my attention, give me a different point of view, make me think, or make me laugh, provide me with a different perspective, show me another part of the solution.

When I was new I went to meetings with a woman named Marie. One night at the Wilder Group, Marie shared that her brain was still a little foggy and that in order to remember some of the things that she would hear in meetings she had started taking notes.

As a frustrated (and unpublished) writer, I loved her idea and started doing the same thing ~ or at least my interpretation of what I heard Marie describe. I'd make notes about things that I heard people say that helped in my recovery or at least seemed to help in theirs. Eventually I wound up with several notebooks full of one-liners that I had heard in meetings that I later put together into a little tome called "As We See It."

I was reminiscing with some friends about this recently when we were talking about A.A. literature. What I know today is that much of what I initially found so amazingly profound from the long-timers when I came in can be found in the books of our program. This, of course, only goes to prove a former sponsor's adage that "if you want to hide something from an alcoholic, put it in the Big Book."

As most of us know, very little of what we hear in these rooms is original. I find myself sharing my story and using lines from the long-timers that were here when I came to the program. Some of what you find in *Walk Softly* are things you may have heard in the meetings you attend. Some you will find in our literature (perhaps presented in slightly different words) and some will be new for you to share with others.

I don't know what ever happened to Marie, but thirty years later, I know that she did what we do in these rooms. She carried a message to someone that suffers, a message that I still use every day of my recovery.

Penny P.
List Owner for As We See It   http://health.groups.yahoo.com/group/AsWeSeeIt/
An on-line daily thought for the day for those in recovery.

There's no elevator. You have to take the Steps.

Section One: *Slogans, Sayings, and Super One-liners*

This section is organized alphabetically by topic. Some listings will be under several headings because the message and emphasis is equally divided between concepts. Take this slogan: *Turn fear into faith through fellowship.* It is listed under *three* headings--Fear, Fellowship, and Faith.

Other sayings or phrases, even when they contain words that we have headings for, may not be under that heading because they are not about that subject...for example: Under the heading "Think" is the saying: *It's a lot easier to react than it is to think.* "Thinking" is clearly in the core of this saying. Another slogan: FOCUS FIRST, doesn't even contain the words "thinking" or "thought" but again has the act "to think" as its core theme. But take this saying: *You're probably an alcoholic if you think spilling beer is alcohol abuse.* The verb "thinking" facilitates the idea, but the saying is not about thinking so this one is not listed under the "Think" heading. It will be found under Abuse, Alcoholic, and Beer.

These slogans were popularized by YOU—so enjoy.

AA (Alcoholic's Anonymous): *Also see* Slogans *and* Program Generic-Mix & Match
AA does not teach us how to handle drinking it teaches us how to handle sobriety.
AA God Squad
Alcoholic: If you drank enough to get to AA, you drank enough.
Alcoholism is a disease of degradation, AA is a process of regeneration.
All the God's send their drunks to AA.
Eventually every alcoholic will have his last drink. Those of us in AA get to talk about ours.
From Alcoholics Obvious to Alcoholics Anonymous.
God liked the first AA meeting so much, He hasn't missed one since.
High and Dry: An AA member who thinks they can still take drugs.
People who say you can't talk about drugs in an AA meeting are usually on them.
Protected by Smith & Wilson.
Soak up AA the way you used to soak up alcohol.
The Grapevine is the Swiss army knife of AA.
The highest you can get in AA is sober.
There are no "Big Shots" in AA, 'cause one shot, and we're all shot!
Worst feeling in the world: A head full of AA and a belly fully of booze.

Abstinence:
Abstinence makes the heart grow fonder.
Abstinence leads to sobriety. The program and 12 Steps lead to recovery.
Untreated abstinence will make our past our future.
White knuckle it.

Abuse:
Bullyproof yourself.
Drug-Use Is Life Abuse
Drug-Use Is Self-Abuse
If you always have to walk on eggshells around your partner, that's fowl play.

1

If you are constantly being mistreated, you are probably co-operating with the treatments.
If you can't love everybody today, at least try not to abuse everybody.
No abuse excuse!
Pain heals; abuse scars.
Refuse to be abused.
Take the bully by the horns.
The worst abuse excuse: it's not that bad *yet*.
Use your wit to amuse, not to abuse.
Walking on eggshells is for the birds.
It takes two to tangle.
When we abused mind-affecting chemicals, we abused people and when we abused people, we abused mind-affecting chemicals.
You're probably an alcoholic if you think spilling beer is alcohol abuse.

Accept(ance): *Also see* Let Go
Accept change because the possibilities are infinite.
Acceptance is about what IS, not about what ISN'T.
Acceptance is forgiveness.
Acceptance is knowing the past will never get better.
Acceptance is the answer to all my problems today. Page 449. (From the Big Book, 4th edition—now Page 417 from the 5th edition)
Acceptance is the Answer.
Acceptance is the Key
Acceptance is transcendence.
Acceptance: Life is 10% what you make it and 90% how you take it.
Acceptance: Stop barking and start biting.
Acceptance: They're just doing it, they're not doing it *to you*.
Do you expect a reward for accepting the greatest gift of your life?
Everyone must row with the oars they have.
Everything will be ok in the end. If it's not ok, it's not the end.
Gratitude and acceptance always help, no matter what the circumstances.
If you refuse to accept anything but the best, you very often get it.
If you resist, it gets worse; if you accept, it gets better.
It ain't OK till it's OK just the way it is.
Just accept, don't expect.
Misery is an option. But acceptance and gratitude did not come as standard equipment either.
No decision (right or wrong) is complete until it is fully accepted.
People who relapse usually do so because they accepted the things they could have changed.
Reality can be as painful to accept as it was to escape.
Remember yourself as the whole person you are and accept yourself as you are.
SHIFT HAPPENS
Take two aspirin and adjust!
This too shall pass, out!
This too shall pass.
Unless you accept your faults, you will be overwhelmed with your virtues.
Unless you accept your virtues, you will be overwhelmed with your faults.
Until you make peace with who you are, you'll never be content with what you have.
Wear life as a loose garment.

What is, is.
What will be...will appear.
What you resist persists.
When the horse dies, dismount.
When you accept others, you accept yourself.
Willingness is the key to acceptance.
You are right where you are supposed to be.

Accident(s):
Accidents aren't planned—slips are.
Live life on purpose, not by accident
Nothing is by accident.
Sobriety is never an accident.

ACOA (Adult Children of Alcoholics):
Act, don't react.
Adult Child of Alien Invaders.
ALL "shoulds" are a lie.
Be Kind to Yourself
Boundaries create freedom.
Come out of the closet, you've been hung-up long enough.
Don't "Should" on yourself.
Don't just do something. Stand there!
Feelings are not facts.
Focus on the program, not the problem.
Formula for failure: try to please everyone.
How important is it?
How you respond is your responsibility.
If you are eating a shit sandwich, chances are, you ordered it.
In order for someone to "give" you a bad day, you have to "take" it.
Never, ever criticize yourself.
Nobody 'gives' you a bad day without your permission.
Pain heals; abuse scars.
Practice makes it better.
Refuse to star in their psychodrama.
Rule 62: Never take yourself too seriously!
Set boundaries: keep boundaries.
TRUST HAPPENS
We're responsible for the effort, not the outcome!
When in doubt, leave it out.
When the horse dies, dismount.
When we remove *me* from "blame" all that's left is bla. bla, bla....
When you feel needy, feel needy.
You deserve more.
You matter.

Act(ions): *Also see* Inaction *and* Reaction(s)
Act as if...

Act the way you want to be, so that one day you will be the way you act.
Act, don't react.
Action alleviates anxiety.
Action Not Distraction
Action: Utilize, don't analyze.
Actions speak louder than words.
Align your actions so they are in agreement with the picture you paint of yourself at meetings.
An action beats a feeling.
Being an alcoholic does not give you the excuse to act alcoholically.
Change your action; change your attitude.
Courage is fear in action.
Courage is not the absence of fear; it is the ability to act in the presence of fear.
Faith is spelled: A C T I O N
Faith without action is like sitting on a dictionary to learn how to spell.
For every action, there is an equal and opposite criticism.
Good actions, not good acting.
If faith without works is dead then; willingness without action is fantasy.
If it is to be, it is up to me.
If you take right actions, you'll get right results.
It is when you act on faith that you actually have it.
Just because you're an alcoholic doesn't mean you have to act like a drunk.
Learn to act as if…and eventually you're not acting any more.
Listening is love in action.
Love is less a feeling than a thousand tiny acts of kindness.
Make it happen.
Never mistake motion for action.
Put one foot in front of the other.
Service is gratitude in action.
Sometimes our individual actions damage the group.
Stay put and act your own best interest.
Step over bodies if you have to.
Take responsibility for your attitude, not my actions.
Take the action and turn over the results.
The difference between feeling grateful and being grateful is action.
This is a program of action.
We find that the smallest deed is better than the grandest intention.
You can't think yourself into right action, but you can act your way into right thinking.
You have to act right in order to feel right, not feel right in order to act right.
You reap what you sow.

Addict(s): *Also see* Alcoholic(s)
Addicts end up in one of three houses: The Big House, the Bug House, or the Ice House.
Alcoholics and addicts – fast talkers, slow thinkers.
Alcoholics and addicts are in a class by themselves. Everyone else has graduated.
An addict alone is slumming.
An addict is a sick person trying to get well, not a bad one trying to be good.
An addict is someone who wants to be held while isolating.
An addict is someone whose feet are firmly planted in thin air.

An addict may be helpless at times, but never hopeless as long as they keep a phone list of people in the fellowship.

Few alcoholics or addicts blame themselves before exhausting all other possibilities.

If you wonder if you're an addict, you probably are.

It's all right to have castles in the air, but addicts move into them, family members clean them and counselors collect the rent!

NA: We are not reformed junkies–but informed addicts.

Once an addict, always an addict.

Practicing addicts aren't afraid to die. They're afraid to live.

That no addict seeking recovery need ever die...

The three most dangerous words for an addict, "I've been thinking".

There is only one thing worse for an addict or alcoholic than bad fortune – good fortune.

Addict(ion): *Also see* Alcoholism

Addiction is a lifestyle whereby we love things and use people. Recovery is a lifestyle whereby we love people and use things.

Addiction is an equal opportunity destroyer and the 12 Step Program is an equal opportunity restorer.

Addiction is not a sentence; it is only a word.

Addiction is the leading cause of relapse.

Addiction is the only disease that tries to convince you that you don't have it.

Addiction: Touched by an angle. Recovery: Touched by an angel.

Cunning, Baffling, Powerful, and Persistent.

If you think life's lessons are hard, try addiction.

The definition of addiction..."Anything that takes the place of my relationship with my Higher Power."

When we use, addiction makes all our decisions.

Admit(ed):

Everybody makes mistakes. Fools repeat them; the weak excuse them; only the wise admit and profit from them.

Own what's yours.

To err is human but you need to admit it.

When you know you are wrong, admit it. When you know you are right, shut your mouth.

Adult:

Stay out of your head, there's no adult supervision up there.

You have to ask yourself, "What would an adult do in this situation?"

Afraid: *Also see* Fear

Act as if you are not afraid.

Angry people are the most afraid.

Don't be afraid to ask dumb questions they are more easily handled than dumb mistakes.

Don't be afraid to try something for fear you will fail; if you have not the will to try you have already failed.

Don't be afraid you will drink and die. Be afraid you will drink and live.

Practicing addicts aren't afraid to die. They're afraid to live.

Religion is for people who are afraid they'll go to hell. Spirituality is for people who have been there.

To be afraid is to have more faith in evil than in good.

What you are afraid to do is a clear indicator of what you should do next.

Aftercare:
Aftercare—the beginning of life!

Agnostic(s):
If you don't believe in God we suggest you change your mind.

Pray to the God of your misunderstanding

Al-Anon: *Also see* Co-dependency
Al-Anon chorus: It's not *that* bad, yet.

Al-Anon doesn't give us the choice between feeling good or feeling bad—it gives us the choice between feeling and not feeling.

Al-Anon handshake: Wag your finger at the person to correct their behavior.

Al-Anon is a kissing cousin to invention because they were both born of necessity.

Al-Anon: known in Ireland as the Provisional Wing of AA.

Before engaging your mouth, put your mind in gear.

Cleaning the house IS spiritual cleaning

Detach with Love.

Detach; don't disappear.

Detachment is neither kind nor unkind.

Don't force solutions.

Don't just do something. Stand there!

Don't love them to death.

Don't romance the "What if…"

Don't care. You don't have to.

Double Winner: a member of both AA and Al-Anon.

Everyone needs to be loved…especially when they do not deserve it.

Give up control, *but never give up hope.*

Having it our own way—isn't winning.

Highest good of all concerned

If you have to say it more than once, it's nagging.

If you think handling everything is too much, try letting go.

If you want to find out what your character defects are, marry an alcoholic.

I'm a Friend of Lois W.

It's Al-Anon, not Ala-Mom.

It's not *your* business to keep *their* secret.

Keep your eyes on yourself.

Learn the difference between being responsible to others and being responsible for others.

Let it go, it was never yours to begin with.

Letting go is not caring for, but caring about.

Mind Your Own Business

Misery is optional.

My serenity, my pace, my choice.

No matter how long you are in this program, you will never rise above the level of human being.
Put down the microscope and pick up the mirror.
Put down the weapons, pick up the tools.
She has a black belt in Al-Anon.
Stark Raving Sober.
Stay in your own square.
Sweep your own side of the street.
Take responsibility for your attitude, not their actions.
The mother of an addict/alcoholic: Ala-Mom.
The road to resentment is paved with expectation.
Their disease is alcoholism and ours is alamomism
Their disease is alcoholism and ours is alanonism.
They don't say things to make me angry, they say things that make me angry.
Today do something for someone you love: Leave them alone.
What you say or do has nothing to do with me.
When you constantly need to help someone, they constantly need to be helpless.
You can detach with anger, detach with apathy, or detach with love.

Alcohol: *Also see* Booze
Alcohol and drugs are solvents; they remove everything from your life.
Alcohol is a perfect solvent; it dissolves marriages, families, and careers.
Alcohol is a silent killer; it destroys little by little until there is nothing left to devour.
Alcohol is like virginity, once you've given it up, you wonder why you kept it as long as you did!
Alcohol is patient; it waits forever for us to return.
Alcohol was not my problem—it was my solution; my problem was alcohol*ism*.
Alcohol: It provokes the desire but takes away the performance.
Alcohol: Liquid courage that turns us into cowards.
Alcohol: What you thought was the solution became the problem.
Changing from alcohol to marijuana was like switching deck chairs on the *Titanic*.
Humans invented alcohol; God invented the ocean. Whom do you trust?
Most things can be preserved in alcohol; dignity, however, is not one of them.
No one has discovered a way to preserve dignity with alcohol.
Not all accomplishments are rum and games.
The chains of alcohol are too light to be felt until they are too strong to be broken.
We didn't use drugs and alcohol; they used us.
We're not against alcohol; we're for sobriety.
You're ready for sobriety when the alcohol doesn't work anymore.

Alcoholic(s) *Also see* Addict(s)
A periodic *is* an alcoholic.
A recovering alcoholic without a sponsor is like leaving Dracula in charge of the blood bank.
A sober alcoholic is like a turtle on a fence post: You know it had help.
Alcoholic thinking keeps us in rebellion and slavery.
Alcoholic: Makes plans for the past and regrets for the future.
Alcoholics and addicts: fast talkers, slow thinkers.
Alcoholics are just like everyone else, only more so.
Alcoholics are life-long loners who cannot stand to be alone.

Alcoholics don't have relationships; they take hostages.
Alcoholics go from no self-esteem to low self-esteem.
Alcoholics make pour choices.
Alcoholics suffer from sick self-preoccupation.
Alcoholics suffer from terminal uniqueness.
Alcoholics think every day should be perfect.
All-coholic: One who is addicted to drugs and alcohol.
An alcoholic by himself is in bad company.
An alcoholic can be in the gutter, yet still look down on people.
An alcoholic is an egomaniac with an inferiority complex.
An alcoholic is someone who finds something that works, and then stops doing it.
An alcoholic is someone who treats loneliness with isolation.
An alcoholic is someone whose feet are firmly planted in thin air.
An alcoholic only knows one note on the scale: Me, Me, Me.
Being a "little bit alcoholic" is like being a "little bit pregnant."
Being an alcoholic does not give us an excuse to act alcoholically.
Being recovered from alcoholism is like getting a gunshot wound. You can recover from it, but it does NOT make you bulletproof.
Better to go through life sober, thinking you're an alcoholic, than go through life drunk thinking you're not.
Even if you're not an alcoholic, joining AA is the best damn mistake you'll ever make.
Eventually every alcoholic will have his last drink. Those of us in AA get to talk about ours.
Few alcoholics or addicts blame themselves before exhausting all other possibilities.
First AA birthdays are wonderful. Every alcoholic should have one.
First, the alcoholic takes the drink, then the drink takes a drink, then the drink takes the alcoholic.
For an alcoholic, something's wrong when nothing is.
For the alcoholic, too much is not enough.
Forgetting how to smile is part of an alcoholic's memory loss.
Grateful alcoholics don't drink, and drinking alcoholics aren't grateful.
If only—What if—As if—The three "realities" of the alcoholic.
If you think you are an alcoholic, chances are, you are.
It's not so important why you are an alcoholic, but rather what are you going to do about it?
Once an alcoholic, always an alcoholic.
Pain is the greatest gift God gives to the alcoholic.
Some people move when they see the light; alcoholics move when they feel the heat.
Sponsorship—the art of helping an alcoholic grow up without putting them down.
Take the "alcohol" out of the "alcoholic" and you're left with the "ic". Are you an untreated "ic"?
Talk to another alcoholic *before*, not after, you have a drink.
The alcoholic is always the last to know.
The most natural state of an alcoholic is irritable, restless, and discontented.
The paradox of recovery is a sober alcoholic.
The smallest package in the world is an alcoholic all wrapped up in himself.
The three most dangerous words for an alcoholic: "I've been thinking..."
The three stages of drinking alcohol: Impulsive, compulsive, repulsive.
There are only three possible outcomes for alcoholics: Locked up, Covered up, or Sobered up!
There is no such thing as justifiable anger to an alcoholic.
There is only one thing worse for an addict or alcoholic than bad fortune – good fortune.

There's no amount of effort alcoholics won't expend to destroy anything that is good in their lives.

We all have the same last name, "Alcoholic"!

"Yes But........." is the mating call for an alcoholic.

You can carry the message, but not the alcoholic.

You're probably an alcoholic if you think spilling beer is alcohol abuse.

Alcoholic's Anonymous: *See* AA

Alcoholism: *Also see* Addiction

Alcohol was not my problem—it was my solution, my problem was alcoholism.

Alcoholism doesn't come in bottles; it comes in people.

Alcoholism is a disease of degradation. AA is a process of regeneration.

Alcoholism is a disease of denial.

Alcoholism is a physical allergy combined with a mental obsession.

Alcoholism is a physical compulsion coupled with a mental obsession.

Alcoholism is a self-diagnosed disease.

Alcoholism is an equal opportunity destroyer and the 12 Step program is an equal opportunity restorer.

Alcoholism is an equal opportunity destroyer.

Alcoholism is an incurable disease; loneliness is not.

Alcoholism is being on a first name basis with all the clerks at the liquor store

Alcoholism is for people who have an adverse reaction to reality.

Alcoholism is like making love to a gorilla—you're not done until the gorilla says you are.

Alcoholism is not a spectator sport. The whole family gets to participate.

Alcoholism is the only disease known where you must treat the symptom before you treat the disease.

Alcoholism is the only disease that tries to convince you that you don't have it.

Alcoholism, treatable but not curable.

Every recovery from alcoholism began with the first sober hour.

It's not alcohol*wasm*; it's alcohol*ism*.

The victims of alcoholism are those around us.

Too often, alcoholism is treated as a tranquilizer deficiency.

Alone (Lonely):

A recovering addict by himself, is not by himself.

Alcoholics are life-long loners who cannot stand to be alone

Alcoholism is an incurable disease; loneliness is not.

Alone, in bad company.

An alcoholic drinks alone no matter where he is.

An alcoholic is someone who treats loneliness with isolation.

Being alone does not mean you have be lonely.

If you are lonely when you're alone, it's probably because you are in poor company.

Lonely is a choice.

Solitude, not Isolation

When you feel left out, reach out.

You alone can do it, but you can't do it alone.

You are not alone.

You get lonely when you build walls instead of doorways.
You never have to be alone again.
You never have to be lonely again.
Your mind is like a bad neighborhood, you should never go in there alone.

Amend(s): *Also see* Step 4

If we make half-assed amends, we'll half-way recover.
Making amends is a good way to have the last word!
Making amends is about cleaning up *your* side of the street.
Making amends is like taking an inside shower.
Sweep your own side of the street.
The most important amends are those you need to make to yourself.
We believe in "Living Amends" not "I'm sorry" amends.
When making amends, a subtle shift occurs in our thinking. We go from thinking we *are* a mistake to acknowledging we *made* a mistake.

Analyze:

These are not the Steps we discussed, or memorized, or analyzed. These are the Steps we took.
Paralysis by analysis.
Utilize, don't analyze

Anonymity(mous):

A coincidence is when God performs a miracle and decides to remain anonymous.
Anonymity is so important it's half our name.
Anonymity: The second A in AA is precious; it is the word in our name that sets us apart from all other alcoholics.
Coincidences are God's way of staying anonymous.
From Alcoholics Obvious to Alcoholics Anonymous.
God does his best work anonymously.
It's Anonymo-us, not Anonymo-me.
Respect the anonymity of others.
There are no coincidences, only situations where God chooses to remain anonymous.
We wanted to be famous and God made us anonymous.
Who you see here, what you hear here, let it stay here.

Anger(y): *Also see* Temper

A closed mouth gathers no foot.
A person is only as big as what makes him angry.
An angry person doesn't even like himself.
Anger blows out the lamp of the mind
Anger is a condition in which the tongue works faster than the mind.
Anger is but a mask for fear.
Anger is just one letter short of danger.
Anger is not a solution.
ANGER... An acid that does more damage in the vessel that it is stored, than on anything it is poured!
Anger: from grateful to hateful in a second.

Angry people are the most afraid.

Be flexible so you don't get bent out of shape.

Control your anger or it will control you.

Depression is anger turned inward.

Depression: anger without enthusiasm.

Don't develop a relationship with anger.

For every minute you are angry with someone, you lose 60 seconds of happiness that you can never get back.

If we were to live—we had to be free of our anger.

If you are right, you don't need to be angry; if you are wrong, you can't afford to be angry.

If you're that angry, the thing to do is to write it down and look at it tomorrow.

Justifiable anger is not justifiable.

Never trust your tongue when your heart is bitter.

Nothing pays off like restraint.

Resentment is when you didn't get your way yesterday. Anger is when you don't get your way today. Fear is when you won't get your way tomorrow.

Self-righteous anger is character assassination.

Speak when you are angry and you will make the best speech you will ever regret.

The clenched fist never receives.

The greatest remedy for anger is delay.

There are no good reasons for anger, only excuses.

There is no such thing as justifiable anger to an alcoholic.

They don't say things *to* make you angry, they say things *that* make you angry.

Those who anger you, conquer you.

We are only as big as the smallest thing that makes us angry.

Anniversary *See* Birthday

Answer(s): *Also see* Solution(s)

Acceptance is the Answer.

All the answers to all of our problems are contained in the sharing in the meetings.

Ask the right question, get the right answer.

Having all the answers is not the answer.

If using is the answer, what is the question?

One of the best ways to get your prayers answered is to get up off your knees and go to work.

Prayers are us calling God. Intuition is when God answers.

Prayers that get answered are Prayers with feet.

Praying is asking God for help, meditating is listening for God's answer.

The answer is in the Steps.

The answers are there, have you just refused to look for them?

There are no stupid questions, only stupid answers.

There is an answer to everything: it's just a matter of finding it.

There is an easy answer to your problem that is neat, plausible, and wrong.

Apology(ize): *Also see* Amends *and* Sorry

An apology is like superglue, it can repair just about anything.

Argue(ment):
Hot words make a cool friendship.
You don't have to attend every argument you're invited to.
The fastest way to end an argument is to give up being right.
We can disagree without being disagreeable; we can argue without being difficult.
When the mouth stumbles, it is worse than the foot.

Ask: *See* Questions

Ass(holes):
Don't let assholes rent space in your head.
Don't use even if your ass falls off.
For Women: A male sponsor will pat your ass and a female will save it.
If we make half-assed amends we'll half-way recover.
If you meet more than three assholes in one day, you need a meeting.
If you pass, it's your ass.
If your ass falls off, put it in a paper bag and take it to a meeting.
If your ass falls off, put it in a wheelbarrow and take it to a meeting.
Instant A-hole. Just add alcohol.
Opinions are like assholes, everyone has one.
Some day we'll look at this and laugh our ass off.
We came to the program to save our ass, and found out our soul was attached.
You can't save your face and your ass at the same time.

Atheist(ism):
There are no atheists in a foxhole.
Atheism is a non-prophet organization.

Attitude(s):
Attitude: You get what you expect in life.
Attitudes are contagious. Is yours worth catching?
Change your attitude and change your life.
Either you control your attitude or it controls you.
If you change your action, your attitude will change.
It isn't the load that weighs us down, it's the way we carry it.
It may not be your attitude problem, but their perception problem.
Keep an attitude of gratitude.
Life is not so much a matter of position as of disposition.
Put latitude in your attitude.
Take charge of your attitude. Don't let someone else choose it for you.
Take responsibility for your attitude, not my actions.
The only thing you can control in your life is your attitude.
When you have gratitude, you don't have attitude.
You can't change reality, but you can change your attitude towards it.
Your Attitude almost always determines your Altitude in life.

Attraction:
Attraction not Promotion.

Pedal the pedals—don't peddle them. (Attraction not Promotion)
You attract what you are, not what you want.

Bad(ly):
A drunk is a sick human being trying to get well, not a bad one trying to be good.
Acquire good habits; abandon bad habits.
An addict is sick trying to get well, not bad trying to be good.
An alcoholic by himself is in bad company.
Are you going to let bad times make you bitter or make you better?
Do the best you can—that's bad enough.
Good feelings or bad feelings are the same; it's feeling that's uncomfortable.
Hope is knowing the good in us will overcome the bad.
If you treat people badly today, you get to reap the benefits tomorrow.
If you've never been to a bad meeting, then you're not getting to enough.
Just because you're having a bad day doesn't mean you're having a bad life.
Nothing is all good and nothing is all bad.
Nothing is so bad, a drink won't make it worse.
Seemingly bad days are usually days when we don't get our own way.
The alcoholic's mind is like a bad neighborhood, don't go there alone.
There are no "bad" meetings.
There is a bit of good in the worst of us and a bit of bad in the best of us.
There's only one thing worse to an alcoholic than bad fortune, and that's good fortune.
Two things that are bad for the heart: running up hill and running down people.
What starts out bad, can't end up good.
When bad times come you can let them make you bitter or use them to make you better.
When things are going great, sobriety is good. When things are going bad, sobriety is better.
When you are having a bad day, lower your expectations and start over!
Whether we think good things about ourselves or whether we think bad things about ourselves, mostly we are thinking about ourselves.
You used to be good at being bad. Now you're going to get good a being good.
You were not that good at being bad.

Bar(tender):
A bartender is just a pharmacist with a limited inventory.
Gossip, rumors, backbiting, loose tongues, verbal altercations: sometimes AA meetings are like the corner bar, without the alcohol.
In a bar, we got sympathy--as long as our money lasted. In AA, we get understanding for nothing.
Sitting in a bar and asking yourself not to drink is like trying to sneak sun-up past a rooster.
We'd rather hear you share about the same thing a thousand times in meetings than learn you were sharing it in a bar.

Beer: *Also see* Alcohol
Beauty is in the eye of the beer-holder.
Deja Brew: The feeling you've had this hangover before.
If you drink near beer, consider yourself near drunk, and then consider yourself near sober.
Nonalcoholic beer is for nonalcoholics.
The Bud stops here.

This Bud's NOT for me!
When do I need a meeting? At beer-thirty.
You're probably an alcoholic if you think spilling beer is alcohol abuse.

Beginner: *See* Newcomer(s)

Behavior: *Also see* Action(s)
Be better than you were!
Change your behavior to meet your goals, not your goals to meet your behavior.
Do something. Lead, follow, or get out of the way.
Do the next right thing.
Do unto others as you would have them do unto you.
Do what you did and get what you got.
God does not want you to do extraordinary things; He wants you to do ordinary things extraordinarily well.
Half measures availed us nothing.
If it's to be, it's up to me!
If you keep doin' what your doin' you'll keep gettin' what your gettin'.
It's easier to change your behavior in advance than to change your reputation afterward.
Keep doing what keeps you here.
Move your body, change your mind.
My behavior, my responsibility; your behavior, your responsibility.
Remember yourself as the whole person you are and accept yourself as you are.
The smallest deed—is better than the grandest intention.
There are three kinds of behavior for the practicing alcoholic: Compulsive—Impulsive—Repulsive.
When does it get better? It gets better when your behavior changes.
When you know that you don't know, then you know!
You are still becoming.
You can do hard.
You're not responsible for your disease, but you are responsible for your behavior.

Belief(lieve):
Believe in your magic.
Believe only half of what you hear. And after you have been around awhile, you will know which half.
Believing is seeing.
Believe it to receive it!
Believe that life is worth living and your belief will create the fact.
Believe those who are seeking the truth and doubt those who have found it.
Do not believe in miracles. Rely on them.
Don't believe everything you think.
Faith is capitalizing on the belief of others.
Faith is not belief without proof, but trust without reservation.
We came, we came to, we came to believe
If you are having trouble believing in a power greater than yourself just try believing in a power other than yourself.
If a thought or belief doesn't serve you, let it go.

If you believe the Big Book, live it.
If you don't believe in God we suggest you change your mind.
If you don't believe, than make believe.
It pays to believe in miracles. In Alcoholics Anonymous we experience them.
People may not always believe what you say, but they will always believe what you do.
Make believe until you can believe.
Our program will work for people who believe in God. Our program will work for people who don't believe in God. Our program will not work for people who believe they are God.
Some things have to be believed to be seen.
Sometimes you have to believe it before you can see it.
What if there is no God? Believe anyway.
What you conceive and believe, you can achieve.
Worry comes from your belief that you are powerless.
You'll see it when you believe it.

Big Book: *See* Book(s)

Bill W.:
Bill W. did it sober.
Bill W. rode a Harley.
Friend of Bill W's
Graduate from Smith-Wilson University
Protected by Smith & Wilson

Birthday (Anniversary): *See also* Chip(s)
Don't count the days; make the days count.
Double digit midget

Blackout(s):
Blackout like you mean it.
Blackouts are not such a bad thing—the stuff we remember is bad enough!
Drinking is all about "out." Knocked out, kicked out, passed out or blacked out
Remember your blackouts!
Seen it all, done it all, can't remember most of it.
Waking up in strange places with strange faces.

Blame:
As long as you blame your past, you're not free to claim your future.
At the end of BLAME is ME.
Becoming aware of our character defects lead naturally to the next step: blame our parents.
Blaming our parents, is the perfect excuse for our shortcomings.
Do not point a finger at another because there are always three pointing back at you.
Expect nothing. Blame no one. Do something.
Failures always blame someone else.
Few alcoholics or addicts blame themselves before exhausting all other possibilities.
In order to forgive, you have to have blamed.
The reason people blame other people is because there is only one alternative.
When we remove *me* from blame all that's left is bla. bla, bla....

When you look into a mirror, take a good look, because this is the guy that got you here.
You can't blame anyone but yourself if you stumble over the same stone twice.

Blessing(s):
Any problem blesses us when we learn the lesson it teaches.
Be Blessed
Can't sleep? Try counting your blessings.
Count your blessings so your blessings count.
If we look closely, we will see we are given even amounts of blessings and sorrows.
May you be blessed with a slow recovery.
Our lives become different once we learn to magnify our blessings the way we do our troubles.
The proof is not in the bottle, but in the blessing.
Too blessed to be stressed.
Write a gratitude list and count your blessings.

Books: (Note, the book *Alcoholics Anonymous* is nick-named the "Big Book," the book *Narcotics Anonymous* is nick-named the "Basic Text," and the book *Chemically Dependent Anonymous* is nick-named the "First Edition")
A pencil, paper, and a Big Book can straighten out a whole nest of mind snakes.
Be careful what you do or say, you may be the only Big Book some people ever read.
By reading the black and white pages of the Big Book, you color your life beautiful.
Chapter Five is called "How It Works," not "Why Me?"
Don't try to change the Big Book, let the Big Book change you.
First Edition suggestion: Read the black parts.
If you don't have a Basic Text, get one.
If you believe the Big Book, live it.
If you believe the First Edition, live it.
If you read the Big Book, believe it.
If you want to hide something from an AA member, put it in the Big Book.
It works it really does! (page 88, line 8 in the Big Book)
One of those rare books that gets smarter every time you read it.
Prevent truth decay—read your Book.
Read the black stuff on the pages of our recovery Book, not the white stuff in between.
Recovery comes with instruction manuals: The Big Book, the Basic Text, the First Edition
The AA Big Book, the NA Basic Text, and the CDA First Edition do not need to be rewritten; they need to be reread.
Chapter Six is not "Into Thinking" or "Into Feeling," it's "Into Action."
The First Edition is like a cookbook – you can read it all day long and starve.
The shortest sentence in the Big Book "It works." .
The shortest sentence in the First Edition: "It works!"
Walk softly and carry a Big Book.
When all else fails, read the Basic Text. Or take the short cut and read it first.
When all else fails, read the Big Book. Or take the short cut and read it first.
When all else fails, read the First Edition. Or take the short cut and read it first.
When all else fails, the directions are in the Book.
You don't need the latest self-improvement bestseller. You have the classic in your hands.
You may be the only copy of the Basic Text some people ever see.
You may be the only copy of the Big Book some people ever see.

You may be the only copy of the First Edition some people ever see.
You may be the only copy some people ever see.
Your Big Book is your sponsor too.

Booze: *Also see* Alcohol
A belly full of booze and a head full of AA don't mix.
Booze: a body snatcher.
Booze and Lose - or - Grin and Win
Booze taught me to fly, then took away the sky.
Born to Booze.
Bottom: When the last thing you lose or the next thing you are about to lose is more important to you than booze.
Deja Booze: The feeling that somehow, somewhere, you've been kicked in the head like this before.
If GOD drives you out, BOOZE will bring you back.
It's a shame that booze doesn't turn off one's mouth at the same time it turns off the brain.
You booze, you loose.

Bored(dom):
Beware of Boredom
Boredom is the feeling that everything is a waste of time; serenity, that nothing is.
If you're lucky, life in recovery can be really boring.
What we used to call boredom, we now call serenity.

Bottom: *Also see* Hitting Bottom
At the bottom of one glass, there's only the top of another.
High bottoms have trap doors.

Boundary(ies):
Set boundaries: keep boundaries.
Boundaries create freedom.

Brain(s): *Also see* Mind
At five years you get your brains back, at ten years you learn how to use them, and at fifteen you realize you didn't need them in the first place.
It takes one month of sobriety for every year of drinking and using just to get our brains out of hock.
It takes time to get your brains out of hock.
It's a shame that booze doesn't turn off one's mouth at the same time it turns off the brain.
It's 11:00, do you know where your brain is?
Some people say that the 12 Steps brainwash us. Thank God, because that's how we get clean!
You can't fix the brain you've got with the brain you've got.

Bug:
Sometimes you are the wind; sometimes you are the bug; sometimes you are the windshield.

Bumper Sticker: *Also see* Slogans
Bumper Sticker Recovery
Actions speak louder than bumper stickers.
Dumber Stickers
Dunker Stickers
Never judge a member of the fellowship by their bumper sticker.
Program bumper stickers belong on the dashboard, not the bumper.

Busy:
Daily meditation for about 20 minutes is recommended for all in recovery; unless, of course, you're *very* busy, then you should meditate for an hour.
Happiness is that certain something you acquire while you're too busy to be miserable.
If you are too busy to pray, you are too busy.
Quick Doesn't Stick
Yesterday is gone; forget it. Tomorrow never comes; don't worry. Today is here; get busy.

CA (Cocaine Anonymous) *Also see* Slogans/Program Generic-Mix and Match
If you snorted enough to get to CA, you snorted enough.

Care:
Always remember we are being taken care of.
If you don't take care of yourself, why should anyone else?
My gratitude speaks when I care and share the NA Way
There is no limit to what you can accomplish if you do not care who gets the credit.
Today, take care of yourself. Tomorrow you can worry about them.
We don't care if you came from Yale or jail, Park Avenue or a park bench.
We don't care why you're here, it's why you stay.
Your kindness is a gift to another and the tag reads, "Handle with tender loving care."

Cause:
If you don't like the effect, don't produce the cause.
Is alcohol the cause of my problems or the result?
You are the cause of everything that happens to you. Be careful what you cause.
You didn't cause it; you can't control it; you can't cure it.

CDA (Chemically Dependent Anonymous) *Also see* Slogans/Program Generic-Mix and Match
CDA Uncensored
Chemically Dependent: If you used enough to get to CDA, you used enough.
Honest Sobriety
I will to will Your Will. (CDA Third Step Prayer)
In CDA we Can Discuss Anything.
Veins full of Vicodin and a head full of CDA bust brain chemistry.
Worst feeling in the world: a head full of CDA and a medicine cabinet full of prescriptions.

Censor(and Uncensored):
CDA Uncensored
Regarding 12-Step rules: Blessed are the censors, for they shall inhibit the Earth.

Chance(s):
Choice, not chance, determines destiny.
Keep your hands in your pants and give the newcomer a chance.
Many meetings, many chances; few meetings, few chances; no meetings, no chances
Remember, "fat chance" and "slim chance" mean the same thing.
Revenge is so disturbing to the alcoholic's "peace of mind" it bars his chances for "Contented Sobriety."

Change(s):
A fanatic is one who can't change his mind and won't change the subject.
Accept change because the possibilities are infinite.
All you have to do is change everything.
All you have to do to change your life, is change your mind.
Be the change you want to see in our service structure.
Change is a process, not an event.
Change is inevitable; growth optional.
Change is not painful; resistance to change is painful.
Change only happens when the pain of holding on is greater than the fear of letting go.
Change is mandatory, progress optional.
Change the way your treat others before you question the way God treats you.
Change your action; change your attitude.
Change your attitude and change your life.
Change your behavior to meet your goals, not your goals to meet your behavior.
Doing one thing different can make the difference.
Don't resist change; there's no way to progress without it.
Don't try to change the Big Book; let the Big Book change you
Don't waste time thinking about what thinking can't change.
Everyone thinks of changing the world, but no one thinks of changing himself.
God grant me the courage to change the things I cannot accept.
If nothing changes, nothing changes.
If you don't believe in God we suggest you change your mind.
If you don't change, you will drink. If you don't drink, you will change.
If you don't change, nothing changes.
If you don't change, you'll be begging for change.
If you don't change, your clean date will.
If you fail to change the person you were when you came in, that person will take you out!
If you keep doing the same thing over and over, you'll keep getting the same thing over and over.
If you want to change who you are, change what you do.
If you want what you never had, you have to do what you've never done.
It is not change that is painful, it is *resistance* to change that is painful.
It's easier to change your behavior in advance than to change your reputation afterward.
Learn to change and change to learn.
Make no major changes in the first year.
Move your body, change your mind.
No pain, no change.
Not everything that is faced can be changed, but nothing can be changed until it is faced.
Nothing changes if nothing changes!

On the pity pot? Change a thought, move a muscle.
People who relapse usually do so because they accepted the things they could have changed.
Practice these principles in all your affairs, or change your affairs.
Prayer changes things; worry changes nothing.
Prayer does not change the situation, it changes the person who prays.
Prayer does not change what you are praying about. Prayer changes you.
Real change requires real change.
Right thought changes things.
See patterns and choose change.
SHIFT HAPPENS
Situations don't change so much as our perception.
Some of us change when we see the light, most of us change when we feel the heat.
Surrender Allows Change
The drunk you were will always drink. *You* need to change.
The essence of all growth is a willingness to change for the better.
There are only two things an alcoholic doesn't like: the way things are, and change.
There is absolutely no pain in change or growth. The pain is in the resistance to the change or growth.
We are not in recovery to change the world. We are in recovery to learn to function within the world.
We must change our old playgrounds, playmates and playthings.
We should all know how to adjust to changed circumstances in order to capitalize on new opportunities.
When does it get better? It gets better when your behavior changes.
When we're through changing—we're through.
When what one needs to do becomes what one wants to do, change becomes simple.
You can change any thought that hurts into a reality that hurts even more.
You must be the change you wish to see in the world.
Your Higher Power makes your life uncomfortable when it's time for you to change.
Your life can be changed in a matter of hours by people who don't even know you.

Character: *Also see* Character Defect(s)
Character is how we act when we think no one is watching.
Character is what you really are, while your reputation is merely what others think you are.
Character shows as we respond to difficulty.
Cynicism is a character defense.
Reputation is what people think of us. Character is what God knows about us.
Self-righteous anger is character assassination.

Character Defect(s): *Also see* Defect(s) *and* Shortcoming(s)
Character defects are like seeds, they are always there waiting to sprout.
Fear is the mother of all character defects.
Having a relationship in early recovery is like pouring Miracle Grow on your character defects.
If you want to find out what your character defects are, fall in love.
Our defects of character are the bars of a cage. The central point is not to study the bars, but to get out of the cage.
You are unconditionally guaranteed to have defects of character.

Chemical Dependency(ent): *Also see* Addict *and* Addiction *and* Alcoholism *and* Alcoholic
Chemical Dependent: If you used enough to get to CDA, you used enough.
Some people think chemical dependency is a two-fold disease--more and right now.
There are no chemical solutions to spiritual problems.

Child(hood):
It is never too late to have a happy childhood.
Your inner child might be an inner juvenile delinquent.
Do not let the newcomer's inner child run our meetings. This is not play therapy.

Chip(s), Token(s), & Medallions:
*Note: Many groups use a marker system to help denote progress in recovery. The markers
vary considerably in form (poker chips, wooden nickels, metallic coins, key chains). Each
group, program and geographical region define their own system and significance to each
marker. The markers are usually called chips, tokens, medallions, and key chains. The first
marker given is generally called the "Desire Chip" and is given to people who want to join the
program. After the desire chip may follow a 30 day marker, 90 day marker, 6 month marker, 9
month marker, and one year. Some areas even give markers for each 30 days in the first year.
At one year of abstinence, group members are often given medal medallions followed each
successive year with another medal medallion. Some groups wean members from receiving so
many markers in the first year by giving an 18 month marker. Below are some of the one-liners
said when giving out the different chips. We do not include what timeline the markers denote
because it varies so much within programs, regions and groups.*
Aluminum chip: made from recycled beer cans.
Blue chip: Best blue chip stock that money can't buy.
Chip Chick: The female that gives out the tokens at a meeting.
Chips: Learn and earn.
Desire Chip = Sponsorchip
Desire chip: (usually white) surrender chip.
Desire chip: Give up the high cost of low living.
Desire chip: Sick & tired of being sick and tired?
Desire chip: Stop throwing up and start growing up.
Desire chip: We give you this one for free, the rest you have to earn.
Double Digit Chip
Double Digit Midget
Double Digit Sobriety
Green chip: Go and grow chip.
Green chip: Keep your recovery green.
If you've had a nip, you need a chip.
Is everybody in chip-shape?
Join us on the road to "L." (*Roman numeral "L" on a chip denotes 50 years.*)
Nine month chip: Pregnant chip, you either are or you aren't one of us.
One year token: Moving into heavy metal.
Put your chip under your tongue and when it dissolves you can go get a drink.
Put the chip in your pocket, not on your shoulder.
Red chip: Danger chip.
Red chip: Stop sign. Don't stop going to meetings.
Token Takers Take It (Meeting Makers Make It)

White chip of surrender.
Yellow chip: Sunshine chip
Yellow chip: Urine chip, by now your urine is clean and you can pass the piss test.
Yellow chip: Urine chip, you'r 'n the right place.
Weiner chip: the 18 month chip to wean people off the frequent chip taking during the first year.
Whiner chip: the 18 month chip because the old-timers whine that they didn't get one when they had 18 months (they didn't have 18 month chips 20 years ago)

Choice(s): *Also see* Decide(cision)
Adrenaline is my drug of choice.
Awareness is a choice.
Choice, not chance, determines destiny.
Choose Calm over Chaos
Choose your life, don't let it choose you.
For our suggestions you have two choices: Take it or leave it.
If we have a rat in the cellar, we have a choice: go down there and feed it or starve it.
In recovery, my drug of choice is anxiety.
It may not be your fault but it's your choice
Lonely is a choice.
Make better choices.
My drug of choice was "more."
My recovery, my pace, my choice.
My serenity, my pace, my choice
Once you choose to use, you can no longer use your choice.
Our drug of choice is actually a drug of No Choice.
People in recovery are creatures that, told "thou shalt not," have no choice but to do it.
See patterns and choose change.
The choice you make today will usually affect tomorrow.
Today we have a *choice!*
You can chose to do right, you can choose to do wrong; with enough wrong choosing, your choices will be gone.
You have the power to choose, if you choose to.
Your only powerless over the first drink, but not powerless over your choices.

Classic 12 Step Slogans:
Easy Does It
Expect Miracles.
First Things First
I Can't, He Can, I think I'll Let Him
Just For Today
Keep Coming Back
Keep It Simple
KISS (Keep it Simple Stupid)
Let Go and Let God
Live and Let Live
One Day at a Time
More Will Be Revealed

Progress Not Perfection
Stick with the winners
There but For the Grace of God
Think Think Think
This Too Shall Pass
Turn it Over

Clean(ing): *Also see* Clean (Clean and Sober)
(_____) Anonymous: When you clean up after your group, you leave the signature of your group behind you.
After each meeting, clean up the wreckage of the present.
After the meeting, clean up the wreckage of your presence.
Cleaning the house IS spiritual cleaning.
Don't drink, clean house, and help another alcoholic.
If you want to feel better, clean house. If you want to get better, find God.
It's all right to have castles in the air but addicts move into them, family members clean them, and counselors collect the rent!
Making amends is about cleaning up *your* side of the street.
The Steps: Give up. (Steps 1,2,3) Clean up. (4,5,6) Make up. (7,8,9) Keep up. (10,11,12).
The Twelve Steps: One to three: Clear up; Four to Nine: Clean up; Ten to Twelve: Group up.
Trust God, Clean house, and Work with Others.

Clean (Clean and Sober):
A day clean is a day won.
Being clean and sober won't keep you clean and sober.
Clean and Serene
Clean n' Crazy
Clean then Serene
Do it clean.
Don't let anything make you change your clean date.
God, help me stay clean and sober today.
If you are clean and sober, the miracle has already happened. Stick around, the impossibilities take a little longer.
If you don't pick up, you will have clean time. If you work the steps, you will have recovery.
If you don't change... your clean date will.
If you want to stay clean, make the coffee.
My worst day clean is better than my best day high.
The paradox of recovery is a clean addict.
www.CDAweb.org - where clean and sober people click.
www.narcoticsanonymous.org - where clean people click.
You have to be clean to learn to live clean.
You woke up this morning clean and sober. That's your spiritual awakening.
Your worst day clean is better than your best day high.

Cocaine:
Turn your back on crack.

Co-dependence(y) & COSA: (Co-dependent on Sex Addicts) *Also see* Al-Anon

A loss in life is not a loss of life.

Awareness is a choice.

Beware of the "Geographic cure" and the simple "Spouse-ectomy."

Change the thought, and the feeling must go.

Claim full "response-ability."

Codependency: You're drowning and somebody else's life flashes in front of your eyes.

Controlling life isn't the answer, it's the problem.

Decisions aren't forever.

Disease to please

Don't care! You don't have to.

Don't do unto others what they can undo for themselves.

Don't drive when you're not driving.

Don't just do something. Stand there!

Don't let your overdoing be your undoing.

Enforce "Respect-me rules"

Honesty without kindness is cruel and kindness without honesty is co-dependence.

How you respond is your responsibility.

If you are eating a shit sandwich, chances are, you ordered it.

It's not your business to keep their secret.

It's not: *Don't take it out on your partner*, it's: *Don't take it in.*

Keeping their secret keeps you sick.

Know your no's.

Letting go is not caring for, but caring about.

Mind your own business

No is a complete sentence.

Nobody 'gives' you a bad day without your permission.

People can't walk over you until you lie down.

Precious and Free

Refuse to be abused.

See patterns and choose change.

Set boundaries: keep boundaries.

Stay put and act in your own best interest.

Sweep your own side of the street.

Take responsibility for your attitude, not their actions.

The bad news: there are a lot of incompetent people out there. The good news: they are no longer your problem.

The bigger the secret, the more dangerous.

The main business of the mind is to mind its own business.

The road to resentment is paved with expectation.

They shouldn't be taking it out on us and we shouldn't be taking it in.

Today do something for someone you love: Leave them alone

Today, take care of yourself. Tomorrow you can worry about them.

Trust your Trust

When in doubt, check it out.

When you constantly need to help someone, they constantly need to be helpless.

When you feel needy, feel needy.

When you feel out of control, thank God.

Why are you suffering someone else's pain?
You don't say things to make me angry, you say things that make me angry.
You had a right to your anger, now you have a right to your joy.
You have done no wrong, still you are sorry.
You matter.
Your serenity, your pace, your choice.

Coincidences:

A coincidence is when God performs a miracle and decides to remain anonymous.
Coincidence—is the word God uses when He wants to be anonymous.
Coincidence—is the word God uses when He wants to be autonomous.
Coincidences are God's way of staying anonymous.
God-incidence
If you can't expect a miracle, at least expect a coincidence.
Is it odd or is it God?
There are no coincidences in (___) A.
There are no coincidences, they say, only God-incidences.

Comfort(able):

AA is a program that comforts the disturbed and disturbs the comfortable.
Any measure of comfort requires rigorous honesty.
Comfort the disturbed and disturb the comfortable.
Complacency kills.
Don't get too comfortable.
Don't make the pity pot too comfortable.
Never attach strings to the comfort you give someone else.
The willingness to be uncomfortable leads to being comfortable.
We drink to be comfortable with being uncomfortable.
You do not need to conform to be comfortable. "Comfortable" is conscious contact, not conscious copycat.

Committee

Itty bitty shitty committee.
How's the committee? (Has it come to a meeting of the mind recently?)

Compare:

Don't compare—identify; don't intellectualize—utilize
Don't hurry. Don't worry. Don't compare.
Identify, don't compare.
Satisfaction begins when comparison stops.
Share, don't compare.
What lies in front of you and what lies behind you is insignificant compared to what lies within you.

Compulsive:

The alcoholic compulsion to have everything done right this minute is usually balanced by a rare talent for procrastination.

There are three kinds of behavior for the practicing alcoholic: Compulsive—Impulsive—Repulsive.

Confidence:
Confidence is the feeling you have before you understand the situation.
Confidence is unattainable without some humility.

Confront:
Not everything that is faced can be changed but nothing can be changed until it is faced.
The death of our addiction forces us to confront life.
What you are afraid to do is a clear indicator of what you should do next.
Whatever you are trying to avoid, we won't go away until you confront it.

Conscience:
A clear conscience makes a soft pillow.
A practicing addict has no conscience.
If you can't get to sleep for three nights, check your conscience.
The best sleeping pill is a clear conscience.

Conscious Contact:
You do not need to conform to be comfortable. "Comfortable" is conscious contact, not conscious copycat.

Contempt:
Addicts are the only people who can be laying in the gutter looking down on people.
Contempt Prior to Investigation
Contempt is not a spiritual gift.
Walk on soles, not on souls.
To be little is to be little.
Contempt and success are both difficult to handle, but one is ultimately more enjoyable.

Control(ling):
Be a harmony freak instead of a control freak.
Control your anger or it will control you.
Control your controlling.
Controlling life isn't the answer, it's the problem.
Don't drive when you're not driving.
Either you control your attitude or it controls you.
Having control over yourself is almost as good as having control over others.
If it's you controlling them, stop it. If it's them controlling you, stop it.
If you have to control your drinking, it must be out of control.
If you have to control your drinking, what's the point of drinking?
The one who controls the least, controls the relationship.
The only thing you can control in your life is your attitude.
When a man tries to control his drinking he has already lost control.
When we couldn't dominate, control, or manipulate, we would ask for terms and conditions.
You can't control—without being controlled.
You didn't cause it; you can't control it; you can't cure it.

Counselor(s): *See* Professionals

Courage: *Also see* Fear
Alcohol: Liquid courage that turns us into cowards.
Courage is not the absence of fear; it is the ability to act in the presence of fear
With the first three steps, you get the courage to work the rest. When you work the rest, you get rid of the garbage so you can work the first three
Courage is fear in action.
Courage is fear that has said its prayers.
God grant me the courage to change the things I cannot accept.

Crazy: *Also see* Insanity
Be kind to your enemies. It will drive them crazy.
Crazy-making is what you make of it.
Drunkenness is nothing but voluntary madness.
My sponsor told me they don't lock you up for being crazy, only for acting crazy.
When you see "CRAZY" coming, hurry up and cross the street!
You can *think* crazy as long as you *act* sober.

Crisis(es):
Alcoholics don't need chaos in their lives; they demand it.
Don't make a mole hill out of a mountain.
Learn the difference between a crisis and an inconvenience.
One needn't make a crisis out of an incident.
Show us a crisis and we'll show you a happy alcoholic.
Try moderation, not magnification.
We can handle the most awful situations, yet we'll drink over a broken shoelace.

Criticize(m): *Also see* Judge(ing)
Don't point a finger; point the whole hand (reach out).
For every action, there is an equal and opposite criticism.
It is much easier to be critical than it is to be correct.
Never ever criticize yourself.
Rather than giving others a piece of your mind, don't—and have peace of mind.
The trouble with most of us is that we would rather be ruined by praise than saved by criticism.
To belittle is to be little.
Walk on soles, not on souls.
Write criticism a letter and tell him to leave you alone.

Cure *Also see* Geographical Cure
You didn't cause it; you can't control it; you can't cure it.

Day(s)(aily) *Also see* Yesterday, Today, & Tomorrow
A day clean is a day won.
A day hemmed in prayer is less likely to unravel.
A day without sunshine is like night.
A lie a day keeps sobriety away.
A meeting a day keeps the demons at bay.

A meeting a day keeps the detox away.
Another day, another recovery!
Carpe Diem. Seize the day!
Day By Day.
Don't "have" a nice day, MAKE a nice day.
Don't count the days, make the days count.
Each Day A New Beginning
Each day, you are either a step farther from your last drink or a step closer to your next.
Every day above ground is a good day.
Every day is perfect. The problem is, you don't know until tomorrow.
Have a nice day, *unless* you have other plans.
In AA the years go by quickly. We seem to have problems with the days.
It is One Day At A Time - In A Row!
It's a daily program: Yesterday's home run may not be enough to win the game today.
Judge each day not by the harvest you reap but by the seeds you sow.
Just because you're having a bad day doesn't mean you're having a bad life.
Life sucks! (but in NA, life sucks one day at a time).
Live each day the best that you can.
Most addicts are only stoned on the days that end in y.
My worst day clean is better than my best day high.
My worst day sober is better than my best day drunk.
New Day, New Way.
One Day at a Time
One day at a time, remember: The mighty oak was once a little nut that held its ground.
One day takes time.
Seven days without a meeting—makes one weak.
Take care of the days and the years will come by themselves.
There are good days and great days. On a good day nothing goes wrong and you don't drink.
On a great day *everything* goes wrong and you don't drink.
Today is a very important day—it's the only day you have.
When you're feeling overwhelmed, remember to take things one at a time—one day at a time.
You can start your day over anytime.
You can't carry a board 365 feet long, but you can carry a one foot board every day for 365 days.

Death: (Die)
A resentment is like drinking poison and expecting the other person to die.
Anybody can die, not everybody can live.
Death, Insanity, or Recovery
Don't love them to death.
Fear not that your life shall come to an end but rather that it shall never have a beginning.
Feed your faith and your doubts will starve to death.
Grateful I'm not dead.
He who dies with the most toys, is, nonetheless, still dead.
How you get to be an old-timer: Don't drink; don't drug; don't die.
Maybe you didn't die because of H & I.
Nobody dies without God's permission.
Recovery isn't a death sentence, it's a life sentence.

Talk or die.
The death of our addiction forces us to confront life.
The Only HOPE in DOPE is DEATH
The secret to long term sobriety: Don't drink, don't die.
Two things you have to do to become an old-timer: don't use and don't die.
Walking drunk man.
We don't have to drink to die.
We've known plenty of people who have died on their way to somebody else's bottom.
When an old-timer dies a library is lost.
When the horse dies, dismount.

Decide(decision): *Also see* Choice(s)
Constant decision making is the price on freedom.
Decide to be satisfied with any results your efforts may bring.
Decide what you want to be, pay the price, and be what you want to be.
Deciding to get sober is the most important decision you will ever make.
Decisions aren't forever.
Each meeting has two types of newcomers: Beginners and visitors. Beginners have made a decision.
Life does not begin at any particular age, but only when you decide to live it.
Most (___)A people spend more time deciding where to have lunch than in choosing a sponsor.
No decision (right or wrong) is complete until it is fully accepted.
Our spiritual possibilities are unlimited when we willingly decide to live them.
Suicide is such a long term decision, while living has so many more variables.
There are no fatal decisions, as long as you don't pick up that first fix, pill, or drink.
There are very few decisions that cannot wait 24 hours.
When you dance with a gorilla, it's the gorilla who decides when to stop.
You can be about as happy as you decide to be.

Defect(s) *Also see* Fault(s) *and* Character Defect(s) *and* Shortcoming(s)
A meeting a day keep my defects at bay.
Do you really want to give up the defect? Or do you just want to give up the result of the defect?
God does not make junk, but some of the goods do have defects.
The most natural state of an alcoholic is irritable, restless, and discontented.

Denial:
Alcoholism is a disease of denial.
Alcoholism is the only disease that tries to convince you that you don't have it.
Better living through denial.
Denial, is not just a river in Egypt.
Denial is not a river in Egypt, but you can drown in it.
If you saw myself as others see you, would you deny it?
If it wasn't for denial my life would be shit.
The back half of the room at meetings is known as the denial section.
Whatever you are trying to avoid, we won't go away until you confront it.
When you are being here now, you don't have to cover up anything.

Depression(DA-Depressed Anonymous):
Depression is a Defense, not a Disgrace.
Depression: anger without enthusiasm.
Depression: when you're taking more than you're giving.
Depression is anger turned inward.
Repression without expression, leads to depression.
Repression causes depression.
When you're down, take a Step and then the Step takes you.

Desire: *Also see* Chip(s), Token(s), & Medallions
A slip occurs when the desire to drink is stronger than the desire not to drink.
Alcohol: It provokes the desire but takes away the performance.
Gratitude is not the word but the desire to say the word.
The basic ingredient of all humility is a desire to seek and do God's will.
Ya gotta wanna.

Detach(ment):
Detachment comes with the development of spiritual trust.
Detachment is neither kind nor unkind.
Detach with love
Detach, don't desert

Detox: *Also see* Rehab *and* Withdrawal
A meeting a day keeps the detox away.
Detox: Spin Dry
Forgiveness detoxifies.

Devil:
New Level; New Devil.
What the devil presents to you is always a real pretty picture. But there is always one hellava price to pay.

Die: (See *Death*)

Difference(s) *Also see* Unique(ness)
AA: Experience the difference, where the difference is experience.
Doing one thing different, can make the difference.
Here is a thought that kills a lot of chemical dependents: *That may be true for you, but I'm different.*
No matter what predicament you find yourself in today, tomorrow can be different.
Our lives become so different once we learn to magnify our blessings the way we do our troubles.
Recovery process: Different ways of doing the same thing.
Things got worse, things got better, and things got different.
We are not different from others, God just made us special.
What we have in common are more important than our differences.
What you think makes you unique and different, are the things you have most in common with other alcoholics and addicts!

Difficulty(ies) *See* Tough Times

Dignity:
Most things can be preserved in alcohol; dignity, however, is not one of them.
No one has discovered a way to preserve dignity with alcohol.
Standing on your own dignity makes for very poor footing.

Disagree:
In AA, we learn how to disagree without being disagreeable.
Your Higher Power may be using people who disagree with you.

Disappointment:
Some of the greatest disappointments in life have come from that which we insisted upon having.

Disease: *Also see* Sick
Alcoholism doesn't come in bottles; it comes in people.
Alcoholism is a disease of degradation, AA is a process of regeneration.
Alcoholism is a disease of denial.
Alcoholism is a self-diagnosed disease.
Alcoholism is an incurable disease; loneliness is not.
Alcoholism is the only disease known where you must treat the symptom before you treat the disease.
Alcoholism is the only disease that tries to convince you that you don't have it.
Being uncomfortable is the dis-ease of the disease.
If the cure works, chances are, you have the disease.
It's a threefold disease: physical, mental, and spiritual.
Recovery is a disease we catch from our ears.
Some people think chemical dependency is a two-fold disease—more and right now.
Turn "dis-ease" to a sense of ease.
We are not what we are in spite of our disease; we are what we are *because* of it.
We know how to be dedicated to our disease. Dedication to sobriety seems less clear.
When you are in a meeting, your disease is in the parking lot doing push-ups.
While you are asleep, your disease is working out with a personal trainer, your inner addict.
Your disease progresses even when you are not drinking.
You're not responsible for your disease, but you are responsible for your behavior.

Do it:
(__)A. is a self-help program but you can't do it by yourself.
CDA is *not* for people who need it. CDA is *not* for people who want it. CDA is for people who do it.
Do something. Lead, follow, or get out of the way.
Don't figure it out. Just do it.
Easy Does It (but do it!).
God didn't do it!
How to get honest: If it's not yours—don't take it. If it's not true—don't say it. If it's not right—don't do it.
If you don't do it, you won't get it!

If you don't have the time to do something right, when will you have the time to do it over?

If you don't know it can't be done, you can do it.

If you keep doin'g what your doin'g you'll keep gettin'g what your gettin'g.

If you let other people do it for you, they invariably will do it to you.

If you want to have what you have not, you must do what you do not.

Just do it!

People in recovery are creatures that, told "thou shalt not," have no choice but to do it.

Remember that a wrong act will prey upon your mind until you either do something to rectify it or get drunk.

The happiest people are those who discover that what they should be doing and what they are doing are the same thing.

There is no way to know God's Will unless you do it.

Well done is better than well said.

What you do may seem insignificant, but it is very important that you do it.

You alone can do it, but you can't do it alone.

Doors:

Faith is a lit doorway; doubt is a dark hall.

Fear knocked on the door. Faith answered; there was no one there.

God never closes one door without opening another…but the draft in the hallway can be hell!

God will not close one door without opening another.

High bottoms have trap doors.

Limitations are opportunities to open new doors.

The doors swing both ways.

The Twelve Steps are like wrenches in a toolbox – they'll fit any nut that walks in the door.

When one door closes, another door opens. It's being in the hallway that's hell.

With drinking there are three doors to choose from; bad, worse and terrible.

Dope:

Dope: Think about it.

Experience, Strength, and hope, not opinions, bullshit, and dope.

From a hopeless dope fiend, to a dopeless hope fiend.

Hope not Dope

Open-minded not Dopen-minded

The Only HOPE in DOPE is DEATH

Dream(ing):

Dream!

Drugs Destroy Dreams!

Remember yesterday, dream of tomorrow, but live for today.

Wet dream—dreaming about drinking.

Who looks outside, dreams. Who looks inside awakens.

Drink(ing,): *Also see* Alcohol

A drink is only an arm's-length away.

A free drink is often the most expensive.

A resentment is like drinking poison and expecting the other person to die.

AA does not teach us how to handle drinking it teaches us how to handle sobriety.

An alcoholic drinks alone no matter where he is.

An alcoholic is someone who drinks more than us.

An alcoholic who reads about the evils of drink, will give up reading.

At the bottom of one glass, there's only the top of another.

Be as enthusiastic about (___) A as you were about your drinking.

Before he got to A.A., he was dying for a drink.

Call before you drink and we will help you stay sober. Call after you drink and you will help us stay sober.

Call your sponsor before, not after, you take the first drink.

Don't be afraid you will drink and die. Be afraid you will drink and live.

Don't drink, clean house, and help another alcoholic.

Don't drink, don't think, and go to meetings.

Don't drink, even if your rear falls off.

Don't fight drink, strengthen sobriety.

Don't romance the drink.

Don't think about the cold one going down but the warm one coming up!

Don't worry about taking the first drink, worry about the first drink taking you.

Don't say, "I can't drink"; say instead, "I CAN not drink".

Drinking is all about "out." Knocked out, kicked out, passed out or blacked out.

Drinking and thinking is worse than drinking and driving.

Drinking is your right, even if everything turns out wrong.

Drinking won't drown your problems, it will irrigate them.

Each day, you are either a step farther from your last drink or a step closer to your next.

Eventually every alcoholic will have his last drink. Those of us in AA get to talk about ours.

Every alcoholic's favorite brand: More!

Every drink you drank got you here. Every drink you don't drink keeps you here.

Everything is either a step toward a drink or a step away.

First the man takes a drink, then the drink takes a drink, then the drink takes the man (Japanese proverb).

Getting drunk interferes with our drinking.

Go to enough meetings and you still may not stop drinking; your drinking, however, will be ruined.

Grateful alcoholics don't drink, and drinking alcoholics aren't grateful.

Having a resentment is like drinking poison and expecting someone else to die.

He did his drinking from Park Avenue to a park bench.

Hope for the best, but prepare for the thirst.

How you get to be an old-timer: Don't drink; don't drug; don't die.

However many years away from your last drink, you are only Twelve Steps away from your next one.

If drinking were our only problem, rehabs would turn out winners.

If life was a problem to be avoided, drinking was the perfect solution.

If we knew which drink would cause "wet brain," we'd stop just before it.

If you can't remember your last drink, you haven't had it yet.

If you come into an AA meeting looking for recovery, you will find exactly that. If you come looking for a reason to continue drinking, you'll eventually find that, too.

If you don't change, you will drink. If you don't drink, you will change.

If you don't drink or use again, you don't have to go back where you came from.

If you drink at the bad news you got today, you'll never know you could get through it without drinking.

If you drink near beer, consider yourself near drunk. Then consider yourself near sober.

If you have to control your drinking, it must be out of control.

If you have to control your drinking, what's the point of drinking?

If you take a drink, you take your will and life back.

If you think you have a drinking problem, chances are, you do.

If you want to be proud of yourself, don't chose drinking as the subject of your pride.

If you want to drink and drug, that's your business; if you don't, that's ours.

If you're not moving away from a drink, you're moving closer to it

It takes one month of sobriety for every year of drinking and using just to get our brains out of hock.

It took every drink to get you here.

It's alright to drink like a fish provided you drink what a fish does.

It's not the fifth drink that gets you drunk, it's the first.

It's not what leads you to drinking, it's where the drinking leads you.

It's not what or how much you drank, it's what it did to you.

It's OK not to drink.

It's the first drink that gets you drunk.

Keep it Simple, Breath In- Breath Out, Don't drink or drug in between Breaths.

Keep the plug in the jug.

Make it a rule—"Don't drink while you're sober."

Make the solution so big, the problem does not exist.

My worse day sober is better than my best day drinking.

No one was ever arrested for driving while drinking too much coffee.

Nobody can make me drink, but there are some people who really make me thirsty.

Normal people don't wonder if they have a drinking problem.

Not drinking is a symptom of your recovery.

Nothing is so bad that a drink or drug won't make it worse.

On the first drink: When you get hit by a train, which kills you, the engine or the caboose?

Once you pick up a drink, the steps are totally bewildering.

Once you take the drink, you have thoroughly completed the slip.

One drink =one drunk

One drink may make you feel like a new person. Then the new person has to have a drink.

One is too many and more not enough.

One is too many, a thousand never enough.

One thing about sobriety, if you don't drink, it lasts a lonnnnng time!

Our program does not teach us how to handle drinking and drugging. It teaches us how to handle recovery.

Pick up the phone before you pick up a drink.

Poor me, poor me, pour me a drink.

Problem drinkers? Every time we drank, we had a problem.

Put your chip under your tongue and if it dissolves, you can take another drink.

Recovery can't begin until the drinking stops!

Sitting in a bar and asking yourself not to drink is like trying to sneak sun-up past a rooster.

Sobriety ruins your drinking.

Stinking thinking leads to stinking drinking which causes stinking problems.

Stinking thinking precedes drinking.

Take the fifth or drink a fifth.

Talk to another alcoholic *before*, not after, you have a drink.

The further you are from your last drink, the closer you are to the next one.

The good news is, we don't *have* to drink anymore.

The insanity of this disease is that when you keep getting drunk, then you're drunk and insane.

The person you were will always drink. You *need* to change.

The secret to long term sobriety: Don't drink, don't die.

The Spirit within you is Stronger than the Spirits you pour in you.

The ultimate defense against the first drink is a spiritual one.

The way to become an old-timer: don't drink and don't die.

There are a million reasons to drink, but no *good* reason.

There are good days and great days. The good days are when everything goes our way and we don't drink. The great days are when *nothing* goes our way and we don't drink.

There are no "big" deals. If you drink—there are "no" deals.

There are no reasons for drinking, only excuses.

There is no tragedy bad enough that a drink or drug won't make it worse and there is no success good enough that a toast won't toast you.

They didn't make a glass big enough for us to have one drink.

Think of what you did to pursue a drink. Now pursue *not* drinking with the same fervor.

Think the drink through.

Think, think, think before you take that drink.

To an alcoholic taking one drink, is like stepping off a roof and only expecting to fall one floor.

Tore up from the floor up.

We came for our drinking and stayed for our thinking.

We came to these rooms not because we drank a lot, but because we drank too much.

We can all stop drinking. Staying stopped is the problem.

We can remain recovered as long as we remain recovering. We are not drink proof.

We come here for our drinking and stay here for our thinking.

We don't drink or use, *no matter what*.

We don't drink even if our ass falls off; we pick it up and take it to a meeting.

We don't have to drink to die.

We don't want to drink like gentlemen; we want to drink like pigs and be treated like gentlemen.

We don't want to drink like ladies; we want to drink like pigs and be treated like ladies.

We drank to drown our sorrows but our sorrows learned how to swim.

We drank to get over the effects of drinking.

We drink to be comfortable with being uncomfortable.

We have a choice not to drink again until we take the first drink. Then we have no choices.

We turned the bottle up because we couldn't turn it down.

Wet dream—dreaming about drinking.

When a man tries to control his drinking he has already lost control.

When God is holding your right hand and AA is holding your left, you have no hands with which to pick up a drink.

When the going gets tough, the tough get drinking.

When you make a 12-Step call and you don't drink, it is successful.

With drinking there are three doors to choose from; bad, worse and terrible.

You are only a wrist away from a drink today.

You are only one drink away from a drunk, one hit away from a high.

You don't get drunk watching another drink. You don't get serenity watching others do the Steps.

You may have another drink in you, but you may not have another recovery.

You may not have been born an alcoholic, but when you took the drink, the alcoholic was born.

You must learn to pick up a program, not just set down a drink!

You only have to give up one drink.............the next one.

You won't lose anything sober you can get back by drinking.

You're one drink away from a drunk.

Drug(s/ing): *Also see* Alcohol *and* Mind-affecting Chemicals

A drug is only an arm's length away.

Adrenaline is my drug of choice.

Alcohol and drugs are solvents; they will remove everything from your life.

All-coholic: One is addicted to drugs and alcohol.

Don't fight drugs, strengthen recovery.

Don't mistake a substance for substance.

Drugs Destroy Dreams!

Drugs vs. alcohol: It doesn't matter which side of the Titanic you're on.

Drug-Use Is Life Abuse

Drug-Use Is Self-Abuse

Egotism is the drug that soothes the pain of stupidity.

High and Dry: an AA member who thinks they can still take drugs.

How you get to be an old-timer: Don't drink; don't drug; don't die.

If the drugs don't kill you, the lifestyle will.

If you have to control your drugging, it must be out of control.

If you have to control your using, what's the point of using?

If you want to drink and drug, that's your business; if you don't, that's mine.

Nothing is so bad that a drink or drug won't make it worse.

One is too many and more not enough.

Our program does not teach us how to handle drinking and drugging. It teaches us how to handle recovery.

People who say you can't talk about drugs in an AA meeting are usually on them.

Reality is for people who can't handle drugs.

Recovery delivers everything drugs promised.

Switching from one drug to another is like switching seats on the Titanic.

There is no tragedy bad enough that a drink or drug won't make it worse and there is no success good enough that a toast won't toast you.

We don't have to drug to die.

We're not against drugs, we're for recovery.

When you're home by yourself you're behind enemy lines.

You are only one drink away from a drunk, one hit away from a high.

You must learn to pick up a program, not just set down a drug!

Drunk:

A drunk alone...is in poor company.

A drunk is a sick human being trying to get well, not a bad one trying to be good.

A newcomer at his first meeting: "Where are all the drunks?"

Anyone can be a drunk. It takes an effort to be an alcoholic even a bigger effort to be a sober alcoholic.

Anything you did drunk, you can do better sober.

Better to have someone sober and hating you because you told them the truth, rather than drunk and liking you because you told them a lie.

Carry the message, not the drunk.

Confucius say, "Never get in a pissing contest with a skunk." (or as we say, "a drunk.")

Driving drunk: Drive hammered, get nailed.

Drunkenness is nothing but voluntary madness.

If you drink near beer, consider yourself near drunk, and then consider yourself near sober.

If you hang around those that drink, they'll get you drunk before you get them sober.

If you take a drunken horse thief and sober him up, you have a sober horse thief.

If you think it's easy being a drunk, drink again.

If you want to see who the drunk is, look for who's shouting for the manager.

It's the first drink that gets you drunk.

One drink =one drunk

Remember that a wrong act will prey upon your mind until you either do something to rectify it or get drunk.

Some say if you can't remember your last drunk, you may not have had it.

Stopping drinking is easy, it's staying stopped that's hard.

The first drink gets you drunk.

The worst day sober is better than the best day drunk.

There will always be problems, whether you're drunk or sober.

Those who quarrel with a drunk injure the absent.

Walking drunk man.

When the pain of staying sober becomes less than the pain of getting drunk, you'll stay sober.

You don't get drunk watching another drink; you don't get serenity watching another do the steps.

You may have another drunk in you, but another recovery?

Your best thinking got you drunk.

Your job is to carry the message, not deliver the drunk.

Dry:
Detox: Spin Dry

High and Dry: An AA member who thinks they can still take drugs.

It counts, wet or dry, if it gets you high.

The only boat that doesn't rock is the one in dry dock!

Wet or dry, you get high.

White knuckle it.

Easy (Does it):
Cooperating with God *is* the easier softer way.

Easy does it – Lazy doesn't.

Easy does it (but do it).

Everything is going to be All Right.

It may be a simple program, but it's not easy.

It's a lot easier to react than it is to think.

It's easier to stay out of trouble than it is to get out of trouble.

It's easy to be loving. What takes work is to be kind.

Nothing is as easy as it seems.

Oozy Does It

Recovery really is simple, it's just not always easy.

Staying sober is simple, not easy.

Stopping drinking is easy, it's staying stopped that's hard.

The easier, softer way is one through twelve.

There is no speeding in the "trudging" zone.

When 'easy' does it—sometimes it is only half done!!!

When things get easy, it's easy to stop growing.

Ego:

Advice is the least heeded when most needed.

Alcoholics' Anthem: "I Was Always on My Mind."

An alcoholic is an egomaniac with an inferiority complex.

An alcoholic only knows one note on the scale: Me, Me, Me.

At the end of the game, the Queen and the Pawn go into the same box.

Being a part of something is more important that being the center of attention.

Do not climb the mountain so that you can look down on others.

Don't let your ego be the first thing people see when you walk onto a room.

Don't let your newcomer ego get tied up in being an "Old-timer."

EGO = "I" Strain

Ego is our separation from God and others.

Egotism is that certain something that enables a man in a rut to think he's in a groove.

Egotism is the drug that soothes the pain of stupidity.

Egotism isn't necessarily thinking a lot of yourself—just thinking of yourself a lot.

Lego your Ego

Members who think they know it all are especially annoying to those of us who do.

My ego: K-mart insides and Gucci outsides.

None are so empty as those who are full of themselves.

The definition of an addict: an egomaniac with an inferiority complex.

The only block between you and God, is your ego.

The smallest package in the world is an alcoholic all wrapped up in himself.

Time is the ego's enemy, not love's.

Two things alcoholics have in common: We are all alcoholics, and we all think we're smarter than everyone else.

We are all important, but not for the reasons we think.

When your head begins to swell your mind stops growing.

Whether we think good things about ourselves or whether we think bad things about ourselves, mostly we are thinking about ourselves.

Emotion(s): *Also see:* Anger, Alone, Hate, Fear, *and* Feel(ings):

Emotional security is a process—not a goal.

Emotions aren't facts.

Emotions destroy intelligence.

Fear is not a shortcoming, it's an emotion. Our reaction to it can be the shortcoming.

My emotional circumstances often keep me from seeing my spiritual possibilities.

NO self-pity. The moment this emotion strikes, do something nice for someone less fortunate than you.

Spiritual and emotional growth does not depend so much upon success as it does upon failures and setbacks.

The good news is you get your emotions back; the bad news is you get your emotions back.

You don't have to get emotional about your feelings.

You're in trouble when you get emotionally involved with yourself.

Enabling(er): *Also see* Al-anon

Don't let your overdoing may be your undoing.

"No" is a complete sentence.

They can't walk all over you unless you lay down.

Try not to be a persecutor, victim or enabler.

Enjoy: *See* Joy(ous, ful, enjoy):

Enthusiasm (astic):

Be as enthusiastic about (___) A as you were about your using.

Depression: anger without enthusiasm.

Enthusiasm makes life enjoyable. Generate some!

Evil:

An alcoholic reading about the evils of drink, will give up reading.

Don't assume evil motives for what stupidity can explain.

'Evil' is 'live' spelled backwards.

See no evil, hear no evil, date no evil.

To be afraid is to have more faith in evil than in good.

Example(s):

A self sponsored person is a good example of unskilled labor.

Few things are harder to put up with than the annoyance of a good example.

If you can't be a good example, then you'll just have to be a horrible warning.

Excuses:

Blaming our parents is a perfect excuse for our shortcomings.

Do not become one of these people who have two excuses for everything: one excuse for what you don't do and another for what you don't have.

Don't be good at making excuses.

Everybody makes mistakes. Fools repeat them, the weak excuse them, only the wise admit and profit from them.

Everything after "but" is BS.

Everything after the word "But" cancels out everything before it.

Heredity is a perfect excuse for our shortcomings.

Hoping and wishing are excuses for doing nothing.

If you really don't want to find a solution, you will find an excuse.

The worst abuse excuse: it's not that bad yet.

There are a million excuses to drink, but no *good* reason.

There are no good reasons for anger, only excuses.

There are no good reasons for drinking, only excuses.

Expectation(s):
A resentment is like drinking poison and expecting the other person to die.
Attitude: You get what you expect in life.
Concepts like *slow* and *late* are always relative to expectations.
Do you expect a reward for accepting the greatest gift of your life?
Doesn't expecting the unexpected make the unexpected become the expected?
Expect a miracle.
Expect nothing. Blame no one. Do something.
Expectations are premeditated resentments.
Expectations are resentments waiting to happen.
Experience is what you get when you were expecting something else
Faith is confident expectation.
If you can't expect a miracle, at least expect a coincidence.
If you start your day with the expectation that nothing meaningful will occur, you won't be disappointed.
Insanity is doing the same thing over and over again and expecting different results.
Just accept, don't expect.
My sanity is inversely proportional to my expectations.
Plan Plans, Not Results.
Serenity comes when you stop expecting and start accepting.
The problem relationship: excessive demands coupled with unrealistic expectations.
The road to resentment is paved with expectation.
We are given the lesson of humility when we least expect or want it.
When you are having a bad day, lower your expectations and start over!
You get what you expect.

Experience:
AA: Experience the difference, where the difference is experience.
Experience is something you don't get until *after* you need it.
Experience is the name everyone gives to their mistakes.
Experience is the thing that enables you to recognize a mistake when you make it again.
Experience is what you get when you don't get what you want.
Experience is what you get when you were expecting something else.
Experience the 12-Steps, don't examine them.
It pays to believe in miracles. In Alcoholics Anonymous we experience them.
Life should be a pattern of experiences to savor, not to endure.
Nothing is a waste of time if we use the experience wisely.
Share your experience, strength, and hope.
There is a difference between sharing our experience and imposing our opinions on someone.

Facts:
Although thoughts are things, they are not actions; although feelings are real, they are not facts.
Believe that life is worth living and your belief will create the fact.
Facts can be stubborn things. Emotions aren't facts.
Feelings are not facts.

God wants for you what you would want for yourself, IF you had all the facts.
There is a difference between factual information and honesty.

Fail(ure):
A man may fall many times, but he is not a failure unless he thinks somebody keeps pushing him.
Any failure will tell you—success is nothing but luck.
Count the lessons learned from failures as rungs upon the ladder of progress.
Dishonesty and reservations precede failure.
Don't be afraid to try something for fear you will fail; if you have not the will to try you have already failed.
Failure is a necessary pathway to success.
Failure is success if you learn from it.
Failure is the easier softer way.
Failure isn't fatal; success isn't permanent.
Failure isn't in falling down, it's in failing to get back up.
Failures always blame someone else.
Follow success and you will be successful; follow failure and you will fail; stick with the winners and you will be a winner.
Formula for failure: trying to please everyone.
God won't fail you (people will).
He who fails to plan, plans to fail.
If you have never failed, you have never risked.
It's the things you do wrong, your failings that are often the bridge to other people.
Many of us fail to recognize "opportunity" because most of the time it is disguised as hard work.
No person is a failure who has friends.
Nothing beats failure like a try.
Our imperfections and failures are as much a blessing from God as our successes and talents.
Spiritual and emotional growth does not depend so much upon success as it does upon failures and setbacks
Success and failure share a common denominator; both are temporary!
Success is never fatal; failure is never final.
The only mistakes that become failures are the ones we don't learn from.
The only time you *don't fail* is the last time you try anything - and it works.
The two hardest things in life to handle are success and failure.
There is no such thing as failure; there is only feedback.
We are not failing as long as we are trying.
When all else fails try God. Or you can take the shortcut and start with Her.
When all else fails, follow directions.
When everything else fails, working with another will save the day.

Fair:
'Life ain't fair' is the war cry of the slipper.
Life isn't fair, life isn't just, life is just what it is.
Life may not be fair, but God is.

Faith:
Excuses are simply a lack of faith.
Faith can't be taught; it can only be caught.
Faith chases away fear.
Faith conquers fear.
Faith gives us that feeling of protection.
Faith is a lit doorway; doubt is a dark hall
Faith is capitalizing on the belief of others.
Faith is confident expectation.
Faith is fear that has said it's prayer's.
Faith is hope in things unseen.
Faith is not belief without proof, it is trust without reservations.
Faith is our greatest gift. Sharing it with others is our greatest responsibility.
Faith is seeing light with your heart, when all your eyes see is the darkness ahead.
Faith is spelled a-c-t-i-o-n.
Faith should be our steering wheel, not our spare tire.
Faith was the first medicine known to man.
Faith without action is like sitting on a dictionary to learn how to spell.
Faith without works is dead.
Faith: If you don't believe, than make believe.
Fear is the absence of faith.
Fear knocked on the door. Faith answered; there was no one there.
Feed your faith and your doubts will starve to death.
God gives us problems—not to test our faith but to strengthen our faith.
God knows the strength of your faith. You're the one who needs reminding.
Have faith in the things you have not seen because of the things you have.
If faith without works is dead then; willingness without action is fantasy.
If you are questioning your faith, God already has you working on the problem.
If you have faith in God, it doesn't make much difference if you have faith in yourself.
It is when you act on faith that you actually have it.
Keep the fear down and the faith up.
Procrastination is fear in five syllables. Patience is faith in two.
Sorrow looks back. Worry looks around. Faith looks up.
To be afraid is to have more faith in evil than in good.
We who have done so little with so much now find with "Faith" we can do anything with nothing.

Fake it:
Fake it 'til you make it.

Family's Anonymous:
Addiction is not a spectator sport. The whole family gets to participate.
Alcoholism is not a spectator sport. The whole family gets to participate.
Before engaging your mouth, put your mind in gear.
Choose Calm over Chaos.
Do not do for them what they can do for themselves.
Don't just do something. Stand there!
Don't let your overdoing be your undoing.

Don't love them to death.
Don't care. You don't have to.
Formula for failure: try to please your kids.
Give up control, *but never give up hope.*
Highest good of all concerned
If you're not part of the solution, you're part of the precipitate.
Insanity is hereditary. You get it from your kids.
It helps to learn the difference between being responsible to others and being responsible for others.
Just Say Know.
Know your "NOs."
Letting go is not caring for, but caring about.
No is a complete sentence.
Rule 62: Never take yourself too seriously!
They must claim their "response-ability."
TRUST HAPPENS
Wash his mouth out with hope.
What are you doing, suffering someone else's pain?
You deserve more.
You either face the issue or you face destruction.

Faults: *Also see* Defect(s)
Accept your virtues or be overwhelmed with your faults.
Almost all of our faults are more pardonable than the methods we think up to hide them.
Criticism and finding fault are not spiritual gifts.
God looks beyond our faults to see our needs.
It is not your job to point out other people's faults.
It may not be your fault, but it's your choice.
People who seek a sponsor without faults, will be without a sponsor.
People who seek friends without faults, will be without friends.
The greatest fault of all is to be conscious of none.
When looking for faults use a mirror, not a telescope.
Your fault, my mistake.
Your feelings aren't somebody else's fault.

Fear: *Also see* Afraid
All fear is about either not getting what you want or losing what you already have.
Anxiety is fear of oneself.
Anxiety is fear that has not yet been identified.
Change only happens when the pain of holding on is greater than the fear of letting go.
Courage is fear that has said its prayers.
Courage is not the absence of fear, but the ability to overcome it.
Courage is not the absence of fear; it is the ability to act in the presence of fear
Don't fear taking a big step when one is needed. You can't cross a chasm in two small jumps.
Don't let fear fool you.
Faith chases away fear.
Faith conquers fear.
Faith is fear that has said it's prayer's.

Fear exists only when you are running from it.
Fear faced is fear erased.
Fear has no power unless you give it power.
Fear is just a four letter word.
Fear is not a shortcoming, it's an emotion. Our reaction to it can be the shortcoming.
Fear is the absence of faith.
Fear is the darkroom where negatives are developed.
Fear is the mother of all character defects.
Fear is what keeps you from God's plan for you.
Fear of expressing ourselves makes us prisoners of our thoughts.
Feelings of "inferiority" & "superiority" are the same. They both come from fear.
If you have a sense of impending doom, it could be that doom is impending.
It is only when we are relieved of our fear of the results that we have a choice.
Keep the fear down and the faith up.
Living in fear is like paying interest on a loan you don't own.
Love the best in others and never fear their worst.
Nothing about life is to be feared; it is only to be understood.
People with fear of commitment have trouble subscribing to a magazine for more than one year.
Procrastination is fear in five syllables. Patience is faith in two.
Resentment is when you didn't get your way yesterday. Anger is when you don't get your way today. Fear is that you won't get your way tomorrow.
The fear of feeling the pain is worse than the pain itself.
Turn fear into faith through fellowship.
UFO's Unidentified Fear Objects.
We all suffer from self-centered fear.
We fear the things we want the most.
When you judge others you are revealing your own fears and prejudices.
When you think of yesterday without regret and tomorrow without fear, you are on the road to recovery.
Worry is interest on fear.

Feel(ings): *Also See* Emotion(s)
Al-Anon doesn't give us the choice between feeling good or feeling bad; it gives us the choice between feeling and not feeling.
Although thoughts are things, they are not actions; although feelings are real, they are not facts.
An action beats a feeling.
Be stronger at what you're doing, than your feelings are at what they're doing.
Change the thought, and the feeling must go.
Do the right thing despite how you feel.
Don't listen to your feelings because they lie to you.
Don't take everything personally.
Don't worry about finding your feelings; they will find you.
Don't judge yourself by the way you feel.
Feel, Deal and Heal (Feel it, Deal with it and then Heal from it).
Feelings are data. They tell you something about yourself.
Feelings are nine times more powerful than the intellect.

Feelings are not facts.

Feelings of inferiority and superiority are the same. They both come from fear.

Feelings won't kill you, but killing your feelings will.

Good feelings or bad feelings are the same; it's the feeling that's uncomfortable.

Hope is the feeling you have that the feeling you have isn't permanent.

How you feel is rarely an indication of how you're doing.

If you don't deal with your feelings. They'll deal with you.

If you want to feel better, clean house. If you want to get better, find God.

If you want to keep feeling how you're feeling, then keep doing what your are doing.

It is easier to live your way into good feeling than to feel your way into good living.

Love is less a feeling than a thousand tiny acts of kindness.

Move your feet; the feelings will follow.

Name it, Claim it, Tame it!!!

Numb is dumb; feel to heal.

The good news is, your feelings come back. The bad news is, your feelings come back.

Think, Think, Think. Not-Feel, Feel, Feel!

We are responsible for what we do, no matter how we feel.

When you feel left out, reach out.

When you practice principles, how you feel is not the point.

You are not responsible for their feelings, just your behavior.

You cannot feel your way into better behavior. You must behave your way into better feelings.

You don't have to get emotional about your feelings.

Your feelings aren't somebody else's fault.

Fellowship:

I can't... We can...

If you don't want what we have, we will cheerfully refund your misery.

If you have one hand in the fellowship and one hand in God's, you can't get drunk today.

It's AnonymoUS, not AnonymoME.

Never judge a member of the fellowship by their bumper sticker.

People in our fellowships who think they are too big to do little things are perhaps too little to be asked to do big things.

The fellowship is full of willing people. Five percent are willing to do the work and ninety-five percent are willing to let them.

There are people with money and there are rich people. In the fellowship we are indeed rich.

This is a "We" program, not a "Me" program.

Today, "we" have a choice.

Turn fear into faith through fellowship.

We are a fel*low*ship because we fell low.

We don't care why you're here, it's why you stay.

We may not have it all together, BUT together we have it ALL!

What we have in common are more important than our differences.

You never *have to be* alone again.

Fight

Am I finished with fighting?

Conflict cannot survive without your participation.

Don't fight drink, strengthen sobriety.

Don't fight drugs, strengthen recovery.
Fight the urge to fight: replace it with surrender.
If you keep fighting yourself and keep losing, you are the winner!
It's not the size of the dog in the fight, but the size of the fight in the dog.

Find(found):
Believe those who are seeking the truth and doubt those who have found it.
Find humility before it finds you.
If you can't find God, who moved?
If you do not find "the peace of mind" you keep hearing about in AA, try working the Steps.
If you don't have a God, let mine stand in until you find your own.
If you find a path with no obstacles, it probably doesn't lead anywhere.
If you want to feel better, clean house. If you want to get better, find God.
If you want to stay sober, you will find a way. If not, you will find an excuse.
It's not a question of finding the right person, but becoming the right person.
People who don't go to meetings don't find out what happens to people who don't go to meetings.
Sometimes you have to stop looking to find what you need.
Stop looking, you've found it.
When you can't find the solution to a problem, look for the soulution to the problem.
When you find yourself in a hole, stop digging.
Where do you find recovery? Twelve steps past any lengths.

First: *Also see* First Fix, Pill, or Drink *and* Steps
A newcomer at his first meeting: "Where are all the drunks?"
Don't commit suicide during the first five years sober (you'll be killing the wrong person.)
First Aid First
First Things First
God liked the first 12-Step meeting so much He hasn't missed one since.
Have patience with all things, but first with yourself.
It's more important to get it right, than get it first.
Sponsor: In the first year, it's my way or the high way and I do mean *high.*
The first step in overcoming mistakes is to admit them.
The first thing you put ahead of your sobriety will be the second thing you lose.
The first year is free.
The first-time sober is a gift; why waste it?
The only meeting you are ever late for is the first one.
When someone hugs you let them be the first to let go.
You can't be first, but you could be next.

First Fix, Pill, or Drink:
If you take the first drink then your PAST becomes your FUTURE!
Just Don't Pick Up the First One
There are no fatal decisions, as long as you don't pick up that first fix, pill, or drink.
There's no problem that can't be made worse by picking up a fix, pill, or drink.
Thirst things first
We are without a defense against the first drink; our defense must come from a power greater than ourselves.

Force:
If you have to force the solution, then it's not the solution.
Don't force solutions.
May the Force be with you.
The death of our addiction forces us to confront life.

Forget: *Also see* Blackout
A short version of the serenity prayer: Forget it!
Forgetting how to smile is part of an alcoholic's memory loss.
Please Lord, teach us to laugh again, but, God, don't let us ever forget that we cried.
The nights you can't remember are the nights you'll never forget
Yesterday is gone; forget it. Tomorrow never comes; don't worry. Today is here; get busy.
You live, you learn; you drink, you forget.

Forgive(ness):
Acceptance is forgiveness.
Forgiveness detoxifies.
Forgiveness is giving up hope for a better past!
Forgiveness is not an event – it's a process.
Forgiveness of others is a gift to yourself.
Going to any length means forgiving the person who has injured you the most.
In order for us to forgive someone else, we must first forgive ourselves.
Learning to forgive takes practice.
On final judgment day, do you want what you deserve or do you want a forgiving God?
Practice forgiveness for your own sake, if not for others.
The flip side to forgiveness is resentment.
The number one way to relieve pain is to forgive.
To forgive is to set a prisoner free and to discover that the prisoner was you.
You accept God's forgiveness by extending it to others.
You cannot learn to love yourself until you can learn to forgive yourself.
You don't have to forgive people, places, and things, if you don't blame people, places, and things.

Free(dom):
And the truth shall set you free, but not 'till it's finished with you.
As long as you blame your past, you're not free to claim your future.
By releasing resentment, we set ourselves free.
Constant decision making is the price of freedom.
If we were to live—we had to be free of our anger.
Remember, we were all born to be happy, joyous, and free.
Ride sober, live free.
Serenity is not freedom from the storm, but peace within the storm.
The suggestions are free. You only have to pay for the ones you don't use.
The truth will set you free but first it may piss you off.

Friends: *Also see* Relationships
A true friend will put a finger on your faults without rubbing it in.
Best vitamin for making friends: B1

Friends don't let friends drive naked.
Hot words make a cool friendship.
If you hang around those that drink, they'll get you drunk before you get them sober.
Measure others by their best moments, not their worst.
People who seek friends without faults—will be without friends.
Probably any one of us can get along with perfect people, but our task is to get along with imperfect people.
Real friends are those who, when you feel you've made a fool of yourself, don't feel you've done a permanent job.
Stand by the coffee pot. It's a good way to meet people.
The people you hang with are the people you hang with.
There are friends for a reason, a season, or a lifetime.
We don't have to change friends if we understand that friends change.
When I accept you as you are and me as I am, then we can be friends.
When you think about how hard it is to change yourself, you should know how hard it will be to change your friends.

Fun(ny): *Also see* Humor
There is nothing funnier than a holier-than-thou recovering alcoholic—unless it is a holier-than-thou nonrecovering alcoholic.
You know what's funny about alcoholics? We think we're not.

Future: *See* Past, Present, & Future

GA (Gambler's Anonymous):
Act your wage.
Too much * Too often * Too long

Game(s):
Not all accomplishments are rum and games.
Only losers can win this game.

Generous:
Generosity Generates

Geographical Cure:
Beware of the "Geographical cure" and the simple "Spouse-ectomy."
Don't run from, run to.
No matter how fast or how far you go, you can't out run yourself.
No matter how fast or how far you go, you can't outrun God.
Wherever you are, be there.
Wherever you go, there you are.
You can't run from God, so let God run you.

Gift(s):
Criticism and finding fault are not spiritual gifts.
Faith is our greatest gift. Sharing it with others is our greatest responsibility.
Forgiveness of others is a gift to yourself.

Guilt: the gift that keeps on giving.
Our Higher Power gives us many gifts in sobriety. We just have to remember to unwrap them.
Pain is the greatest gift God gives to the alcoholic.
Sobriety is a gift.
Sobriety is a grant, not a gift. A gift is something we get to keep forever. A grant is contingent on us doing something to keep it.
Sobriety is God's gift to me; what I do with it is my gift to God.
The first-time sober is a gift; why waste it?
The talents you have are God's gift to you; what you do with those talents is your gift to God.
Today is a gift; that's why it's called the present.
Yesterday is but a dream, tomorrow but a vision. Today well lived is a gift, that's why they call it the Present.
Yesterday is history, tomorrow is a mystery, but today is a gift—that's why they call it the present.
Your kindness is a gift to another and the tag reads, "Handle with tender loving care."
Your kindness is a gift to another and the tag reads, "Handle with tender loving payer."
Your willingness to listen is your gift to others.

Give(ing):
Depression: when you're taking more than you're giving.
Don't go to a meeting looking for what you can get; look for what you can give.
Give drugs an inch, and they will become your ruler.
Give time, time.
Give to God and God will give to you.
Give us ninety days and if you don't want what we have, your misery will be cheerfully refunded.
Give your program what's right, not what's left.
God will never give you more than you can handle.
Guilt, the gift that keeps on giving.
If you continually give, you will continually have.
In order for someone to "give" you a bad day, you have to "take" it.
In order to keep it, you have to give it away.
It is characteristic of the humor in the Universe that we are given free will and then told to give it back!
Love isn't love until you give it away.
Pain is the greatest gift God gives to the alcoholic.
The barometer of where your are in your life, is not what you have, but what you can give.
The best way to keep recovery is to give it away.
The greatest gift you can give anyone is your full attention.
The harder it is to give something up, the more you know you should.
The only thing we take from this world when we leave is what we gave away.
The people you most need to give love to, will seem like the ones who deserve it the least.
There is plenty to go around of what you give away.
We keep what we have by giving it away!
We know that God has a sense of humor. He gives us free will and then asks us to give it back.
We make a living by what we get. We make a life by what we give.
We must give away what we cannot keep so we might receive what we cannot lose.

What a big difference there is between giving advice and lending a hand.
You came here demanding justice and you were graciously given mercy.
You can't give away something you don't have.
You can't keep it unless you give it away.
You have received without cost, now give without charge.
You have to give it away to keep it.
You need all the help you can give.

Give Up
An alcoholic reading about the evils of drink, will give up reading.
Desire chip: Give up the high cost of low living.
Do you really want to give up the defect? Or do you just want to give up the result of the defect?
Don't give up before the miracle happens.
Forgiveness is giving up hope for a better past!
Give up control, *but never give up hope.*
Never give up on anybody. Miracles happen every day.
Surrender is victory. We win by giving up the fight.
The fastest way to end an argument is to give up being right.
The only way to get to be right is to give up being right.
The steps: Give up. (Steps 1,2,3) Clean up. (4,5,6) Make up. (7,8,9) Keep up. (10,11,12).
You can keep going after you think you can't.
You give things up, you get things.
You only have to give up one drink............the next one.

God: *Also see* Higher Power *and* God's Will *and* Prayer *and the* Chapter: Higher Power Pages
A 12-step meeting is God's workshop.
All in God Time.
Ask God not for things to enjoy life, but rather life that you may enjoy all things.
Be more concerned with what God thinks about you than what people think about you.
Call on God, but row away from the rocks.
Change the way your treat others before you question the way God treats you.
Coincidence—is the word God uses when He wants to be anonymous.
Cooperating with God is the easier softer way.
Difficulties are God's errands.
Do your best, God does the rest.
Don't expect God to use you as a *Lighthouse* somewhere else if he can't use you as a *Candle* just where you are!
Don't put anyone in God's spot.
Envision yourself as God envisions you.
Everything we have is on loan from God.
Few of us realize God is all we need, until God is all we have.
Found God? He wasn't the one that was lost.
God can't give you anything new until you let go of the old.
God can't use your light if you're trying to burn everyone with your brilliance.
God didn't save you from drowning to beat you up on the beach.
God does for us what we can't do for ourselves.
God does for you what you can't do for yourself, not what you can.

God does not live inside of you. You live inside of God.
God does the impossible after you've done what is possible.
God doesn't make junk, but some of the goods do have defects.
God doesn't make junk.
God doesn't need much; whatever you have left is enough.
God gave you two ears and only one mouth for a reason.
God gives us faces; we create our own expressions.
God has three answers to everything: yes, no, and if you insist.
God helps those who let Him do His job.
God is closer to you than you are to yourself.
God is not an outside issue.
God is the answer. Now what is the problem?
God is upstairs in church on Sunday morning, but at night He's in the basement at the AA meeting.
God lends us people when we need them.
God liked the first 12-Step meeting so much He hasn't missed one since.
God plus one is always a majority.
God speaks through people, don't worry about which ones.
God wants spiritual fruit, not religious nuts.
God won't fail you (people will).
God works through people and gets twice the result for the same amount of work – for both are helped.
God, would not have put us through the wringer if He did not think we were worth laundering.
God's business is making miracles and you are one of them.
God's last name isn't "Damn."
He who kneels before God can stand before anyone.
Helping hands are God's hands.
Humans invented alcohol; God invented the ocean. Whom do you trust?
If the GOD talk drives you out, BOOZE will bring you back.
If you can't find God, who moved?
If you don't believe in God, we suggest you change your mind.
If you don't have a God, let mine stand in until you find your own.
If you have faith in God, it doesn't make much difference if you have faith in myself.
If you have one hand in the fellowship and one hand in God's, you can't pick up today.
If you think you are having a problem with God, just try to imagine the problem She is having with you!
If you want to feel better, clean house. If you want to get better, find God.
Instead of defining God for yourself, let God define Himself for you.
Is it odd, or is it God?
It's a God thing.
Let go and let God.
Listen to your heart often, God lives there.
Looking for God is like a fish looking for water.
Most people want to serve God, but only in an advisory capacity.
Nervousness is just God trying to shake the truth out of you.
No God, No Peace. Know God, Know Peace.
No God, No Recovery   *   Know God, Know Recovery.
Nothing is impossible in God's world.

On final judgment day, do you want what you deserve or do you want a forgiving God?
Our need is God's opportunity.
Pain is the greatest gift God gives to the alcoholic.
Patience is giving God space.
Rather than using God to solve your problems, use your problems to get closer to God.
Re: God. There is one, and it's *not you*.
Recovery leads us to God, and God leads us to ourselves.
Recovery, on loan from God.
Rejection is God's protection.
Relax. God is in charge.
Religion is man talking to man about God. Spirituality is God and Man talking.
Remember, God still makes house calls.
Reputation is what people think of us. Character is what God knows about us.
Responsibility: Your response to God's ability.
See God in someone else or you will never see God in yourself.
Serenity is God's garden. The entrance is though our hearts.
Sobriety is God's gift to you; what you do with it is your gift to God.
Sobriety, on loan from God.
Thank God for what you have, TRUST GOD for what you need.
The character of God is not determined by your opinion of Him.
The difference between us and God is that God knows the end of the story.
The main difference between God and you is that God doesn't think he is you.
The most important relationship you have is between God and yourself.
The person who looks up to God, rarely looks down on anyone.
The Spirit within is stronger than the Spirits poured in.
There are no coincidences, only situations where God chooses to remain anonymous.
There are no coincidences, they say, only God-incidences.
There are really only two choices: worry or trust God.
There is nothing we can do to make God love us more than God already does.
There is nothing we can do wrong that will make God love us any less.
There is only one thing you need to know about God, you are not He/She/It!
Think God
Trust God, Clean house, and Work with Others.
We are not different from others, God just made us special.
What if there is no God? Believe anyway.
When God made time, He made plenty of it.
When God measures us, He puts the tape around the heart instead of the head.
When we get tangled up in our problems, be still. That way God can untangle the knot.
Who is LARGE and in CHARGE?
You accept God's forgiveness by extending it to others.

God's Will (God's Plan) *Also see* Guide(ance):
Everything in God's time (and God doesn't wear a watch.)
Everything that is happening is God's plan for you today.
God can't do *what*? Ha ha ha ha ha…
God did not bring you this far only to drop you on your face.
God didn't do it!
God does Her best work anonymously.

God does not hurry.

God does not want you to do extraordinary things; He wants you to do ordinary things extraordinarily well.

God does not work well under supervision.

God doesn't make mistakes.

God is my employer...

God is never late.

God may be slow, but never late.

God may give you these seeds, but you have to plant them yourself.

God never asks about our ability or our inability, just our availability.

God wants for you what you would want for yourself, IF you had all the facts.

God will never give you more than you can handle, but He didn't count on you piling on yesterday and tomorrow.

God will never give you more than you can handle.

God will not close one door without opening another.

God's will for us is our well being.

God's will: you've turned it over. Self-will: you've over turned it.

God's will: You can't do His will, your way.

God's will: You can't sit in a closet and pray to God to bring you a hot dog.

I will to will your will. ~ CDA First Edition, Page 48

If God takes you to it, He will walk you through it.

If it's something you want, it's your will. If it's something that happens to you, it's God's will.

If you don't remember what God did for you yesterday, you'll have trouble trusting Him today.

If you pray for a Porsche and God sends you a jackass, *ride it.*

If you want to know God's will, spend time with Him.

Let God do for you what you can not do for yourself.

Life may not be fair, but God is.

No matter how fast or how far you go, you can't outrun God.

Nobody dies without God's permission.

Nothing in God's world happens by mistake.

Recovery is God's will for you.

Removing your life and will from God is not as easy as you may think.

Start here

Surrender means following the direction God's finger is pointing.

The basic ingredient of all humility is a desire to seek and do God's will.

The nice thing about calling God? You know you will not get His answering machine.

The will of God will never take you where the grace of God will not protect you

There is no way to know God's Will unless you do it.

There's your plan and there's God's plan. Yours doesn't matter.

Turn your life over to God and take it out of the hands of an idiot.

We know that God has a sense of humor. He gives us free will and then asks us to give it back.

What will be...will appear.

When all else fails, try God. Or you can take the shortcut and start with Him.

Where God guides, He provides.

You are exactly where God wants you to be.

You can't run from God, so let God run you.

You may not always know God's will. But you ALWAYS know what it is NOT!

Good:
A drunk is a sick human being trying to get well, not a bad one trying to be good.
A good life is of more value than good living.
A good marriage means falling in love many times—always with the same person.
Don't be good at making excuses.
Every good thought is a prayer.
Few things are harder to put up with than the annoyance of a good example.
For romance in AA, the odds are good and goods are odd.
God does not make junk but some of the goods do have defects.
Good enough never is.
Good feelings or bad feelings are the same; it's the feeling that's uncomfortable.
Good things get better when they are shared.
Hope is knowing the good in us will overcome the bad.
If you can't be a good example, then you'll just have to be a horrible warning.
Nothing is all good and nothing is all bad.
Show genuine willingness to God through good actions and not good acting.
Sobriety is like sex. If it doesn't feel good, you're not doing it right.
Some people are so successful in A.A. they turn out almost as good as they used to think they were when they were drinking.
Sometimes the good is the enemy of the best.
The good news is, we don't *have* to drink anymore.
There are a million excuses to drink, but no *good* reason.
There are good days and great days. The good days are when everything goes your way and you don't drink. The great days are when *nothing* goes your way and you don't drink.
There is a bit of good in the worst of us and a bit of bad in the best of us.
There's only one thing worse to an alcoholic than bad fortune, and that's good fortune.
To an alcoholic, if one is good, one in every color is better.
To be afraid, is to have more faith in evil than in good.
We never obsess about anything good.
What starts out bad can't end up good.
When things are going great, sobriety is good. When things are going bad, sobriety is better.
When you do good, you never know how much good you do.
You are heading towards a slip when you remember the good times more than the bad.
You used to be good at being bad. Now you're going to get good a being good.

Gossip:
If anyone speaks badly of you, live so no one will believe it.

Grace:
Co-operate with Grace
From Shame to Grace
Grace is getting what you don't deserve and mercy is *not* getting what you do deserve.
Our reprieve from using is a daily grace contingent upon a spiritual base.
The will of God will never take you where the grace of God will not protect you
There but for the grace of God, go I.
When I am grate-full, I am grace-filled.

Gratitude (Grateful): *Also see* Thank(ful)
Anger: from grateful to hateful in a second.
Be grateful you have been given two ears and only one mouth.
Grateful addicts don't drink and drug and drinking and drugging addicts aren't grateful.
Grateful alcoholics don't drink, and drinking alcoholics aren't grateful.
Grateful I'm not dead.
Gratitude and acceptance always help, no matter what the circumstances.
Gratitude gratifies
Gratitude is not the word but the desire to say the word.
Gratitude, that's the attitude.
If you are not grateful for your sobriety, you will not stay sober.
If you are treated today as you deserve to be, be grateful.
If you can't make a list of all you are grateful you have, make a list of all you are grateful you don't have.
If your heart is full of gratitude, there is no room for resentment.
It's hard work taking everyone else's inventory. Worst of all, they seldom seem grateful!
It's hard to be Grateful when you're Hateful.
Keep an attitude of gratitude.
Misery is an option. But acceptance and gratitude did not come as standard equipment either.
My gratitude speaks when I care and share the NA Way
No two of us are alike, that should make us grateful!
Reason to be grateful: you learn to wake up instead of coming to.
Replace guilt with gratitude.
Service is gratitude in action.
Some people grumble because the roses have thorns instead of being grateful that the thorns have roses.
The difference between feeling grateful and being grateful, is action.
When you have gratitude, you don't have attitude.
When you're filled with regrets of yesterday and worries about tomorrow, you've lost today in which to be grateful.
Write a gratitude list and count your blessings.
You can't be grateful and hateful at the same time because you can't serve two masters.

Grave:
From Rave to Grave
Share with your sponsor the "take it to the grave" stuff.
The difference between a rut and a grave is its depth.

Group(s): *Also see* Meeting(s)
Heard it through the group-vine.
If you are looking for the perfect group before you join a home group, you are going to be homeless.
One Group, One Vote, One family
Sometimes our individual actions damage the group.
The steps are to get us well. The traditions are to get the group well. Since we are part of the group, we must also work the traditions.

Growth:
All growth is not painful but all pain can be growthful.
Growing old is mandatory, growing up is optional.
Growing old is natural... Growing up is spiritual...
If small things make you angry-how big are you?
In order to keep growing, like a plant, we cannot be potted or plastic.
It's hard to see the growth in ourselves; it's much easier to see it in others.
Learn to grow and grow to learn.
Pain is the touchstone of growth.
Self-centeredness is a casualty of spiritual growth.
Show up to grow up.
The growth process is worth the pain as you transform into the person you have always pretended to be.
The only difference between stumbling blocks and stepping stones is how we use them.
The pain of growth is a good sign, not a stop sign.
There are only two sins: To stand in the way of someone else's growth, or to stand in the way of your own.
There is absolutely no pain in change or growth. The pain is in the resistance to the change or growth.
We grow only when we push ourselves beyond what we already know.
When things get easy it's easy to stop growing.
When you try to impress others with your growth, your halo becomes a noose!
When your head begins to swell, your mind stops growing

Grudge(s): *Also see* Resent(ments)
A Grudge is a heavy thing to carry.
Warning: Carrying a grudge can be hazardous to your health.

Guide(ance) *Also see* God's Will (God's Plan):
A sponsor is a push when stalled, a guide when you're lost, a smile when you're sad—and love.
A rudder will not guide a boat until the boat is moving.
Guidance shows us which is the right side—not which side is right.
My problems are guidelines, not stop signs.
Where God guides, He provides.

Guided Visualization: See also Vision(alize)
Picture yourself "recovered."

Guilt(y):
Guilt is a sure sign your thinking is unnatural.
Guilt is concerned with the past. Worry is concerned about the future. Contentment enjoys the present.
Guilt: the gift that keeps on giving.
Take a vacation instead of a guilt trip.
Try to replace guilt with gratitude.
When all else fails, feel guilty.
You are not guilty; you are accountable.

Habit(s):
Acquire good habits; abandon bad habits.
The best way to break a habit is to "drop" it.

Half-measures:
Half measures do not avail us half, they avail us nothing.
Half-measures avail us nothing.
There are no shortcuts.

Hangover:
Deja Brew: The feeling you've had this hangover before.
Hangover: the wrath of grapes.

Happy(iness):
Do not search for happiness. Search for right living, and happiness will be your reward.
Do you want to be right or do you want to be happy?
Don't put off being happy until you are perfect.
For every minute you are angry with someone, you lose 60 seconds of happiness that you can never get back.
Happiness begins when comparison stops.
Happiness is a by-product of right living.
Happiness is an inside job.
Happiness is appreciating what you have, not getting what you want.
Happiness is contagious. Don't wait to catch it, be a carrier.
Happiness is falling in love with what you've got.
Happiness is found along the way, not at the end of the road.
Happiness is not a place you arrive at, it is a way you travel.
Happiness is pretty much independent of our circumstances.
Happiness is that certain something you acquire while you're too busy to be miserable.
Happiness is wanting what you have, not having what you want.
Happiness isn't getting, but giving.
Happy memories never wear out....relive them as often as you want.
Happy, Joyous, & Free
Happy, sober, and me.
If you are not happy today, what day are you waiting for?
If you are not happy with what you have, what makes you think you would be happy with more?
If you're happy, notify your face. If you're not, notify your sponsor.
It is never too late to have a happy childhood.
It says in the Big Book: "*We insist on being happy.*"
It's not your position in the world that will make you happy. It's your disposition.
It's not easy to find happiness in ourselves and it's impossible to find it elsewhere.
Remember, we were all born to be happy, joyous, and free.
Share your happiness.
Show me a crisis and I'll show you a happy alcoholic.
The best way to multiply happiness is to divide it.
The happiest people are those who discover that what they should be doing and what they are doing are the same thing.

True happiness comes to the person who seeks and finds how to help others.
True happiness is found in service.
Would you rather be right, or happy?
You aren't responsible for anyone's happiness but your own.
You can be about as happy as you decide to be.
You have a right to be happy, sober and you.

Hate(full):
Anyone can hate. It costs to love.
Hate binds you to the thing you hate.
If you are hating somebody, you might as well call them up in the middle of the night because they are sleeping like a log while you are the one losing sleep!
It's hard to be hateful when you're being grateful.
Life is a mirror: That which we hate in ourselves is what we hate in others.
You cannot be honest, open-minded, and willing if any part of you is blind including, love, hate, fear, and faith.

Head: *Also see* Mind *and* Brain
A belly full of booze and a head full of AA don't mix.
Do not rent space in your head to other people's sicknesses.
Don't let people, places and things live rent free in your head.
Fill your head with positive thoughts and there won't be room for the negative.
Resentment is like letting someone live rent-free in your head.
Stay out of your head, there's no adult supervision up there.
The liar's punishment is not that he/she is not believed, but that he/she can believe no one else.
There are twelve inches between your head and your heart, but they're not always connected.
Use your head—it's the little things that count.
When God measures us, He puts the tape around the heart instead of the head.
When you are living inside someone's head, you are out of your mind.
You get sober not with your head, but with your feet.

Heal(ing):
Feel, Deal and Heal (Feel it, Deal with it and then Heal from it)
God has no reproach for anything that God has healed.
God will heal your broken heart, if you will give Him all the pieces.
If you're paining...you're gaining; if you're feeling...you're healing.
Numb is dumb; feel to heal.
Pain heals; abuse scars.
When the pain is of no more value, the healing is instantaneous.
Your sick mind cannot heal your sick mind.

Health(y):
Don't try to be normal; try to be healthy.
Take care of your body. If you don't, where else are you going to live?
Warning: Carrying a grudge can be hazardous to your health.
We are only as healthy as our honesty.

Heart:
A good exercise for the heart is to bend down and help another up.
Abstinence makes the heart grow fonder.
If you have happiness in your heart notify your face, if you don't, notify your sponsor.
If you want to know what's in your heart, listen to your mouth.
If your heart is full of gratitude, there is no room for resentment.
Listen to your heart often, God lives there.
Never trust your tongue when your heart is bitter.
Serenity is God's garden. The entrance is though our hearts.
There are twelve inches between your head and your heart, but they're not always connected.
Two things that are bad for the heart: running up hill and running down people.
When God measures us, He puts the tape around the heart instead of the head.

Hell:
Home for the Hellidays
Religion is for people who are afraid they'll go to hell. Spirituality is for people who have been there.
Religious people hope to avoid hell; spiritual people have been there.
Sobriety doesn't open up the gates of heaven to let us in, but it sure opens the gates of hell to let us out.
The quickest way to CDA: go all the way to hell and make a U-turn.
We have to be hellthy in active addiction to learn how to be healthy in recovery.
When one door closes, another door opens. It's being in the hallway that's hell.

Help(ing): *Also see* Working with Others
Ask for help. Don't help unless asked.
Asking for help is NOT a bad thing.
Call before you drink and we will help you stay sober. Call after you drink and you will help us stay sober.
Don't drink, clean house, and help another alcoholic.
Don't look down on another person unless you are leaning over to help them up.
God helps those who let Him do His job.
Help is only a phone call away.
Helping hands are God's hands.
If you want to feel better right away, ask God to help you be of service.
Praying is asking God for help, meditating is listening for God's answer.
Rather than getting even with those that hurt you, the challenge is to get even with those that help you.
Taped to a bathroom mirror: Good morning; this is God; I will not be needing your help today.
The only time we should look down on another person is when we are bending over to help them.
The shortest prayers are "Thank you" and "Help."
We are sent helpers, friends, and lovers.
When a drunk reaches out for help, step on their fingers.
You are not obligated to pay it back when people help you, you are obligated to pay it forward.
Your sponsor helped you up. Don't let them down.

Hero(es):
Heroes are the people who do what has to be done when it needs to be done, regardless of the consequences.

High:
Don't pick up and you won't get high.
Get high and get bye.
You are only one drink away from a drunk, one hit away from a high.

Higher Power: *Also see* God
Are you Higher Powered today?
Do what you can, let go of what you can't, and leave the results to a Higher Power.
Don't worry about tomorrow, your Higher Power is already there.
If you are having trouble believing in a power greater than yourself just try believing in a power other than yourself.
If you don't understand the concept of a Higher Power, go down to the ocean and try to hold back the waves.
If you don't have a Higher Power, borrow mine.
If your Higher Power can handle eternity, you can surely handle now!
If your prayers don't mean anything to you, they mean even less to your Higher Power.
Instead of worrying about what you can't do, think about what your Higher Power can do.
Is your program powered by Will Power or Higher Power?
Match your will to your Higher Power's and not your Higher Power's will to yours.
My Higher Power exists. _____Yes _____No
My Higher Power LOVES to extend itself.
Our Higher Power does the impossible, after we've done what is possible.
Our Higher Power gives us many gifts in sobriety. We just have to remember to unwrap them.
Pain gives me willingness; my Higher Power gives me recovery.
The definition of addiction..."Anything that takes the place of my relationship with my Higher Power."
The definition of addiction..."anything that takes the place of your relationship with your Higher Power.
What would my Higher Power do?
Willpower: our willingness to use a Higher Power.
Your Higher Power makes your life uncomfortable when it's time for you to change.
Your Higher Power may be using people who disagree with you.

Hit(ting): *Also see* Hitting Bottom
Easy Does It does not mean counting to ten before hitting someone.
Hit it with a prayer, not a chair!
When someone's pushing your buttons, hit the "MUTE" on your remote.
You are only one drink away from a drunk, one hit away from a high.

Hitting Bottom:
Bottom: No one comes to a 12 Step program on a good day.
Bottom: When the last thing you lose or the next thing you are about to lose is more important to you than booze.
Bottom: When things get worse faster than you can lower your standards.

BOUNCE when you hit BOTTOM !
Don't deny a drunk their bottom.
High bottoms have trap doors.
Hitting bottom happens when reality speaks to you clearly.
Hitting bottom means you have only one way to go from there.
Success is how high you bounce when you hit bottom.
The bottom is where you put the shovel down.
When you hit bottom, there's only one place to go from there.
When you're flat on your back, there's no way to look but up.
You hit bottom; you bounce back.
You hit your bottom when you quit digging!
Your bottom just may be six feet under.

Holiday(s):
Don't try to do Thanksgiving; just do Thursday
Home for the Hellidays

Honesty/Dishonesty:
Any measure of comfort requires rigorous honesty.
Cash-register honesty
Dishonesty is like a boomerang. About the time you think all is well, it hits you in the back of the head.
Honest Sobriety
Honesty in little things is not a little thing.
Honesty without kindness is cruel and kindness without honesty is co-dependence.
Honesty, Open-mindedness, Willingness
How to get honest: If it's not yours—don't take it. If it's not true—don't say it. If it's not right—don't do it.
If you pray for honesty, the chances of your lying go 'way up.
It is better to have someone sober and hating you because you told them the truth, rather than have someone drunk and liking you because you told them a lie.
No matter the consequences, those who are honest with themselves, get further in life.
No one is easier to deceive than yourself.
Practice Rigorous Honesty
The liar's punishment is not that he/she is not believed, but that he/she can believe no one else.
There is a difference between factual information and honesty.
We are only as healthy as our honesty.
We are only as sick as our secrets; we are only as healthy as our honesty.
With all the bull-shit—who needs Miracle Grow?

Hope(less):
Experience, strength, and hope.
Experience, Strength, and hope, not opinions, bullshit, and dope.
For addicts, self-will leads to a hopeless end and recovery leads to an endless hope.
Forgiveness is giving up hope for a better past!
Hope not dope.
Hoping and wishing are excuses for doing nothing.

Hope for the best, but prepare for the thirst.
Hope is the feeling you have that the feeling you have isn't permanent.
Hope is knowing the good in us will overcome the bad.
From hopeless dope fiend, to dopeless hope fiend.
From hopelessly dope-full...to dopelessly hopeful.
Nothing is as sweet as the smell of hope in the air.
The Only HOPE in DOPE is DEATH
Worry is an ironic form of hope.

HOW: Also *see* Open-minded
"How it works" works for me.
"Why" questions keep me in the problem while "How" questions keep me in the solution.
Chapter Five is called "How It Works," not "Why Me?"
How important is it?

Hug(s):
A hug is a great gift, one size fits all.
A pat on the back is a mobile hug.
Hug often, hug well.
Hugs, not drugs.
No one hugs a drunk—*drunk*.
We came here for our drugging and stay, in part, for hugging.
When someone hugs you, let them be the first to let go.

Humility:
Always try to be humble - and be damn proud of it!
Be humble and you will not stumble.
Before you become too proud to be a member of (__)A, make sure (__)A is proud to have you
as a member.
Being humble means being teachable.
Confidence is unattainable without some humility.
Don't be so humble, you're not *that* great.
Find humility before it finds you.
Get humble, or be made humble.
Halos can turn into nooses.
Humility doesn't mean thinking any less of yourself, just less often.
Humility is being a part of the whole, not apart from the whole.
Humility is humanity.
Humility is mandatory, humiliation is optional.
Humility is not humiliation.
Humility is not so much thinking less of yourself, as it is thinking of yourself less.
Humility is that virtue which reduces a man to the proper size without degrading him, thereby
increasing him in statue without inflating him.
Humility is that which reduces you to your proper size without degrading you.
Humility is the soil in which all other virtues grow.
If you are having trouble getting down on your knees to pray in the morning, put your shoes
under the middle of the bed the night before.
Just when you think you have humility, you've lost it.

Medication for humility: swallow your pride.
The basic ingredient of all humility is a desire to seek and do God's will.
The difference between a demand and a request, is humility.
True humility is accepting myself without embellishment and without embarrassment.
We are given the lesson of humility when we least expect it or want it.
When you feel it's your job to *humble* others, you may be in for a ... stumble, fumble, or crumble.
You can't save your face and your ass at the same time.

Humor: *See Also, Laugh*
It is characteristic of the humor in the Universe that we are given free will and then told to give it back!
Lighten up by enlighting up.
Some things are so serious that you can only joke about them.
To see the most hilarious alcoholic, look in the mirror.
Use your wit to amuse and not to abuse.
We know that God has a sense of humor. He gives us free will and then asks us to give it back.

Hurry:
Don't hurry. Don't worry. Don't compare.

Hurt: *Also see* Pain
Hurt people, hurt people.
If you can't love everybody today, at least try not to hurt anybody.
It doesn't hurt to try.
No matter how good a friend someone is, they're going to hurt you every once in a while and you must forgive them for that.
Rather than getting even with those that hurt you, the challenge is to get even with those that help you.
You can change any thought that hurts into a reality that hurts even more.

Inaction: *Also see* Action
If you're coasting, you're going downhill.
On the pity pot? Change a thought, move a muscle.
Our problem is not lack of information or insight, it is lack of action.

Idea(s):
All our old ideas had to be smashed.
Don't get a new set of old ideas.
If you think you have a good idea you might want to get second opinion from your sponsor.
Let go of old ideas.
Most good ideas are simple.
Sometimes you might want to share your "brilliant idea" with friends before you take action.
Sponsors are like Ford; they have a better idea.

Identify:
Don't identify out.

Don't compare---identify, don't intellectualize----utilize.

Identify, don't compare.

When I look into a mirror, I take a good look, because this is the guy that got me here.

Indian:

Drinking is not Indian.

Drugging is not Indian.

Insanity: *Also see,* Crazy *and* Sanity

Alcoholics don't need chaos in their lives; they demand it.

Death, Insanity or Recovery.

Drunkenness is nothing but voluntary madness.

Insanity is doing the same thing over and over again and expecting different results.

Insanity is not doing the same thing over and over again expecting different results; insanity is doing the same thing over and over again knowing full well what the results will be!

Insanity is the seeming inability to learn from past mistakes.

My mind is out to get me.

Our insanity got us things we did not need, with money we did not have, to impress people we did not know.

Plead contemporary insanity.

The program fixes it so we don't have to suffer from insanity anymore. Now we can enjoy it!

Time-for-a-meeting clue #128: Feeling that you're "going insane."

Unsound in mind, unsound in action—what better definition of insanity?

You are a sane person in an insane situation.

Insight:

Our problem is not information or insight, it is lack of action.

Uncover...Discover...Discard

We do not see things as they are. We see things as we are.

When you look into a mirror, take a good look, because this is the guy that got you here.

When you know that you don't know, then you know!

When you're flat on your back, there's no way to look but up.

Insult:

Don't insult the alligator until after you have crossed the river.

We used to think being called an alcoholic was an insult.

Intention(s):

Good intentions are often checks drawn on accounts with insufficient funds.

We find that the smallest deed is better than the grandest intention

Integrity:

People of integrity make an easy target for critics because they stand upright.

Intelligence (lectualize):

Don't compare—identify, don't intellectualize—utilize

Emotions destroy intelligence.

Emotions destroy intelligence.

Feelings are nine times more powerful than the intellect.
Nobody ever got sober as a result of an intellectual awakening.
We never found anyone too dumb to get this program, but we have found some too smart.
We've never seen someone too dumb to get this program, but there are those who are too intelligent.

Intimacy:
Intimacy: Into-me-I-see.

Inventory: *Also see* Steps—Step 4
Don't just take an inventory; let it take you.
Got a problem? Get a pencil!
If you spot it, you got it.
If you take another person's inventory, who will take yours?
It's hard work taking everyone else's inventory. Worst of all, they seldom seem grateful!
Take your own damn inventory!
You take others' personal inventory 'till you take your own.

Jail: *Also see* Prison(er)
CA is not a sentence, it is a reprieve.
Got here with a nudge from the judge?
There are only three possible outcomes for alcoholics: Locked up, Covered up, or Sobered up!
We don't care if you came from Yale or jail, Park Avenue or a park bench.
We have everyone in CDA, from Yale to jail.

Job: *Also see* Work
A job is something that happens to you on the way to a meeting.
Don't rely on your sponsor to call you. It's your job to call him or her.
God helps those who let Him do His job.
If you haven't been fired yet, then you know you haven't been doing anything very interesting.
If you want to make an easy job seem mighty hard, just keep putting it off.
It is God's job to make miracles and you are one of them.
It is not your job to point out other people's faults.
Recovery is an inside job.
Those who can't laugh at themselves leave the job to others.
You can't be fired for on-the-job sobriety.
You no longer need to punish, deceive, or compromise yourself, unless you want to stay employed.
Your job is to carry the message, not deliver the drunk.

Journey: *Also see* Path(s) *and* Travel(ing)
A journey of a thousand miles begins with the first step.
Embrace the journey.
Put one foot in front of the other.
Recovery is a journey, not a destination. May your journey be long.
Recovery is not a destination, it's a journey.
The journey begins with the first step.
The journey is our destination.

The journey of a thousand miles begins with the first step.
Where ever you go, there you are.
You can go nowhere from where you are not.

Joy(ous, ful, enjoy):
AA is the highest priced club in the world. You "paid the dues," why not enjoy the benefits?
Shared joy is double joy; shared sorrow is half sorrow.
Ask God not for things to enjoy life, but rather life that you may enjoy all things.
Chemically Dependent Anonymous doesn't prevent you from committing a vice—it simply prevents you from enjoying it.
Contempt and success are both difficult to handle, but one is ultimately more enjoyable
Enjoy the moment, in a minute it'll be a memory.
Enthusiasm makes life enjoyable. Generate some!
Guilt is concerned with the past. Worry is concerned about the future. Contentment enjoys the present.
Happy, Joyous, & Free
If the newcomer could see no joy in our existence they would not want it.
If you aren't enjoying your life…then you aren't recovering.
Insist on enjoying life.
Life happens; joy is optional.
Life is only temporary, relax and enjoy it!
Remember, we were all born to be happy, joyous and free.
The opposite of joy is not sorrow, the opposite of joy is cynicism.
The pain of becoming is essential to the "Joy of Being."
The program fixes it so we don't have to suffer from insanity anymore. Now we can enjoy it!

Judge(ing): *Also see* Criticize
Do not condemn the judgment of another because it differs from your own. You may both be wrong.
Don't judge yourself by the way you feel.
If you judge people, you have no time to love them.
Judge each day not by the harvest you reap but by the seeds you sow.
Judge yourself by your insides not by someone else's outsides.
People who judge other people for not doing what they say they are doing are usually not doing what they say they are doing.
People who matter, don't mind; people who mind, don't matter.
Take care of your heart. Do not run up hill and don't run down people.
To belittle is to be little.
When we point the finger at someone else, there are three pointing back at us.
When you judge others you are revealing your own fears and prejudices.
When you live and let live, you teach myself to love.

Junkie:
Carry the message, not the junkie.
Chunky, Funky, Junky
NA: We are not reformed junkies–but informed addicts.

Justice:
Don't pray for justice. Pray for mercy.
You came here demanding justice and were graciously given mercy.
When demanding justice, consider the consequences.

Kill(ing):
Alcohol is a silent killer; it destroys little by little until there is nothing left to devour.
Complacency kills.
Feelings won't kill you, but killing your feelings will.
Here is a thought that kills a lot of chemical dependents: *That may be true for you, but I'm different.*
If the drugs don't kill you, the lifestyle will.
If you commit suicide you're killing the wrong person.
If you're thinking of committing suicide, wait five years; otherwise you will have killed the wrong person.
On the first drink: When you get hit by a train, which kills you, the engine or the caboose?
Secrets kill.
Speed kills.
Speed kills. Don't meth around.
That which doesn't kill you, serves to make you stronger.
When you kill time, remember it has no resurrection.

Kindness:
Be kind to unkind people. It gets to them.
Be kind to your enemies—it will drive them crazy.
Be kinder than is necessary.
Detachment is neither kind nor unkind.
Honesty without kindness is cruel and kindness without honesty is co-dependence.
If there is someone weaker than you, be kind to them. If there is someone stronger than you, be kind to yourself.
Kind is better than right.
Kind words cost so little, but they mean so much.
Kindness is a gift and the tag reads, "Please handle with tender loving care."
Love is less a feeling than a thousand tiny acts of kindness.
Random Acts of Kindness
To the desolate alcoholic, the act of kindness can be the difference between getting "better" or getting "bitter."

Know(ledge):
"No-ing" is not enough and "knowing" is not enough. We must "do."
Don't figure it out. Just do it.
Don't know - BE.
Get to know a stranger, do a 4th step today.
He who knows that enough is enough will always have enough.
If you don't know it can't be done, you can do it.
If you want to know what's in your heart, listen to your mouth.
It's okay to say, "I don't know."
Know God, Know Peace. No God, No Peace.

Knowing why is the booby prize of life.

Many of us knew all about God before coming to AA. But we had to find AA to get to know God.

Members who think they know it all are especially annoying to those of us who do.

Not knowing, is not the problem. Not being OK with not knowing is the problem.

Success is not getting what you want; it's knowing what you don't need.

The alcoholic is always the last to know.

To know what you know and to know what you don't know is knowing what it's all about.

We grow only when we push ourselves beyond what we already know.

When you don't know what to do, don't do anything.

When you talk, you can only say something you already know. When you listen, you may learn something somebody else knows.

You may not always know God's will. But you ALWAYS know what it is NOT!

Laughter: *Also see* Humor *and* Fun(ny)

Comedy is tragedy plus time.

He who laughs, lasts!

Laughter is "Chicken Soup for the Soul"

Laughter is good medicine.

Laughter puts the wrinkles in the right places.

Please Lord, teach us to laugh again, but, God, don't let us ever forget that we cried.

Problems always melt in the face of laughter.

Those who can't laugh at themselves leave the job to others.

When you can laugh at your disease, you know that you're recovering.

You can not feel sorry for yourself and laugh at the same time. So take your levity seriously.

Lead(er):

Abstinence leads to sobriety. The program and 12 steps lead to recovery.

All recovery roads lead to the ability to love and be loved.

Do something. Lead, follow, or get out of the way.

For addicts, self-will leads to a hopeless end and recovery leads to an endless hope.

It's not what leads you to drinking, it's where the drinking leads you.

Leaders are readers.

Our leaders are but trusted servants.

Pain instructs or it leads to more pain.

Repression without expression, leads to depression.

Stinking thinking leads to stinking drinking which causes stinking problems.

The 12 Steps lead us to God, and God leads us to ourselves.

Today you are leading a life. When you were drinking, you were a life being led.

Twelve steps leads to twelve promises and they begin before we are half way through.

When you're out in front, you catch the most arrows.

You can lead a horse to water but you can't make 'em.

Learn(ing):

Any problem blesses us when we learn the lesson it teaches.

As long as you live—keep learning how to live.

At five years you get your brains back, at ten years you learn how to use them, and at fifteen you realize you didn't need them in the first place.

Count the lessons learned from failures as rungs upon the ladder of progress.
Failure is success, if we learn from it.
Faith without action is like sitting on a dictionary to learn how to spell.
If you can't get what you want, learn to want what you get.
It is surprising what we learn after we think we know it all.
It's hard to learn from mistakes you don't acknowledge.
Learn from other's mistakes. You will never live long enough to make them all yourself.
Learn to change and change to learn.
Learn to listen, listen to learn.
Learn to listen. Opportunity sometimes knocks very softly.
Learn to relax without feeling guilty.
Learning to forgive takes practice.
Lessons repeat until learned.
Repetition is the mother of learning. Action is the result.
The most important and timely lesson any of us can learn is that doing our best is as close to perfect as we need to get.
The two ways to learn are the hard way and the harder way.
To teach is to learn again.
We are not in recovery to change the world. We are in recovery to learn to function within the world.
We teach best, what we most need to learn.
We'll love you until you learn to love yourself.
When you do all the talking you can only learn what you already know.
When you think you've learned enough, you haven't.
You can not learn to love yourself until you can learn to forgive yourself.
You cannot get ahead until you learn to be here.
You have to be clean to learn to live clean.
You live, you learn; you drink, you forget.

Lesson(s):
Any problem blesses us when we learn the lesson it teaches.
Count the lessons learned from failures as rungs upon the ladder of progress.
If you think life's lessons are hard, try addiction.
Look for the Lesson
The lesson will repeat until it is learned.
The most important and timely lesson any of us can learn is that doing our best is as close to perfect as we need to get.
We are given the lesson of humility when we least expect it or want it.

Letting Go: *Also see* Surrender
Change only happens when the pain of holding on is greater than the fear of letting go.
Do what you can, let go of what you can't, and leave the results to a Higher Power.
Everything I ever let go of had claw marks all over it.
I finally got a grip when I learned to let go.
If a thought or belief doesn't serve you, let it go.
If you don't let go, you will lose your grip.
If you think handling everything is too much, try letting go.
If you turn it over and don't let go, you will be upside down.

Let Go and Let God.
Let go of old ideas.
Let go or be dragged.
Let it go, it was never yours to begin with.
Letting go is not caring for, but caring about.
Move forward; don't look back
Relax, relate, release
Release for Peace
Release your reservations.
Share your pain and let it go.
The result was nil until we let go absolutely.
Turn it over, don't over turn it.
Turn it over, don't turn it off.
When all you want to do is hang on, let go. When all you want to do is let go, hang on.
When you get to the end of your rope, let go.

Lie(s, liar): *Also see* Honesty/Dishonesty
Everything after the word "but" is a lie.
Like-me lies
Lying means dying.
One lie a day keeps sobriety away.
People who will lie for you, will lie to you.
The liar's punishment is not that he/she is not believed, but that he/she can believe no one else.
WD-40 lies

Life (Live-ing):
A loss in life is not a loss of life.
AA may not add years to your life—but it adds life to your years.
Aftercare, the beginning of life.
Alcohol is a solvent; it will remove everything from your life.
Alcoholics don't need chaos in their lives; they demand it.
All you have to do to change your life is change your mind.
As long as you live—keep learning how to live.
As you go through life, make this your goal - watch the donut not the hole.
Ask God not for things to enjoy life, but rather life that you may enjoy all things.
Believe that life is worth living and your belief will create the fact.
Better living through denial.
By reading the black and white pages of the Big Book, you color your life beautiful.
Change your attitude and change your life.
Choose your life, don't let it choose you.
Controlling life isn't the answer, it's the problem.
Do not search for happiness. Search for right living, and happiness will be your reward.
Don't let life discourage you; everyone who got where he is had to begin where he was.
Don't let people, places and things live rent free in your head.
Don't look at life as a puzzle to be solved, rather as a mystery to be lived.
Encouragement from an old-timer can turn a newcomer's life around.
Everything we have in life right now, we probably drank to get.

Evil is live spelled backwards.

From what we get, we can make a living; what we give, however, makes a life.

Get a sponsor; get a program; get into service; get a Higher Power in your life; get a life; get it right. Wake up and smell the recovery.

God puts assholes in our lives that we may recognize our own potential.

Happiness is a by-product of right living.

If we were to live—we had to be free of our anger.

If you aren't enjoying your life…then you aren't recovering.

If you believe the Big Book, live it.

If you live on the edge of the program, you might fall off.

If you reach out to someone, you just might save your life.

If you think life's lessons are hard, try addiction.

If your life worked so well, what are you doing here now?

Imagination is a preview of life's coming attractions.

In life, the process is perfect.

Insist on enjoying life.

It is easier to live your way into good feeling than to feel your way into good living.

It is only possible to live happily ever after on a day to day basis.

It's not *what* you have in your life, but *who* you have in your life that counts.

Just because you're having a bad day doesn't mean you're having a bad life.

Knowing why is the booby prize of life.

Lead a life. Don't be a life being led.

Learn from the mistakes of others. You can't live long enough to make them all yourself.

Let us live and give the NA way of life.

Life can only be understood looking backward; it must be lived looking forward.

Life does not begin at any particular age, but only when you decide to live it.

Life happens; joy is optional.

Life is a dance if you take the steps.

Life is a mirror: That which we hate in ourselves is what we hate in others.

Life is fragile; handle with prayer.

Life is full of "else's." What else is there?

Life is not a dress rehearsal.

Life is not measured by the number of breaths we take, but by the moments that take our breath away.

Life is only temporary, relax and enjoy it!

Life is too short to be small.

Life isn't black or white. It's black and white.

Life isn't fair, life isn't just, life is just what it is.

Life may not be fair, but God is.

Life must be lived forwards, but it can only be understood backwards.

Life on Life's' Terms.

Life should be a pattern of experiences to savor, not to endure.

Life starts when you stop.

Life sucks! (but in AA, life sucks one day at a time).

Life without recovery: Even roses have thorns. Life in recovery: Even thorns have roses.

Life—is not growing up—it is to complete a journey.

Live and Let Live.

Live as though every thing you do will eventually become known.

Live each day the best that you can.

Live every day as if it were your last, because someday it *will* be.

Live for today. Yesterday's history. Tomorrow's a mystery.

Live in the moment.

Live in the solution!

Live in the solution, not the problem.

Live life on life's terms.

Live life on purpose, not by accident.

Live today as you want to remember your life.

Living well is the best revenge.

Long to live in order to live long.

Look at your life through fresh eyes.

Making a living isn't the same as making a life. If you don't want what we have, go back out to what you had.

Most of the catastrophes you suffer in life, never happen.

My life is none of my business.

No matter the consequences, those who are honest with themselves, get further in life.

Nothing about life is to be feared; it is only to be understood.

Nothing in your life happens *to you*, but *for you*.

Projection: Living in the wreckage of the future.

Recovery is the natural order of life.

Recovery isn't a death sentence; it's a life sentence.

Resentment is like letting someone live rent-free in your head.

Ride sober, live free.

Simply, alcoholics are people whose lives are better if they don't drink.

Sometimes the worst things in life happen after you get what you think you want.

Take care of your body. If you don't, where else are you going to live?

Take your life lightly.

The best things in life aren't things.

The biggest obstacle to a spiritual life is lack of attention.

The death of our addiction forces us to confront life.

The expression of surrender is to live your life in harmony with the universe.

The greatest tragedy in this life is not death but the things that die inside of us while we're still alive.

The only thing you can control in your life is your attitude.

The single most important thing to living life sober, is a term called 'showing up.'

The two hardest things in life to handle are success and failure.

There's no amount of effort alcoholics won't expend to destroy anything that is good in their lives.

Tired of the high cost of low living?

Today you are leading a life. Drinking and drugging, you were a life being led.

Try to live life without adding to your 8th Step list.

We make a living by what we get. We make a life by what we give.

Wear life as a loose garment.

When you are living inside someone's head, you are out of your mind.

Work the program hard; life is easy. Work the program easy; *life is hard.*

You can't think your way into a new way of living…You have to live your way into a new way of thinking.

You cannot think yourself sober, read yourself sober or act yourself sober. You must live yourself sober.

You have to be clean to learn to live clean.

You live, you learn; you drink, you forget.

Your Higher Power makes your life uncomfortable when it's time for you to change.

Your life can be changed in a matter of hours by people who don't even know you.

Light(en):

A candle loses nothing by lighting another candle.

Don't expect God to use you as a *Lighthouse* somewhere else if he can't use you as a *Candle* just where you are!

Enlighten up!

Faith is seeing light with your heart, when all your eyes see is the darkness ahead.

God can't use your light if you're trying to burn everyone with your brilliance.

In recovery, we know that the light at the end of the tunnel is no longer an on-coming train.

Lighten up—the war is over.

Short version of the Serenity Prayer: *Lighten up*

Some people move when they see the light; alcoholics move when they feel the heat.

Sponsors are lighthouses, not foghorns.

Take your life lightly.

Listen(ing):

A good listener is not only popular everywhere but after awhile he knows something.

God gave you two ears and only one mouth for a reason.

If you cannot hear the voice of God, it is because you choose not to listen.

If you want to know what's in your heart, listen to your mouth.

If you're just listening to yourself, you're getting really bad advice.

Learn to listen. Opportunity sometimes knocks very softly.

Learn to listen; listen to learn.

Listen and learn.

Listen more, talk less!

Listen to the message, not the messenger.

Listen to your heart often, God lives there.

Listening is better than hearing.

Listening is love in action.

Listen—or thy tongue will keep thee deaf.

Praying is asking God for help, meditating is listening for God's answer.

Sharing: The opposite of listening is waiting to talk.

Take the cotton out of your ears and put it in your mouth.

The opposite of listening is waiting to talk.

Try to listen sober, your ears work better that way.

When you talk you can only say something you already know when you listen—you may learn something somebody else knows.

You learn more by listening (you already know what you would say).

Your willingness to listen is your gift to others.

Lonely: *See* Alone

Lost:
A sponsor is a push when stalled, a guide when you're lost, a smile when you're sad—and love.
Found God? He wasn't the one that was lost.
If you lose your temper, you've lost.
Just when you think you have humility, you've lost it.
Remember what you have left, not what you have lost.
When a man tries to control his drinking he has already lost control.
When an old-timer dies a library is lost.
When you're filled with regrets of yesterday and worries about tomorrow, you've lost today in which to be grateful.
You don't need to "find God"; He isn't lost.

Love: *Also see* Heart *and* Relationship(s)
A sponsor is a push when stalled, a guide when you're lost, a smile when you're sad—and love.
Alcoholism is like making love to a gorilla—you're not done until the gorilla says you are.
All recovery roads lead to the ability to love and be loved.
Anyone can hate. It costs to love.
Detach with love
Don't love them to death.
Embrace the power of love. Reject the love of power.
Everyone needs to be loved...especially when they do not deserve it.
If love has conditions attached, it's not love, it's barter.
If you can't love everybody today, at least try not to hurt anybody.
If you can't take it, leave it. If you can't leave it, love it.
If you want to find out what your character defects are, fall in love.
It's easy to be loving; what takes work is to be kind.
Just because someone doesn't love you the way you want them to doesn't mean they don't love you with all they have.
Let us love you until you can love yourself.
Listening is love in action.
Love God.
Love is a verb.
Love is all powerful
Love is an action.
Love is everywhere.
Love is less a feeling than a thousand tiny acts of kindness.
Love is not a noun; it is a verb.
Love is not enough...but it sure helps.
Love isn't love until you give it away.
Love like there is no tomorrow.
Marriage is the glue that keeps you together until you fall back in love again.
No one is wrong in the eyes of love. Everyone is doing the best they can.
Practice love and service at work and at home and not just in meetings.
Self-loathing will keep you from love, every time.
The people you most need to give love to are often the people who deserve it the least.
The things we love tell us what we are.

There are people who love you dearly, but just don't know how to show it.
There is nothing we can do wrong that will make God love us any less.
Time is the ego's enemy, not love's.
To open oneself up to love, is to open oneself up to loss.
Today do something for someone you love: Leave them alone.
We receive love and understanding from strangers and we make progress as we in turn give it to new strangers.
We'll love you until you learn to love yourself.
You cannot be honest, open-minded, and willing if any part of you is blind including, love, hate, fear, and faith.
You cannot learn to love yourself until you learn to forgive yourself.
You cannot make someone love you. All you can do is be someone who can be loved. The rest is up to them.
You deserve love.
You should always leave loved ones with loving words. It may be the last time you see them.

Luck(y):
Any failure will tell you—success is nothing but luck.
Many people believe in luck to explain the success of those they don't like.
The harder you work, the luckier you get.

MA (Marajuana Anonymous) *Also see* Slogans *and* Program Generic-Mix and Match
Pot head: If you smoked enough to get to MA, you smoked enough.
Sign in MA meeting: No Smoking
One toke is no joke.

Manipulate:
When we couldn't dominate, control, or manipulate, we would ask for terms and conditions.

Marijuana: *Also see* MA
From a chicken in every pot to a chicken smokin' pot.
Marijuana Maintenance

Mean(ingful):
Not mean, but meaningful
Say what you mean. Mean what you say. But don't say it mean.

Medicine/Medicate(tion):
Faith was the first medicine known to man.
Laughter is good medicine.
Medication for humility: Swallow your pride.
Meditate instead of Medicate

Meditation(s):
Are you doing your meds? Meditations.
Breathe in. Breathe out. REPEAT.
Daily meditation for about 20 minutes is recommended for all in recovery; unless, of course, you're very busy—then you should meditate for an hour.

Deep Peace
Meditate instead of Medicate
Prayer is talking to God; meditation is listening to God.
Praying is asking God for help; meditating is listening for God's answer.
To the mind that is still, the world surrenders.

Meeting(s):*Also see* Sharing *and* Group(s)
20/20: Come 20 minutes before the meeting, stay 20 minutes after.
90 meetings in 90 days.
A 12-Step meeting is God's workshop.
A job is something that happens to you on the way to a meeting.
A meeting a day keep defects away.
A meeting a day keeps detox away.
A meeting lasts from preamble to prayer.
A newcomer at his first meeting: "Where are all the drunks?"
A treatment center is where you go and pay $15,000 to find out that A.A. meetings are free.
After each meeting, clean up the wreckage of the present.
After the meeting, clean up the wreckage of your presence.
Align your actions so they are in agreement with the picture you paint of yourself at meetings.
All it takes to start a new meeting is a resentment and a coffeepot.
At the start of meetings we always ask, "Is there anybody new or coming back?" We should also ask, "Is there anybody old and going out?"
Better to be in a meeting by mistake than out drunk by mistake.
Bring the body and the mind will follow.
"Buts" belong in ashtrays or chairs of Alcoholics Anonymous.
CA meetings work because not everyone goes crazy every day.
Chairman at meeting: "Anybody from out of town? Out of state? Outer space?"
Chairman at meeting: "Anybody from out of town? Out of state? Out of their minds?"
Coffee makers make it.
Do not let the newcomer's inner child run our meetings. This is not play therapy.
Don't drink, don't think and go to meetings.
Don't go to a meeting looking for what you can get, look for what you can give.
Don't shoot up and throw up, suit up and show up.
Don't "keep coming back," just stay.
Don't act out, don't think, and go to meetings.
Double Dipper: Member who shares twice at a meeting.
Each meeting has two types of newcomers: Beginners and visitors. Beginners have made a decision.
Get smart feet; go to meetings.
Go to meetings to listen to what happens to people who don't go to meetings.
Go to meetings when you want to, and go to meetings when you don't want to.
Go to meetings; do the readings.
God is upstairs in church on Sunday morning, but at night he's downstairs in the AA meeting.
God liked the first 12-Step meeting so much He hasn't missed one since.
Gossip, rumors, backbiting, loose tongues, verbal altercations: sometimes A.A. meetings are like the corner bar, without the alcohol.
If you come into an AA meeting looking for recovery, you will find exactly that. If you come looking for a reason to continue drinking, you'll eventually find that, too.

If you go to meetings, even when you don't need a meeting, you will rarely need a meeting.
If you have two addictions, throw two bucks in the basket.
If you meet more than three assholes in one day, you need a meeting.
If you rely on meetings alone to keep you sober, then you must find a 24 hour meeting.
If you think you don't need a meeting, chances are, you do.
If you've never been to a bad meeting, then you're not getting to enough.
If your ass falls off, put it in a paper bag and take it to a meeting.
If your ass falls off, put it in a wheelbarrow and take it to a meeting.
If you're not getting mad at meetings, you're not going to enough meetings.
If you're thinking about going to a meeting, go to the meeting, and then think about it.
It' alright to hold a discussion meeting, as long as you let go of it now and then.
It's a *meeting* or a beating.
It's been a good meeting so far.
It's not what you get *from* a meeting, it's what you take *to* a meeting.
It's the second meeting that's the most important one.
Keep Comin' Back! It gets better, it gets different.
Keep coming back, it gets greater later.
Keep coming' back, it works if you work it.
Keep coming back, it works…don't go away; it works even better!
Keep coming until you hear your story.
Many meetings, many chances; few meetings, few chances; no meetings, no chances
Meeting makers make it.
Meeting: check-up from the neck up.
Meetings are for quitters.
Meetings are not enough.
Meetings, meetings, meetings.
No one who has ever had a slip said she went to too many meetings.
Non-stop talkers can be a constant source of earitation at meetings.
People who don't go to meetings don't find out what happens to people who don't go to meetings.
People who say you can't talk about drugs in an AA meeting are usually on them.
Recovery is not about meetings, but what happens in between meetings.
Respect the anonymity of others.
Seven days without a meeting—makes one weak.
Share experience, strength and hope
Sitting in meetings doesn't make you a member anymore than sitting in a chicken coop makes you a chicken.
Sometimes you don't need a meeting, you need a convention.
Suit up, show up, and grow up!
Suit up, Show up, Sit up, and Speak up!
Suit up, Show up, Sit up, Shut up
Take what you can use and leave the rest.
The back half of the room at meetings is known as the denial section.
The church basements where we meet are prayer-conditioned.
The most productive ups and downs are getting up for a meeting and down to the steps.
The only meeting you're ever late for is your first one.
There are no "bad" meetings.
There are two times when we need to go to a meeting, when we think we need one and when

we know we don't.

They say that you need only one meeting a week but it might be a good idea to go to one every night so you don't miss the one you need!

Thinking about what you'll say before you share, or what you should have said after you share means you missed the meeting.

Those who get around, stay around.

Time-for-a-meeting clue: Feeling that you're "going insane."

Time-for-a-meeting: Feeling under the weather.

Time-for-a-meeting: The feeling of having a lot on your mind.

Token takers take it and meeting makers make it.

Try it for 90 days, and if you don't like it, we'll gladly refund your misery.

We are all here because we aren't all here.

We don't care why you're here, its why you stay.

We don't drink even if our ass falls off; we pick it up and take it to a meeting.

We get something out of each meeting we attend even if it's only resentment.

We *have* to keep going to meetings until we *want* to go to meetings.

We may not have it all together, but *together* we have it all.

What you hear and see here, stays here.

When do you need a meeting? At beer-thirty.

When you are in a meeting, your disease is in the parking lot doing push-ups.

When you lead a meeting, lead.

Who you see here, what you hear here, let it stay here.

With that, I'll take another 24.

You can't be late until you show up.

You only have to go to meetings until you want to go to meetings.

You start to skip, you start to slip.

Message(s):
Carry the drunk to the messengers.

Carry the message, not the drunk.

Carry the message, not the junkie.

Carry the message.

Drinking is like getting a message in a bottle. What's your message?

If you can't be a good example, then you'll just have to be a horrible warning.

Learn to carry the message, not the mess.

Listen to the message, not the messenger!

Sometimes you carry the message; sometimes you are the message.

Sponsors carry the message, not the person.

Sponsors carry the message, not the sponsee.

Take the mess to your sponsor, take the message to the meeting.

The message is in the front row.

The message is under the ashtray.

You carry the message, not the drunk; however, if necessary, carry the drunk to the message.

Your job is to carry the message, not deliver the drunk.

Mind: *Also see* Brain *and* Head *and* Open-minded

A fanatic is one who can't change his mind and won't change the subject.

All you have to do to change your life is change your mind.

An alcoholic is a man who is a legend in his own mind.
Because your mind thinks something, doesn't necessarily make it so.
Before engaging your mouth, put your mind in gear.
Bring the body and the mind follows.
For peace of mind, resign as general manager of the universe.
How's the committee? (Has it come to a meeting of the mind recently?)
If only a closed mind came with a closed mouth.
If you do not find "the peace of mind" you keep hearing about in AA, try working the steps.
If you don't believe in God, we suggest you change your mind.
If you keep giving them a piece of your mind, you won't have anything left for peace of mind.
Itty bitty shitty committee.
Keep an unmade mind instead of a mind made up.
Move your body, change your mind.
Rather than giving others a piece of your mind, don't—and have peace of mind.
Sanity begins with the admission of reality into the mind.
Skid Row is a place in your mind--not a place on the street.
The addict's mind is like a bad neighborhood, don't go in there alone.
The main business of the mind is to mind its own business.
Time-for-a-meeting: The feeling of having a lot on your mind.
To the mind that is still, the world surrenders.
When you are living inside someone's else's head, you are out of your mind.
When your head begins to swell your mind stops growing.
You can speak your mind here. Nobody is paying attention anyway.
Your mind has a mind of its own.
Your mind may be out to get you.
Your sick mind cannot heal your sick mind.

Mind-affecting Chemicals *Also see* Alcohol *and* Drug(s/ing)
Don't pick up and you won't get high.
Four Horsemen of mind-affecting chemicals: Terror, Bewilderment, Frustration, and Despair.
When you abused mind-affecting chemicals, you abused people and when you abused people, you abused mind-affecting chemicals.

Misery:
Give us ninety days and if you don't want what we have, your misery will be cheerfully refunded.
If you don't like it here, we will gladly refund your misery.
Misery is optional.

Miracles:
A coincidence is when God performs a miracle and decides to remain anonymous.
A sober alcoholic is a living miracle.
Don't believe in miracles. Rely on them.
Don't leave before you recognize the miracle.
Don't leave five minutes before the miracle.
Don't quit before the miracle happens.
Expect a Miracle
God's business is making miracles and you are one of them.

If you are clean and sober, the miracle has already happened. Stick around, the impossibilities take a little longer.

If you can't expect a miracle, at least expect a coincidence.

If you have a problem believing in miracles, go to an (___)A meeting and you'll see miracle, after miracle, after miracle.

It is when miracles do not occur that something has gone wrong.

It pays to believe in miracles. In (_____) Anonymous we experience them.

Never give up on anybody. Miracles happen every day.

The miracle of recovery is that no matter where you are, you're here.

We see miracles every night when we attend (__)A meetings.

You will be happy to know that the universal law that created miracles has not been repealed.

Misc:

Don't be a has-been; be a will-be.

I'm not OK. You're not OK. And that's OK.

If you do not know where you are going, then any road will take you there.

If you don't stand for something, they say you will fall for anything.

It will begin with me.

It's a cinch by the inch and a trial by the mile.

Man is the only varmint who sets his own trap—baits it—and then steps in it.

More will be Revealed

None for the Road.

None of us came here on a winning streak.

Nothing is all good and nothing is all bad.

Our journey is our destination.

Remember where you came from.

The law of physics says there is only one way to "coast:" down hill.

The only person you can ever be better than is the person you were yesterday.

Today's mighty oak is just yesterday's nut that held its ground.

Uncover...Discover...Discard.

We are not bullet-proof.

We are very small when the stars come out at night, yet remember that we too, are made of stardust.

When we go too far, it is seldom in the right direction.

Mistake(s):

A mistake is evidence that someone has tried to do something.

Don't be afraid to ask dumb questions; they are more easily handled than dumb mistakes.

Experience is the name everyone gives to their mistakes.

Experience is the thing that enables you to recognize a mistake when you make it again.

God doesn't make mistakes.

If you are not making mistakes, then you probably are not making anything.

If you want to get maximum attention make a big mistake.

Insanity is repeating the same mistakes over and over again and expecting different results.

Insanity is the seeming inability to learn from past mistakes.

It's hard to learn from a mistake you don't acknowledge making.

It's not making a mistake that means anything, it's in never repeating it.

Learn by others' mistakes. You will never live long enough to make them all yourself.

Mistakes are our teachers.

Never mistake activity for achievement.

Nothing Happens in God's World By Mistake

"Opened by mistake" applies to the mouth more often than it does to mail.

The first step in overcoming mistakes is to admit them.

The greatest mistake you can make is to be continually fearing you will make one.

The man who makes a mistake and doesn't correct it, makes two.

The one good thing about repeating your mistakes is that you know when to cringe.

There are some people who learn from the mistakes of others and then there are the rest of us.

There is a big difference between being a mistake and making one.

There is no mistake so great as that of being always right.

We must learn from the mistakes of others because we won't live long enough to make them all ourselves.

When making amends, a subtle shift occurs in our thinking. We go from thinking we were a mistake to acknowledging we *made* a mistake.

You don't make as many mistakes when you keep your mouth shut.

Your fault—my mistake.

More:
Every alcoholic's favorite brand: More!

If one is good, more is better!

More will be Revealed

One is too many and more not enough.

The more that is revealed, the more that is required of us.

The more you have, the more you want.

To an alcoholic, if one is good, one in every color is better.

We're all here because we want more.

Motive(vate):
Don't assume evil motives for what stupidity can explain.

Motivate, don't denigrate.

Mouth:
A closed mouth gathers no foot.

Be grateful you have been given two ears and only one mouth.

If you want to know what's in your heart, listen to your mouth.

It's a shame that booze doesn't turn off one's mouth at the same time it turns off the brain.

"Opened by mistake" applies to the mouth more often than it does to mail.

Take the cotton out of your ears and stuff it in your mouth.

When you are in it up to your ears, keep your mouth shut.

You don't make as many mistakes when you keep your mouth shut.

NA (Narcotic's Anonymous) *Also see* Slogans/Program Generic-Mix and Match
Directions to NA: Just go straight to hell and make a u-turn.

From Narcotic's Obvious to Narcotic's Anonymous.

If you lose, you lose.

If you think you are an NA watchdog, just remember that watchdogs have to bark and bite.

If you used enough to get to NA, you used enough.

Life sucks! (But in NA, life sucks one day at a time).

My Gratitude Speaks When I Care and I Share With Others the NA Way.

NA Nazis

NA: We are not reformed junkies–but informed addicts.

Never Alone

N—Fucking—A

One Disease, One Program

The NA Way

The NA Way is the Swiss army knife of NA.

NarAnon: *Also see* Al-Anon

Addiction is not a spectator sport. The whole family gets to participate.

For every action, there is an equal and opposite criticism.

It's all right to have castles in the air but addicts move into them, family members clean them, and counselors collect the rent!

You'd better stop pleasing the addict, because he cannot be pleased; you'd better start pleasing yourself because, at least, someone will be pleased.

Need: *See* Wants and Needs

Nervous(ness):

Nervousness is just God trying to shake the truth out of you.

Newcomer(s):

A newcomer at his first meeting: "Where are all the drunks?"

Anyone under five years is a newcomer.

At the start of meetings we always ask, "Is there anybody new or coming back?" We should also ask, "Is there anybody old and going out?"

Be nice to newcomers; one day they may be your sponsor.

Do not let the newcomer's inner child run our meetings. This is not play therapy.

Don't be a professional newcomer; why don't you become a real newcomer?

Don't drown the newcomer in program; irrigate them in patience.

Don't let your newcomer ego get tied up in being an "Old-timer".

Don't push a newcomer to do the steps too fast. A heavy downpour runs off, whereas a gentle rain soaks in.

Each meeting has two types of newcomers: Beginners and visitors. Beginners have made a decision.

Encouragement from an old-timer can turn a newcomer's life around.

If the newcomer could see no joy in our existence they would not want it.

Keep your hands in your pants and give the newcomer a chance.

Newcomer meets newcomer in AA is worse than the 13th step; it's more like 26.

The first year is free.

The greatest artist was once a beginner. Hang in there.

There are none so righteous as the newly converted.

We don't care if you came from Yale or jail, Skidmoore or skid row, Park Avenue or a park bench.

What happens to newcomers? Old-timers.

When you share with a newcomer, you are teaching myself.
You can only be a newcomer one time.
You need newcomers to tell you where you came from; old-timers, to tell you where you could go, and a *sponsor* to tell you where you are at.

Normal:
Don't try to be normal, try to be healthy.
My sense of reality has calluses. Insanity is normal for me.
Normal is a cycle on your washing machine, not a cycle in your life.
Why, if we could drink normally, we'd get drunk every night!

Now: *Also see* Past, Present, & Future
Do it now.
God grant me patience. NOW.
Here and now: don't postpone living!
If your Higher Power can handle eternity, you can surely handle right now!
No Where to *Now Here*. It works.
Now is God's gift to you. That's why they call it the 'present.'
NOW turned around is WON.
Right here. Right Now
SERENITY NOW
We only need to work this program thoroughly one time: NOW

OA (Overeaters Anonymous):
Abstinence is the most important thing in my life.
Don't romance the aroma.
Don't romance the bite.
Floss and brush after every meal.
Food thoughts are just thoughts. You don't have to eat.
You won't starve to death between meals.
If you have a problem and eat over it, then you have two problems.
It's about the food until it's not about the food.
Short version of the Serenity Prayer: "Lighten up"
It's not what you're eating, it's what's eating you.
Most folks commit suicide with a knife and fork.
Nothing tastes as good as abstinence.
Only losers can win.
One compulsive bite is too many and 100 bites are not enough.
Put down the fork.
Remember, "fat chance" and "slim chance" mean the same thing.
Service is slimming.
There is no situation so bad that a compulsive action can't make it worse.
What's eating you?
Work the program from the waist up.

Obsess(ive):
Alcoholism is a physical allergy combined with a mental obsession.
Alcoholism is a physical compulsion coupled with a mental obsession.

If you're obsessing about something, try praying instead. It's impossible to concentrate on two things at once.

We never obsess about anything good.

Old:

Don't get a new set of old ideas.

Don't worry about avoiding temptation - as you grow older, it will avoid you.

God can't give you anything new until you let go of the old.

Growing old is mandatory; growing up is optional.

Growing Old is Natural... Growing Up is Spiritual...

Old-timer:

All old timers started as newcomers.

An old-timer makes his time count; he doesn't count his time.

At the start of meetings we always ask, "Is there anybody new or coming back?" We should also ask, "Is there anybody old and going out?"

Don't let your newcomer ego be tied up in being an "Old-timer".

Encouragement from an old-timer can turn a newcomer's life around.

How you get to be an old-timer: Don't drink; don't drug; don't die.

No matter how much sobriety you have, you will never rise above the level of human being.

One thing about sobriety, if you don't drink, it lasts a lonnnnng time!

Take care of the days and the years will come by themselves.

When an old-timer dies, a library is lost.

You need newcomers to tell you where you came from; old-timers, to tell you where you could go, and a *sponsor* to tell you where you are at.

Open-minded(ness):

Don't be so open-minded your brains fall out.

Honest * Open-minded * Willing

Honesty * Open-mindedness * Willingness

Honesty, Open-mindedness, Willingness to Learn.

Keep an open mind, something may fall in.

Keep an open mind.

Minds are like parachutes they won't work unless they are open.

Open-minded not Dopen-minded

Open-mindedness is mandatory for an open mind.

You cannot be honest, open-minded, and willing if any part of you is blind including, love, hate, fear, and faith.

Opinion(s):

A sure way to set yourself up for a "slip" is to be convinced that others will slip if they don't listen to your opinion.

An alcoholic can be counted on to have an opinion on just about everyone and everything at all times.

Group conscience: There's room for more than one opinion and none of them has to be wrong.

Opinions are like assholes, everyone has one.

The character of God is not determined by your opinion of Him/Her.

There is a difference between sharing our experience and imposing our opinions.

Optimist/pessimist:
Don't be a W.C.S. person. That's Worst Case scenario.
None ever ruined their eyesight by looking at the bright side of things.
The pessimist sees only the tunnel. The optimist sees the light at the end of the tunnel.

Opportunity:
Alcoholism is an equal opportunity destroyer and the 12 Step program is an equal opportunity restorer.
In the middle of difficulty lies opportunity.
Learn to listen. Opportunity sometimes knocks very softly.
Limitations are opportunities to open new doors.
Man's extremity is God's opportunity.
Many of us fail to recognize "opportunity" because most of the time it is disguised as hard work.
Our need is God's opportunity.
Watch for big problems, they disguise big opportunities.
When one door shuts, another opens.

Ordinary:
God does not want me to do extraordinary things; He wants me to do ordinary things extraordinarily well.
In sobriety, you are given permission to be ordinary.
The only difference between ordinary and extraordinary is that little extra.

Outcome(s): *Also see* Result(s)
Plan, but don't plan the outcome.
There are only three possible outcomes for alcoholics: Locked up, Covered up, or Sobered up!
We're responsible for the effort - not the outcome!

Pain: *Also see* Misery *and* Hurt
A pain shared is a pain cut in half.
All growth is not painful but all pain can be growthful.
Beauty and truth are admired; pain is obeyed.
Change is not painful; resistance to change is painful.
Change only happens when the pain of holding on is greater than the fear of letting go.
Egotism is the drug that soothes the pain of stupidity.
If you share your pain you cut it in half, if you don't you double it.
If you're paining...you're gaining; if you're feeling...you're healing.
Just because you *have* pain, doesn't mean you have to be one.
No pain, no change.
No pain, no gain.
No Pain; No Gain/Know Pain; Know Gain.
Not facing pain prolongs it.
Pain brings people into the program and pain takes them out. Work the steps.
Pain gives willingness, our Higher Power gives recovery.
Pain heals; abuse scars.
Pain instructs or it leads to more pain.
Pain is inevitable; suffering is optional.

Pain is the arrow coming out, not the arrow going in.
Pain is the difference between what is and what you would like it to be.
Pain is the greatest gift God gives to the alcoholic.
Pain is the touchstone of growth.
Pain: It's either suffering or service.
People who think they know it all, are really a pain in the ass for those of us who do.
Reality can be as painful to accept as it was to escape.
Share your pain and let it go.
Thank you for sharing my pain.
The fear of feeling the pain is worse than the pain itself.
The greatest pain of resentment is that everlasting agonizing rehearsal for retribution.
The number one way to relieve pain is to forgive.
The only avoidable pain is the pain we endure in the process of trying to avoid pain.
The pain of becoming is essential to the "Joy of Being."
The pain of growth is a good sign, not a stop sign.
There is absolutely no pain in change or growth. The pain is in the resistance to the change or growth.
When the pain is of no more value, the healing is instantaneous.
When the pain of staying sober becomes less than the pain of getting drunk, you'll stay sober.
Why are you suffering someone else's pain?

Paradox:
Paradox of the alcoholic: balancing low self-esteem with grandiosity.
The paradox of recovery is a clean addict.
The paradox of sobriety is a sober alcoholic.

Party(ing):
From Rave to Grave
Throw a party instead of a fit.

Past, Present, & Future: *Also see* Yesterday, Today & Tomorrow
(__) Anonymous is like a raffle; you must be present to win.
After each meeting, clean up the wreckage of the present.
Definition of the Alcoholic: Makes plans for the past and regrets for the future.
Don't waste your time reliving the past when you can spend it worrying about the future.
Don't let your past become your future.
Enjoy the moment, in a minute it'll be a memory.
Forgiveness is giving up hope for a better past!
Guilt is concerned with the past. Worry is concerned about the future. Contentment enjoys the present.
If you marry your past, you must divorce your future.
If you take the first drink then your PAST becomes your FUTURE!
Insanity is the seeming inability to learn from past mistakes.
It's okay to look back at the past - just don't stare at it.
It's not the yets we have to worry about, it's the again's.
Never look back unless you intend to go that way.
Projection: Living in the wreckage of the future.
Some worry about the wreckage of the past, some dwell in the wreckage of the future.

The longer you've been in recovery, the more successful you've been in the past.
The past is like a rear view mirror. You have to glance at it on occasion, but if you focus on it, you won't see what's right in front of you.
The wreckage of the past is environmentally safe and bio-degradable.
There is no future in the past.
Today is a gift; that's why it's called the 'present.'
Try to improve the wreckage of the present.
Untreated abstinence will make our past our future.
What lies in front of you and what lies behind you is insignificant compared to what lies within you.
When you have one foot in the past and one foot in the future, you're dumping on the present.
Yesterday is but a dream, tomorrow but a vision. Today well lived is a gift, that's why they call it the "Present."
You cannot be there for someone else if you are not present for yourself.
You must be present to win.

Patience:
Ask for patience, and you're likely to get a traffic jam.
Cultivate patience
Cunning, baffling, powerful, and *patient.*
Don't be impatient with the universe—it sure hasn't been impatient with you!
Don't drown the newcomer in program; irrigate them in patience.
Have patience with all things, but first with yourself.
It's more important to get it right, than get it first.
Patience is giving God space.
Patience is the ability to idle your motor when you feel like stripping your gears.
Patience: Everything in God's time (and God doesn't wear a watch).
Procrastination is fear in five syllables. Patience is faith in two.

Path: *Also see* Journey *and* Travel(ing)
If you find a path with no obstacles, it probably doesn't lead anywhere.
The longer you are sober, the narrower the path.

Peace:
Cultivate peace.
Deep Peace
Do you want to be right or do you want peace?
For peace of mind, resign as general manager of the universe.
If you do not find "the peace of mind" you keep hearing about in AA try working the steps.
No Peace; No God. Know Peace; Know God.
Rather than giving others a piece of your mind, don't—and have peace of mind.
Recovery is education; peace of mind is graduation.
Release for Peace
Until you make peace with who you are, you'll never be content with what you have.

People Please:
Don't "people please", "Higher Power Please."
Formula for failure: try to please everyone.

Stop people pleasing, OK?
You'd better stop pleasing the alcoholic, because he cannot be pleased; you'd better start pleasing yourself because, at least, someone will be pleased.

Perception:
A spiritual awakening does not change your world, it changes your perception of the world. Everything is perception.
If your only tool is a hammer, everything you see will be a nail.
It may not be your attitude problem, but their perception problem.
Our perception of what's happening and what's really happening are two completely different things.
Situations don't change so much as your perception of them.
You don't have a problem unless you think you do.

Perfect(ion):
Alcoholics think every day should be perfect.
Doing our best is as close to perfect as we need to get.
Don't put off being happy until you are perfect.
God gives us tasks to do knowing we are incapable of doing them perfectly, but not incapable of trying.
If life was a problem to be avoided, drinking was the perfect solution.
If you try to be perfect you will be frustrated all the time.
In life, the process is perfect.
Nobody's perfect, not even your sponsor.
People come in a lot of varieties, but perfect isn't one of them.
Practice makes better.
Progress, not perfection.
Strive for perfection; accept progress.
The first step is the only step a person can work perfectly.
The list of "perfect" sponsors, is a blank sheet of paper on the bulletin-board.
The process is perfect; *let it work.*
Today is perfect (the problem is, we'll only find out tomorrow.)
We are not Saints…

Pessimist: *See* Optimist/Pessimist

Pick up:
A slip occurs before you pick up.
Before you pick up a drink, think it all the way through.
Don't pick up and you won't get high.
If you don't pick up, you will have clean time. If you work the steps, you will have recovery.
If you get in the urge to pick up, pick up the phone.
If you have one hand in the fellowship and one hand in God's, you can't pick up today.
Just don't pick up the first one.
Life picks up when we put down.
Once you pick up a drink, the steps are totally bewildering.
Pick up the telephone before you pick up a drink.
Put down the weapons, pick up the tools.

There are no fatal decisions, as long as you don't pick up that first fix, pill, or drink.
When you fall, pick something up.
You must learn to pick up a program, not just set down a drink!

Pills: *Also see* PPA (Prescription Pills Anonymous)
The best sleeping pill is a clear conscience.
Too often alcoholism is treated as a Valium deficiency.

Pity Pot:
Along the road well traveled, there are many pity potholes.
Chapter Five is called "How It Works," not "Why Me?"
Don't allow self-pity. The moment this emotion strikes, do something nice for someone less fortunate than you.
Don't make the pity pot too comfortable.
For some alcoholics, a little whine is more than we need and a lot more than we can handle.
Get off the pity pot.
It's all right to sit on your pit pot every now and again. Just be sure to flush when you are done.
On the pity pot? Change a thought, move a muscle.
Poor me, poor me, pour me a drink.
Self-pity always follows resentment.
Self-pity is just a temper tantrum with God.
Thou shalt not snivel.
Wallowing in self pity? Get off the cross, we need the wood!

Plan(s):
Definition of the Alcoholic: Makes plans for the past and regrets for the future.
Fear is what keeps you from God's plan for you.
He who fails to plan, plans to fail.
If you want to make God laugh, tell him YOUR plans for the day.
Plan Plans, Not Results.
Plan to be spontaneous.
Plan, but don't plan the outcome.
Plan, don't project.
There's your plan and there's God's plan-and yours doesn't matter.
Use the 24-hour plan

Power(less): *Also see* Higher Power
Do not allow others to upset you; their only power comes from your reaction.
Fear has no power unless you give it power.
ME + U is a power greater than ME. U + US is a power greater than U.
Powerless over people, places and things; it's a two-way street.
Strength in powerlessness.
The Power behind us is much greater than the problems in front of us.
We are powerless over people, places, and things.
Worry comes from your belief that you are powerless.
You're powerless over the first drink, but not powerless over your choices.

PPA (Prescription Pills Anonymous) *Also See* Slogans/Program Generic-Mix and Match
In PPA we are Pillers of the community.

Practice:
Anonymous does not work in theory; it only works in practice.
Learning to forgive takes practice.
Practice forgiveness for your own sake, if not for others.
Practice love and service at work and at home, not just in meetings.
Practice makes it better.
Practice makes progress.
Practice Rigorous Honesty
Practice these principles in all your affairs—or change your affairs.
Practice what you preach and share what you practice.
Practicing principles simply put is: There is no right way to do the wrong thing.
Successful living must be practiced daily.
The program does not work in principle. It only works in practice.
When you practice principles, how you feel is not the point.

Pray(er(s): *Also see the chapter:* Higher Powered Pages
A day hemmed in prayer is less likely to unravel.
A lot of kneeling will keep you in good standing.
A meeting lasts from preamble to prayer.
A short version of the serenity prayer: Forget it!
Always pray for willingness.
Ask God not for things to enjoy life, but rather life that you may enjoy all things.
Be careful what you pray for...you just might get it.
Courage is fear that has said its prayers.
Don't pray for justice. Pray for mercy.
Every good thought is a prayer.
Faith is fear that has said it's prayer's.
Foxhole Prayers
He who kneels before God can stand before anyone.
Hit it (him/her) with a prayer, not a chair!
I will to will your will. ~ CDA Book Page 48
If we're not praying, we're not staying.
If you are having trouble getting on your knees to pray in the morning, put your shoes under the middle of the bed the night before.
If you are too busy to pray, you are too busy.
If you pray for a Porsche and God sends you a jackass, ride it.
If you pray for honesty, the chances of you lying go 'way up.
If you pray, don't worry. If you worry don't pray.
If you're obsessing about something, try praying instead. It's impossible to concentrate on two things at once.
If your prayers don't mean anything to you, they mean even less to your Higher Power.
If you're going to worry, why pray?
It pays to pray.
It's hard to stumble when you are down on your knees.
Life is fragile; handle with prayer.

No prayer of despair ever goes unanswered.

Note to self: Remember to pray.

One of the best ways to get your prayers answered is to get up off your knees and go to work.

Only pray for potatoes when you intend to pick up a hoe.

Pray and stay in today.

Pray and wait for the answer. If you don't get an answer, that's the answer.

Pray as if it's all up to God, work as if it's all up to you.

Pray daily, God is easier to talk to than most people.

Pray for a good harvest and go get the plow.

Pray like you mean it.

Pray not for a lighter burden but for a stronger back.

Pray to catch the bus, then run as fast as you can.

Pray. God loves to hear the voice of a stranger.

Prayer changes things, but worry changes nothing.

Prayer does not change the situation, it changes the person who prays.

Prayer does not change what you are praying about. Prayer changes *you*.

Prayer. It helps!

Prayers are us calling God. Intuition is when God answers.

Prayers must have feet.

Prayers that are answered are Prayers with feet.

Praying is asking God for help; meditating is listening for God's answer.

Put a little prayer in your air

Sometimes you have to get on your knees to rise.

Tears are liquid prayers.

The hardest part of The Serenity Prayer is the first word.

There is no "Amen" at the end of the 3rd step prayer, only after the 7th step prayer.

Trying to pray *is* praying.

When we offer prayers up, blessings come down.

Worry is a prayer for something you don't want.

You can pray now and again to get out of trouble or you can pray every day and stay out of trouble.

Present: *See* Past, Present, & Future

Pride (proud):

Be proud of yourself, just don't chose drinking as the subject of your pride.

False Pride: Lying in the gutter, looking down on the rest of the world.

False pride: when one says he has nothing to say and then takes twenty minutes to prove it.

Medication for humility: Swallow your pride.

Pride is like body order: Everyone notices except the person who has it.

Swallow your pride—it's non-fattening.

Swallow your pride—zero calories.

Swallowing one's pride never choked anyone.

Temper gets you into a problem, and pride keeps you there.

When your head begins to swell, your mind stops growing.

You can't save your face and your butt at the same time.

You can't get indigestion from swallowing your pride.

Principle(s):
Examine what is said, not who speaks.
One way to tell how well you're practicing the principles in all of your affairs is to notice how you treat people who can be of no service to you.
Practice these principles in all your affairs—or change your affairs.
Practicing principles simply put is: There is no right way to do the wrong thing.
Principles before Personalities
Principles before Personals

Prison(er): *See Also Jail(s)*
The people you hang with are the people you hang with.
We didn't have relationships, we took prisoners and held hostages.

Problem(s):
A good scapegoat is nearly as welcome as a solution to the problem.
A problem shared is a problem halved.
A smooth sea never made a skillful sailor.
Alcohol was not the problem—it was the solution. The problem was alcoholism.
Any problem blesses us when we learn the lesson it teaches.
Controlling life isn't the answer, it's the problem.
Don't tell your Higher Power how big the problem is; tell the problem how big your Higher Power is.
Every day is perfect. The problem is, you don't know until tomorrow.
Focus on the program-not the problem.
God is the answer. Now what is the problem?
Got a problem? Get a pencil!
If drinking were our only problem, rehabs would turn out winners.
If you are having a difficult time being thankful, the problem may be your memory.
If you think you have a drinking problem, you probably do.
Is alcohol the cause of your problems or the result?
It may not be your attitude problem, but their perception problem.
Live in the solution, not the problem.
Make the solution so big, the problem does not exist.
My problems are guidelines, not stop signs.
Normal people don't wonder if they have a drinking problem.
Others may be responsible for your troubles. You are responsible for your recovery.
Our problem is not information or insight, it is lack of action.
Prior Planning Prevents Problems!
Problems always melt in the face of laughter.
Problems have a high infant mortality rate.
Rather than using God to solve your problems, use your problems to get closer to God..
Recovery may not solve all your problems but it is willing to share them.
Stinking thinking leads to stinking drinking which causes stinking problems.
Suicide is a permanent solution to a temporary problem.
Temper gets you into a problem, and pride keeps you there.
The biggest problem in the world could have been easily solved when it was small.
The Power behind us is much greater than the problems in front of us.
There is an easy answer to your problem that is neat, plausible, and wrong.

There will always be problems, whether you're drunk or sober.

There's no problem that can't be made worse by picking up a fix, pill, or drink.

Today, we have more solutions than problems.

Watch for big problems, they disguise big opportunities.

What you thought was the solution became the problem.

When we dwell on the problem, the problem gets bigger. When we dwell on the solution, the solution gets bigger.

When we get tangled up in our problems, be still. That way God can untangle the knot.

When you look in the mirror, you are looking at the problem, but, remember, you are also looking at the solution.

Why questions keep you in the problem while *How questions* keep you in the solution.

Work the program, not the problem.

Work the Steps. You may still have living problems but you will no longer have problems living.

You are the problem, but you are also the solution.

You don't have a problem unless you think you do.

Your situation is your situation, not your problem.

Procrastinate(ion):

Begin: the rest is easy.

If it were not for the last minute, a lot of things would never get done.

Never put off till tomorrow what you can forget about forever.

Nothing makes a person more productive than the last minute.

Procrastination is fear in five syllables. Patience is faith in two.

The alcoholic compulsion to have everything done right this minute is usually balanced by a rare talent for procrastination.

What is it that makes people suppose they can more easily do twice tomorrow what they didn't do once today?

Why put off today, what you can put off tomorrow?

Professional(s):

It's all right to have castles in the air but addicts move into them, family members clean them and counselors collect the rent!

Remember, the Ark was built by amateurs; the Titanic by professionals.

Program(s): *Also see* Slogans/Program-Generic. Mix and Match *and* Recovery

AA is a program that comforts the disturbed and disturbs the comfortable.

Abstinence leads to sobriety. The program and 12 steps lead to recovery.

An alcoholic is an individual who takes the most simple program and works on it until he has eventually reduced it to its most complicated form.

Are you around the program or in the program?

Don't work my program, or your program, work "the program".

Don't worry, if you don't get the program right away, it *will* get you.

First we work the program because we have to. Then we work the program because we are willing to. Finally we work the program because we want to.

Focus on the program, not the problem.

Garbage in, garbage out - dump yours out regularly.

Get a 100 proof program.

Give the program one hour a day and it'll give you 23 back.

If it's working, don't fix it.

If you are done using, you can't work the program bad enough; if you're not done using, you can't work the program good enough.

If you do what we do, you can have what we have.

If you don't buy the whole package, you are cheating yourself.

If you have one hand in the program and one hand in your Higher Power's, you won't have a hand to pick up with.

If you live on the edge of the program, you might fall off.

If you stop doing the things that keep you in the program, you will go back to doing the things that brought you to the program.

Is your program powered by Will Power or Higher Power?

It may be a simple program, but it's not easy.

It works better if you get into the program instead of just getting around the program.

It works if you work it and won't if you don't.

It works if you work it.

It's a daily program: Yesterday's home run may not be enough to win the game today.

It's a program of attraction, not promotion.

It's a selfish program.

It's a simple program for complicated people.

Look for a way in; not for a way out.

No matter how long you are in this program, you will never rise above the level of human being.

Our program does not teach us how to handle drinking and drugging. It teaches us how to handle recovery.

Our program will work for people who believe in God. Our program will work for people who don't believe in God. Our program will *not* work for people who believe they are God.

Pain brings people into the program and pain takes them out.

Pain is part of the program, suffering is optional.

Step up to the program.

Sweat the small stuff, the big stuff we can handle. It's the day to day crap that messes us up.

Take the program seriously, not yourself.

The 12 Step programs do not have to be your whole life, but they do keep your life whole.

The only question is, are you closer to being the person today that you wanted everyone to think you were?

The program does not work in principle; it only works in practice.

The program does not work in theory. It only works in practice.

The program is education without graduation.

The program is for participants, not spectators.

The program is for those who want it.

The program is like a submarine. It is much better to be in it than around it.

The program is like a swimming pool, and you can't learn to swim until you get in.

There are no grades in this program, just pass or fail and if you fail, you get to come back.

There are no musts in our program, but a lot of "have-to's".

This is a Positive Program for Negative people.

This is a self-help program that you can't do by yourself.

This is a twelve-step-program, not thirteen.

Treatment is discovery and the program is recovery.

Try the program for 90 days. If not satisfied, we will gladly refund your misery.

Use the 24-hour plan.

We only need to work this program thoroughly one time: NOW

When your insides match your outsides, then you're practicing a good program.

Work the program hard; life is easy. Work the program easy*; life is hard.*

Work the program, not the problem.

You don't get drunk watching another drink. You won't get serenity watching others do the Steps.

You must learn to pick up a program, not just set down a drink!

You must work a full program in a half-way house.

You never get your teeth so white that you never have to brush them again.

You're not required to like it, you're only required to DO it.

Progress:
Change is mandatory, progress optional.

Count the lessons learned from failures as rungs upon the ladder of progress.

Don't resist change, there's no way to progress without it.

Even though the right road seems all uphill, I'll never get there if I don't go.

If you're faced in the right direction, and you fall on your face, you've still made progress.

Material well-being always follows spiritual progress, never precedes it.

Most people resist change and yet it's the only thing that brings progress.

Move forward; don't look back

Practice makes progress.

Progress, not perfection.

Progression: The bottom will start falling out faster than you can lower your standards.

Strive for perfection; accept progress.

There's only one way to coast, and that's downhill.

We claim progress, not perfection.

You are either *pro*gressing or *re*gressing. There is no such thing as simply "gressing."

Projection:
A good way to discover your shortcomings is to observe what annoys you in others.

Don't hide from people who aren't there.

You spot it, you got it.

Promise(s):
A winner makes commitments; a loser makes promises.

Recovery delivers everything drugs promised.

Sobriety delivers everything alcohol promised.

Twelve steps lead to twelve promises and they begin before we are half way through.

Purpose:
Do not put the sole purpose of any fellowship above the soul purpose.

Live life on purpose, not by accident.

Question(ing):
"Why" questions keep me in the problem while "How" questions keep me in the solution.

Ask better questions.

Ask questions that lead to exclamations not explanations.
Ask the right question; get the right answer.
If using is the answer, what is the question?
People who ask "Why?" keep others from getting things done. Those who ask "Why not?" get things done.
The only dumb question is the one not asked.
The only question is, are you closer to being the person today that you wanted everyone to think you were?
There are no stupid questions, only stupid answers.
There is only one question you should ever ask yourself, "What is God's will for me today?"

Quit(ing):
Don't quit before the miracle happens.
If you want to quit USING; you are going to have to quit USING.
Meetings are for quitters.
Quit for Good.
Quit quitting and be done.
Quit thinking. (It's what got you here.)
Quit while you're behind.
Quitters never win and winners never quit.
Quitting is easy; it's staying stopped that's hard.
Rehab is for quitters.
Surrender, don't quit.
You hit your bottom when you quit digging!

Rationalize(tion):
Everything after the word "But" cancels out everything before it.
Rationalization is like masturbation, you are only screwing yourself.

React(ion):
Act, don't react.
Alcoholism is for people who have an adverse reaction to reality.
Do not allow others to upset you; their only power comes from your reaction.
Fear is not a shortcoming- it's an emotion. Our reaction to it can be the shortcoming.
It's a lot easier to react than it is to think.

Reality:
Alcoholism is for people who have an adverse reaction to reality.
Do reality, it is the easier softer way.
Don't let your reality check bounce.
Hitting bottom happens when reality speaks to you clearly.
If only—What if—As if—The three "realities" of the alcoholic.
Reality can be as painful to accept as it was to escape.
Reality check: you are here "X."
Reality is a crutch for people who can't handle drugs.
Reality: It's real.
Sanity begins with the admission of reality into the mind.
You can change any thought that hurts into a reality that hurts even more.

You can't change reality, but you can change your attitude towards it.
You either are or you aren't.

Reason(s):
Even if you do the right thing for the wrong reason, it's still the wrong thing to do.
Everything happens for a reason.
If you come into an AA meeting looking for recovery, you will find exactly that. If you come looking for a reason to continue drinking, you'll eventually find that, too.
Reasons that sound good aren't always good sound reasons.
The reason people blame other people is because there is only one alternative.
There are a million excuses to drink, but no good reason.
There are no good reasons for anger, only excuses.
When your only reason for doing something is because you have the right, it usually turns out wrong.

Recover(y):
Abstinence leads to sobriety. The program and 12 Steps lead to recovery.
Addiction is a lifestyle whereby we love things and use people. Recovery is a lifestyle whereby we love people and use things.
Addiction: touched by an angle. Recovery: touched by an angel.
All 12 Step Roads lead to recovery.
Another day, another recovery!
Anything we place in front of our recovery, we'll lose.
Be insistent, consistent, and persistent in recovery.
Beginning Recovery: Ready, Fire, Aim.
Death, Insanity, or Recovery.
Don't let your starting point in recovery ever discourage you. Anyone who gets to be an old timer had to begin where they were.
Every recovery from alcoholism began with the first sober hour.
Recovery is a school in which we are all learners and all teachers
Got recovery?
Having a relationship in early recovery is like pouring Miracle Grow on your character defects.
If it's working, don't fix it.
If we make half-assed amends, we'll half-way recover.
If you aren't enjoying your life…then you aren't recovering.
If you come to a meeting looking for recovery, you will find exactly that. If you come looking for a reason to continue drinking, you'll eventually find that, too.
If you're lucky, life in recovery can be really boring.
In recovery, the years go by quickly. It is the individual days that we have trouble with.
In recovery, you get an owners manual to go with your new life.
It doesn't cost a lot of money for you to recover. It just takes everything you have.
It gets better.
Keep your cock (or cash, or car) out of recovery.
Life without recovery: *Even roses have thorns*. Life in recovery: *Even thorns have roses*.
May you be blessed with a slow recovery.
My recovery, my pace, my choice.
No one floats into recovery on the wings of victory.
Not drinking is a symptom of your recovery.

Others may be responsible for your troubles. You are responsible for your recovery.

Our program does not teach us how to handle drinking and drugging. It teaches us how to handle recovery.

People have the right not to recover.

Picture yourself "recovered."

Plant seeds, reap recovery

Put recovery first and everything you put second will be first class.

Put your recovery first to make it last.

Recovery can't begin until the drinking stops!

Recovery comes with an instruction manual: The Big Book, the Basic Text, the First Edition

Recovery delivers everything drugs promised.

Recovery is a contact sport.

Recovery is a disease we catch from our ears.

Recovery is a journey, not a destination.

Recovery is a school in which we are all learners and all teachers.

Recovery is a stairway, not a landing.

Recovery is an inside job.

Recovery is contagious; we catch it from coffee cups.

Recovery is education; Peace of Mind is graduation.

Recovery is God's will for you.

Recovery is its own reward.

Recovery is like trying to drown and swim at the same time.

Recovery is not a word, it is The Word.

Recovery is not an Event. It is a Process.

Recovery is not the absence of conflict, but the ability to cope with it.

Recovery is safe.

Recovery is the natural order of life.

Recovery is the process of "recovering" who we are.

Recovery isn't a death sentence. It's a life sentence.

Recovery may not solve all your problems but it is willing to share them.

Recovery really is simple. It's just not always easy.

Recovery Unity Service

Recovery, on loan from God.

Recovery: Respect it, Protect it.

Recovery: Try it and see what happens.

Recovery is the easier, softer way

Slipping: Recovery is a lifestyle, not a turnstyle

Slow and sure.

Stay in the main tent, and out of the side shows.

Step over the bodies if you have to.

The best way to multiply recovery: divide it.

The gateway to recovery is always open.

The longer you've been in recovery, the more successful you've been in the past.

The miracle of recovery is that no matter where you are, you're here.

The paradox of recovery is a sober alcoholic.

The quality of your recovery is proportional to the quality of your surrender.

The Road to Recovery is ALWAYS under construction.

The spiritual part of recovery is like the wet part of the ocean.

There are no strangers in recovery – just friends we have never met.
Things got worse, things got better, and things got different.
Treatment is discovery and (__)A is recovery.
Treatment is discovery and the program is recovery.
Two people in recovery trying to have a relationship is like two garbage trucks colliding.
Uncover to Recover.
Unity, Service, & Recovery
We do it the old fashioned way, we earn our recovery.
We have much to recover and we have much to recover from.
We're not against drugs; we're for recovery.
Where do you find recovery? Twelve steps past any lengths.
Worry slows recovery.
You can't speed up your recovery, but you sure can slow it down.
You know you're in recovery when everyone else sees a bum and you see a prospect.
You may have another drink in you, but do you have another recovery?
You may only have one recovery in you.
You're worth it.
You're not responsible for your disease, but you are responsible for your recovery.

Rehab(ilitation): *Also see* Treatment *and* Detox
Rehab Is for Quitters.
If drinking were our only problem, rehabs would turn out winners.

Rejection:
Embrace the power of love. Reject the love of power.
Rejection is God's protection.
You cannot be rejected by another human being – all they can tell you is what their limits are.

Relationship(s): *Also see* Friendship(s)
Alcoholics don't have relationships; they take hostages.
Even if you give 100%, it's still only 50%.
For true intimacy to take place, you must be a whole person forming a partnership, not a broken person seeking another to be whole.
God will heal your broken heart, if you will give Him all the pieces.
Having a relationship in early recovery is like pouring Miracle Grow on your character defects.
Hot words make for a cool relationship.
If you are constantly being mistreated, you are probably co-operating with the treatments.
If you're always walking on eggshells around your partner, that's fowl play.
It takes two to make a relationship and only one to bring it down.
It's not a question of finding the right person, but becoming the right person.
Looking for the right person? Become the right person.
Men are from Earth. Women are from Earth. Learn to live with it.
No matter how bad your heart is broken the world doesn't stop for your grief.
Practice these principles in all our affairs.
Principals before personals
See no evil, hear no evil, date no evil.
The one who controls the least controls the relationship.
This is a twelve-step-program, not thirteen.

To an alcoholic, relationships are like buses-there'll be another one along any time now.
To the world you might be one person, but to one person you just might be the world.
Today do something for someone you love: Leave them alone
Try to become the person you'd like to come home to.
Two people in recovery trying to have a relationship is like two garbage trucks colliding.
We are sent helpers, friends, and lovers.
We don't have relationships, we take hostages.
When newcomer meets newcomer in Narcotic's Anonymous, it is worse than the 13th step-it's more like 26.
You spend more time with yourself than with anyone else. Doesn't it make sense to put something into that relationship?

Relapse: *Also see* Slip *and* Trigger
Addiction is the leading cause of relapse.
An ounce of prevention is worth a gallon of relapse.
Call before you drink and we will help you stay sober. Call after you drink and you will help us stay sober.
Cunning, baffling, powerful, and patient.
Daniel didn't go back to the lion's den to get his hat.
Don't entertain the thought.
Each time you come back, the tuition goes up.
Getting sober is a process; relapsing is a process, too.
If you hang around a barber shop, eventually you're going to get clipped.
Nothing is so bad that relapse won't make it worse.
People who relapse usually do so because they accepted the things they could have changed.
Relapse is a part of addiction.
Relapse is a part of recovery.
Relapse is a part of recovery: NOT!
Relapse is NOT a requirement.
Relapse starts long before the drink is drunk.
The door swings both ways.
There are a million excuses to drink, but no good reason.
There's no grades here. Only pass or fail and if you fail, you get to come back.
Try again - you can't fall out of the gutter.
What (__)A gives back to me could take me out again.
When you dance with a gorilla, it's the gorilla who decides when to stop.

Relax:
Learn to relax without feeling guilty.
Life is only temporary, relax and enjoy it!
Relax, God is in charge.
Relax, Relate, Release

Religious(on):
God wants spiritual fruit, not religious nuts.
Religion is for those who want life after death. Spirituality is for those who want life BEFORE death!
Religious people hope to avoid hell; spiritual people have been there.

Remember:
Always remember we are being taken care of.
As you sponsor others, remember this: If you are trying to recreate someone in your own image, then one of you will be redundant.
Blackouts are not such a bad thing; the stuff we remember is bad enough!
If you don't remember what God did for you yesterday, you'll have trouble trusting Him today.
Just remember, the darkest hour is only sixty minutes long.
Keep it simple and remember to thank yourself.
Live today as you want to remember your life.
Note to self: Remember to pray.
One day at a time, remember: The mighty oak was once a little nut that held its ground.
Remember that a wrong act will prey upon your mind until you either do something to rectify it or get drunk.
Remember that if only through gratitude, we must help others in order to help ourselves.
Remember to listen to the message, not the messenger.
Remember where you came from.
Remember, God still makes house calls.
Remember, the Ark was built by amateurs; the Titanic by professionals.
Remember, we were all born to be happy, joyous and free.
Remember, your best thinking got you here in the first place.
Remember—you are not important, your responsibilities are.
Some say if you can't remember your last drunk, you may not have had it.
To be wronged is nothing unless you insist on remembering it.
We are very small when the stars come out at night, yet remember that we too, are made of stardust.
When you kill time, remember it has no resurrection.
When you're feeling overwhelmed, remember to take things one at a time—one day at a time.
You are heading towards a slip when you remember the good times more than the bad.

Repeat(ing-repetition):
Breathe in. Breathe out. REPEAT.
Everybody makes mistakes. Fools repeat them, the weak excuse them, only the wise admit and profit from them.
From repetition comes recognition.
Insanity is repeating the same mistakes over and over again and expecting different results.
It's not making a mistake that means anything, it's in never repeating it.
Progress is not so much indicated by not making a mistake as in never repeating it.
Repetition—is the mother of learning. Action—is the final result.
The lesson will repeat until it is learned.
The one good thing about repeating your mistakes is that you know when to change.

Repression:
Repression causes depression.
Repression is your disease asking you to come out and play.

Reputation:
Character is what you really are, while your reputation is merely what others think you are.
It's easier to change your behavior in advance than to change your reputation afterward.

Reputation is what people think of us. Character is what God knows about us.

Resent(ment):
A resentment is like drinking poison and expecting the other person to die.
A thorough 4th Step will ruin your ability to hold resentments.
All it takes to start a new meeting is a resentment and a coffeepot.
An expectation is a premeditated resentment.
Better to be a resentment than to have one.
By releasing resentment, we set ourselves free.
Expectation is premeditated resentments.
Expectations are resentments waiting to happen.
If resentment is not relinquished entirely, it is not relinquished at all.
If we have a rat in the cellar, we have a choice: go down there and feed it or starve it.
If your heart is full of gratitude, there is no room for resentment.
Rather than getting even with those that hurt you, the challenge is to get even with those that help you.
Resentment is a cup of poison we pour for our enemy and drink ourselves.
Resentment is from the Latin, meaning to "feel again."
Resentment is like burning down your house to get rid of a rat.
Resentment is like letting someone live rent-free in your head.
Resentment is when you didn't get your way yesterday. *Anger* is when you don't get your way today. *Fear* is that you won't get your way tomorrow.
Resentments are like stray cats: if you don't feed them, they'll go away.
Resentments are like stray dogs: if you don't pet them, they will go away.
Self-pity always follows resentment.
The flip side to forgiveness is resentment.
The greatest pain of resentment is that everlasting agonizing rehearsal for retribution.
The road to resentment is paved with expectation.
To be wronged is nothing unless you insist on remembering it.
Try to be grateful and resentful at the same time, you can't serve two masters.
We get something out of each meeting we attend, even if it's only a resentment.
What fire dies when you feed it?
When you are living inside someone's head, you are out of your mind.
When you tighten the noose of resentment around someone's neck, you choke yourself.
While you're carrying a resentment, the other guy's out dancing.
You may become the person you used to resent!

Resist(ance):
Change is not painful; resistance to change is painful.
Don't resist change; there's no way to progress without it.
Resistance is only a waste of strength.
There is absolutely no pain in change or growth. The pain is in the resistance to the change or growth.
What We Resist – Persists

Respect:
Enforce the "Respect-me rules"
Recovery: Respect it, Protect it.

Respect is for the Respectable.
Respect the anonymity of others.
Self-respect is the most important respect you can earn.

Responsible(ity):
Claim full "response-ability."
Faith is our greatest gift. Sharing it with others is our greatest responsibility.
How you respond is your responsibility.
If it is to be, it's up to me.
If you let other people do it for you, they invariably will do it to you.
It helps to learn the difference between being responsible to others and being responsible for others.
My behavior, my responsibility; your behavior, your responsibility.
Others may be responsible for your troubles. You are responsible for your recovery.
Our background and circumstances may have influenced who we are, but we are responsible for who we become.
Remember—you are not important, your responsibilities are.
Responsibility: Your response to God's ability.
Take responsibility for your attitude, not my actions.
We are not to "blame" if we accept responsibility for our feelings.
We are responsible for what we do, no matter how we feel.
We're responsible for the effort - not the outcome!
You are not responsible for their feelings-just your behavior.
You are responsible for what you think of you. You are not responsible for what others think of you.
You aren't responsible for anyone's happiness but your own.
You're not responsible for your disease, but you are responsible for your recovery.

Results: *Also see* Outcome(s)
If you have never experienced the results of working the 12 Steps, no explanation is sufficient.
If you have experienced the results of working the 12 Steps, then no explanation is necessary.
If you keep doing the same thing over and over, you'll keep getting the same thing over and over.
If you take right actions, you'll get right results.
Insanity is not doing the same thing over and over again expecting different results; insanity is doing the same thing over and over again.
Insanity is repeating the same mistakes over and over again and expecting different results.
Is alcohol the cause of your problems or the result?
Things turn out the best for those who make the best of the way things turn out.
You reap what you throw.

Revenge:
If you want to bury someone with revenge, it is best to dig two graves.
Living well is the best revenge.
Rather than getting even with those that hurt you, the challenge is to get even with those that help you.
Time wasted in getting even can never be used in getting ahead.
What goes around, comes around.

What goes around, goes around.
Whenever you try to get even, you get even worse.
You cannot get ahead when you are getting even.

Right:
Do the next, right thing.
Do the right thing, not the self-righteous thing.
Do you want to be right or do you want peace?
Even if you do the right thing for the wrong reason, it's still the wrong thing to do.
Even though the right road seems all uphill, you'll never get there if you don't go.
Guidance shows us which is the right side—not which side is right.
If something is right, it can be done. If it is wrong it can be done without.
If you are right, you don't need to be angry. If you are wrong, you can't afford to be angry.
If you don't have the time to do something right, when will you have the time to do it over?
If you take right actions, you'll get right results.
If you're faced in the right direction, and you fall on your face, you've still made progress.
In (__)A, it doesn't matter who is right–only who is left.
It takes less time to do something right, than to explain to your sponsor why you did it wrong.
It's more important to get it right, than get it first.
It's not a question of finding the right person, but becoming the right person.
Looking for the right person? Become the right person.
People have the right not to recover.
Practicing principles simply put is: There is no right way to do the wrong thing.
Right place, right time, right here, right now
Right thinker.
The fastest way to end an argument is to give up being right.
The man who says, "I can't", is usually right.
There is no mistake so great as that of being always right.
There is no right way to do the wrong thing.
We can act ourselves into right thinking much earlier than we can think ourselves into right action.
When you are in the wrong place, the right place is empty.
When you are wrong, step forward; when you are right, step back.
When you ask the right question, you get the right answer.
When you know you are wrong, admit it. When you know you are right, shut your mouth.
When your only reason for doing something is because "you have the right!" it usually turns out wrong.
You have the right to be wrong.
You may not know what right is, but now you know what wrong is.
You must allow people to be right, because it consoles them for not being anything else.
You're right where you're supposed to be.

Risk:
A ship that stays in the dock is safe, but that's not what ships are for.
If you have never failed, you have never risked.

Romance:
Abstinence makes the heart grow fonder.

Don't romance the drink.
Don't romance the drug.
For romance in AA the odds are good and goods are odd.
You attract what you are, not what you want.

Run(ner):
Yesterday's home run may not be enough to win the game today.
Highs are short lived. Serenity is a long-distance runner.
Self-will run riot.
Don't run from; run to.
No matter how fast or how far you go, you can't outrun God.
No matter how fast or how far you go, you can't out run yourself.
You can't run from God, so let God run you.

SA: (Sexoholic's Anonymous, Sex and Love Addicts Anonymous, et al)
A drug is a drug is a drug (even sex).
Addictive sex is a perfect solvent: It dissolves marriages, families, and careers.
Friends don't let friends drive naked.
You can lead a horse to water but you can't make 'em.

SA: (Smoker's Anonymous)
In Smokers Anonymous, my sponsor is Nosmo King.
Lengths Become Strengths
Oozy Does It
Pray instead of puff.
Put a little prayer in your air.
Quit for Good.
Quit for yourself.
Smoking is Not an Option
Suck, bite, or chew
To Postpone it, Phone it
You're just one convenience store away from a slip.

Sanity: *Also see* Insanity
My sanity is inversely proportional to my expectations.
Restored to sanity
You are a sane person in an insane situation.

Sarcasm:
Sarcasm is derived from a Greek word meaning to "tear flesh!"
The only weapon that gets sharper when you use it, is the tongue.

Save:
For Women: A male sponsor will pat your ass and a female will save it.
We came to AA to save our ass, and found out our soul was attached .
You can't save your ass and your face at the same time.

Search (& Seek-er):
An alcoholic will steal your wallet. A drug addict will steal your wallet and help you look for it.
Believe those who are seeking the truth. Doubt those who have found it.
Do not search for happiness. Search for right living, and happiness will be your reward.
For true intimacy to take place, you must be a whole person forming a partnership, not a broken person seeking another to be whole.
If you come into a meeting searching for recovery, you will find exactly that. If you come searching for a reason to continue drinking and drugging, you'll eventually find that, too.
If you're looking for God, you'll never see God more at work than at an (__)A meeting.
People who seek a sponsor without faults, will be without a sponsor.
Sometimes you have to stop looking to find what you need.
Stop looking, you've found it.
That no addict seeking recovery need ever die...
The basic ingredient of all humility is a desire to seek and do God's will.
True happiness comes to the person who seeks and finds how to help others.
What you seek—you will not find—unless you share it.
When you can't find the solution to a problem, look for the soulution to the problem.

Secrets:
Come out of your closet. You've been hung up long enough.
It's not *your* business to keep *their* secret.
Keeping their secret keeps you sick.
Secrets kill.
The bigger the secret, the more dangerous.
We are only as sick as our secrets; we are only as healthy as our honesty.
We're only as sick as our secrets.
You're only as sick as your secrets.

Self-centered: *See* Selfish

Self Esteem:
Alcoholics go from no self-esteem to low self-esteem.
Envision yourself as God envisions you.
Esteem-able acts build self-esteem.
If you suffer from low self-esteem, do estimable things.
My net worth is not my "self" worth.
Paradox of the alcoholic: balancing low self-esteem with grandiosity.
Self-esteem comes from doing esteemable things.

Self-help:
(__)A. is a self-help program that you can't do by yourself.
You start getting better when you get out of the self-help section.

Self-pity: *See* Pity Pot

Self-righteous:
Do the right thing, not the self-righteous thing.
Self-righteous anger is character assassination.

When you point a finger at another, remember that three are always pointing back at you.

Self-seeking: *See* Selfish

Self-will:
For addicts, self-will leads to a hopeless end and recovery leads to an endless hope.
God's will: you've turned it over. Self-will: you've over turned it.
Seemingly bad days are usually days when we don't get our own way.
Self will imprisons one far more than bars ever do.
Self-will can get you what you want right now, God's will can provide what you need for eternity.
Self-will cannot be overcome by Self-will.
Self-will run riot.
The best thing you can do is get out of your own way.
Things aren't necessarily going wrong just because they're not going your way.
Turn it over; don't overturn it.
You have got to get out of your way.

Selfish (Self-centered, Self-seeking):
An alcoholic only knows one note on the scale: Me, Me, Me.
It's a selfish program.
Self-centeredness is a casualty of spiritual growth.
Selfish or Serving
The differences between selfishness, self-seeking, and self-centered. Selfishness is: It's all for me. Self-centeredness is: It's all about me. Self-seeking is: What's in it for me?
The healthy person finds happiness in helping others. Thus, for him unselfishness is selfish.
We all suffer from self-centered fear.

Self/Myself/Yourself/Ourselves: *Also see* Selfish (Self-centered, Self-seeking)
Anxiety is fear of oneself.
Be yourself today. You are perfect for the part.
Discover yourself. Everything else has been done.
Don't judge yourself by the way you feel.
Don't take yourself too darn seriously.
Egoism isn't necessarily thinking a lot of yourself—just thinking of yourself a lot.
Feel good about yourself by serving others.
Forgiveness of others is a gift to yourself.
Humility doesn't mean thinking any less of yourself, just of yourself less often.
If you are having trouble believing in a power greater than yourself, just try believing in a power other than yourself.
If you don't take care of yourself, why should anyone else?
If you make yourself available, you'll get what you need when you need it.
If you review your problem closely enough, you will recognize yourself as part of the problem.
It's easy to see the difference between ourselves and our inferiors, but it is much harder to see the difference between ourselves and our superiors.
Keep it simple and remember to thank yourself.
Keep the focus on yourself, but once the picture is taken, move on.
Pray as if everything depended on God; work as if everything depends on ourselves.

Refuse to attack yourself.
Take the program seriously, not yourself.
Thou shalt not 'should' on thyself.
To thine own self be true!
We'll love you until you learn to love yourself.
You cannot learn to love yourself until you learn to forgive yourself.

Serenity:
Boredom is the feeling that everything is a waste of time; serenity, that nothing is.
Clean and Serene.
Everything is as it should be.
Highs are short lived. Serenity is a long-distance runner.
My expectations are inversely proportional to my serenity.
My serenity, my pace, my choice
Serenity comes when you stop expecting and start accepting.
Serenity is God's garden. The entrance is though our hearts.
Serenity is not freedom from the storm but peace within the storm.
Serenity is not the absence of disturbance, it is being okay with that disturbance.
SERENITY NOW
Short version of the serenity prayer: Forget it!
Short version of the Serenity Prayer—"F" it.
Short version of the Serenity Prayer—Screw it.
Sobriety then serenity..
The hardest part of The Serenity Prayer is the first word.
What we used to call boredom, we now call serenity.
When you realize there is nothing lacking, the whole world belongs to you.

Serious(ly):
All slips are serious—some are fatal.
Don't take yourself too darn seriously.
Rule 62: Never take yourself too seriously!
Some things are so serious that you can only joke about them.
Take the program seriously, not yourself.
You cannot feel sorry for yourself and laugh at the same time. So take your levity seriously.

Service:
Get it, give it, grow in it
Give a damn; be a channel.
Give your gift away.
If you serve, you will be served.
If you want to feel better right away, ask God to help you be of service.
It's either suffering or service.
Let It Begin With Me
Pass it on
Pay It Forward.
People in our fellowships who think they are too big to do little things are perhaps too little to be asked to do big things.
Practice love and service at work and at home and not just in meetings.

Reach Out
Recovery Unity Service
Selfish or Serving
Service is gratitude in action.
Service is slimming.
Service Saves Lives!
Shut up, show up and say "yes."
Sober and Serving
True happiness is found in service.
Trust in God, clean house, and work with others.
You know you're in recovery when everyone else sees a bum and you see a prospect!
You received without cost, now give without charge.

Sex: *Also see* SA (Sexoholic's Anonymous *and* Sex and Love Addicts Anonymous, et al)
Addictive Sex is a perfect solvent: It dissolves marriages, families, and careers.
Alcohol: It provokes the desire but takes away the performance.
Before, it was so many women and so little time. Now it's so many defects and so little time.
Keep your cock (or cash, or car) out of recovery.
Keep your hands in your pants & give the newcomer a chance.
"Practicing these principles in all our affairs" is not referring to sex!
Sleazy does it, one lay at a time.
Sobriety is like sex. If it doesn't feel good, you're not doing it right.

Shame:
All slippers are in the shame situation.
From Shame to Grace
It's a shame that booze doesn't turn off one's mouth at the same time it turns off the brain.

Share: *Also see* Meeting(s)
A pain shared is a pain cut in half.
A problem shared is a problem halved.
All the answers to all of our problems are contained in the sharing in the meetings.
Be a channel, not a dam.
Good things get better when they are shared.
How to tell your story. Be sincere. Be Brief. Be seated.
If you don't hear what you need to hear, say what you need to hear.
If you pass, it's your ass.
My gratitude speaks when I care and I share with others the NA Way.
Pass it on!
Practice what you preach and share what you practice.
Share with your sponsor the "take it to the grave" stuff.
Share your happiness.
Share your pain and let it go.
Share, don't compare.
Shared joy is double joy; shared sorrow is half sorrow.
Sharing is caring.
Sharing my past with a newcomer adds value and dignity to my life.
Sharing: The opposite of listening is waiting to talk.

Talk or die.
Thank you for sharing my pain.
There is a difference between sharing our experience and imposing our opinions.
There is plenty to go around of what you give away.
Thinking about what you'll say before you share, or what you should have said after you share means you missed the meeting.
We'd rather hear you share about the same thing a thousand times in meetings than learn you were sharing it in a bar.
What you seek—you will not find—unless you share it.
When you do all the talking, you can only learn what you already know.
When you share with a newcomer, you teach yourself.

Shit
Everything past the "but" is bullshit.
Experience, Strength, and Hope, not opinions, bullshit, and dope.
If it wasn't for denial, my life would be shit.
If you are eating a shit sandwich, chances are, you ordered it.
Most of us can stay sober through the bullshit and the horseshit. It's the chicken shit that gets us.
Sympathy falls between shit and syphilis in the dictionary.
We're not exempt from the shit in life because we are clean.
When you are in it up to your ears, keep your mouth shut.
With all the bull-shit—who needs Miracle Grow?

Shortcoming: *Also see* Character Defect(s)
A good way to discover your shortcomings is to observe what annoys you in others.
Acknowledge your tallcomings along with your shortcomings.
Blaming our parents, is a perfect excuse for our shortcomings.
Fear is not a shortcoming- it's an emotion. Our reaction to it can be the shortcoming.
Heredity is a perfect excuse for our shortcomings.

Sick: *Also see* Disease
Alcoholics suffer from sick self-preoccupation.
An addict is sick trying to get well, not bad trying to be good
Do not rent space in your head to other people's sicknesses.
Sick and tired of being sick and tired?
The slicker, the sicker
We are not bad people trying to be good, we are sick people trying to get well.
We are only as sick as our secrets.
We are only as sick as our secrets; we are only as healthy as our honesty.

Silence:
Alcohol is a silent killer it destroys little by little until there is nothing left to devour.
Cultivate silence.
Silence is often misinterpreted, but never misquoted.
You may often regret your speech, never your silence.

Simple:
An alcoholic is an individual who takes the most simple program and works on it until he has eventually reduced it to its most complicated form.
Appreciate simplicity.
Important things are simple; it's the simple things that are hard.
Keep it simple and remember to thank yourself.
Keep it Simple. Breath in; breath out; don't drink or drug in between breaths.
Most good ideas are simple.
Recovery really is simple; it's just not always easy.
Simple things are often the most satisfying.
Sobriety is simple; it's the people who are complicated.
Staying sober is simple, not easy.
There are no single truths, there are only simple truths.
This is a simple program for complicated people.
When what one needs to do becomes what one wants to do, change becomes simple.

Skid Row:
He got his credentials from skid row, not Skidmore.
Skid Row is a place in my mind--not a place on the street.
We don't care if you came from Yale or jail, Park Avenue or a park bench.

Slip(per): *Also see* Relapse *and* Trigger
A slip is the end of a process.
A slip occurs before you pick up.
A slip occurs when the desire to drink is stronger than the desire not to drink.
A sure way to set yourself up for a "slip" is to be convinced that others will slip if they don't listen to you.
Accidents aren't planned—slips are.
All slippers are in the shame situation.
All slips are serious—some are fatal.
Call before you drink and we will help you stay sober. Call after you drink and you will help us stay sober.
Don't entertain the thought.
Don't watch the "slippers," watch those who don't slip...watch them go through difficulties and pull through.
Each time you come back, the tuition goes up.
If you don't take a 4th, you'll soon pick up a 5th.
If you don't want to slip, stay away from slippery places.
It is those who have slipped the most who think (__)A does not work.
Minor slips are unfinished drunks until you tell your group and sponsor.
No one who has ever had a slip said she went to too many meetings.
On the road to a slip, the first step is to get rid of your sponsor.
People start slipping when they take other people's inventory instead of their own.
Slipping: Recovery is a lifestyle, not a turnstile
The doors swing both ways
There is a SLIP under every skirt.
There is no standing in (__)A. You either forge ahead or slip.
What (__)A gives back to me could take me out again.

When you dance with a gorilla, it's the gorilla who decides when to stop.
When you take the drink you have thoroughly completed the slip.
You start to skip, you start to slip.
You're just one convenience store away from a slip.

Slogan(s): *Also see* Bumper Stickers
Slogans are the Swiss army knives of Recovery.
Slogans are wisdom written in shorthand.
Slogans can be stepping stones or stumbling blocks; it's just a matter of how you view them.
The slogans are Band-aids; the steps are the salve; your Spiritual Source is your safety.
The slogans work much better when we decorate our life with them rather than decorate the walls.
There are no shortcuts.

Slogans/Program-Generic. Mix and Match
Many sayings and slogans that use a fellowship's name or initials, are interchangeable between fellowships. Some are not. The slogans and sayings that are exclusive to a particular fellowship and are not generally interchangeable with another fellowship are listed under their respective names. The generic program slogans that easily adapt from one fellowship to another are listed here. They are designed so that you can fill in the program name or initials of your choice. We will not list each variation—you can mix and match as suits you. Have fun!

(___) A does not open the gates of heaven to let us in, it opens the gates of hell to let us out.
(___) A is not a sentence, it is a reprieve.
(___) A is the highest priced club in the world. You "paid the dues," why not enjoy the benefits?
(___) A will work if you work it.
(___) A: Experience the difference, where the difference is experience.
(___) A: It's (Alcoholics) AnonymoUS, not AnonymoME.
(___) A: We're here for a reason–not for the season.
(___) Anonymous does not have to be your whole life, but it does keep your life whole.
(___) Anonymous does not work theory it only works in practice.
(___) Anonymous doesn't prevent you from committing a vice—it simply prevents you from enjoying it.
(___) Anonymous has no fixed address – you can take it with you.
(___) Anonymous has no musts but it has a lot of "have-to's".
(___) Anonymous is a program that comforts the disturbed and disturbs the comfortable.
(___) Anonymous is a self-help program but you can't do it by yourself.
(___) Anonymous is an education without graduation.
(___) Anonymous is for people who do it.
(___) Anonymous is like a raffle; you must be present to win.
(___) Anonymous is like a shifting spanner...it can be adjusted to fit any nut.
(___) Anonymous is not about meetings but what happens in between meetings.
(___) Anonymous is not for people who need it. (___) Anonymous is not for people who want it., but for people who *do it.*
(___) Anonymous is not my life, but it gives me life.
(___) Anonymous is the highest priced fraternity in the world. If you have paid your dues why not enjoy the benefits.

(___) Anonymous is the only place where you can walk into a room full of strangers and reminisce.

(___) Anonymous leads us to God, and God leads us to ourselves.

(___) Anonymous may not add years to my life—but it has added life to my years.

(___) Anonymous: When you clean up after your group, you leave the signature of your group behind you.

(___) Anonymous: Will be judged by the worst behavior of its' members.

A meeting of (___) Anonymous is God's workshop.

A treatment center is where you go and pay $15,000 to find out that (___) Anonymous meetings are free.

Addiction is a disease of degradation, (___) A is a process of regeneration.

Around (___) A or IN (___) A?

Be as enthusiastic about (___) A as you were about your using.

Before (___) A—I used people and loved things. Since (___) A—I love people and use things.

Before you become too proud to be a member of (___) A, make sure (___) A is proud to have you as a member.

"Buts" belong in ashtrays or chairs of (___) Anonymous.

Don't just go to (___) A, join!

Even if you're not an (_____), joining (__)A is the best damn mistake you'll ever make.

Eventually every addict will have his last fix, pill, or drink. Those of us in (___) A get to talk about ours.

Everyone is useful-no one is unnecessary. The longer I'm in (___) A, I wonder who is helping who.

First (___) A birthdays are wonderful. Every chemical dependent should have one.

For romance in (___) A the odds are good and goods are odd.

Give your (___) A program what's right, not what's left.

God is upstairs in church on Sunday morning, but at night he's downstairs in the (___) A meeting.

If hanging around (___) A doesn't work, try hanging inside (___) A.

If something is between you and your seat in (___) A, that thing has to go.

If you come into an (___) A meeting looking for recovery, you will find exactly that. If you come looking for a reason to continue drinking and drugging, you'll eventually find that, too.

If you do not find "the peace of mind" you keep hearing about in (___) A; try working the steps.

If you stop doing the things that keep you in (___) Anonymous, you will go back doing the things that brought you to (___) Anonymous.

If you're like everyone in (___) Anonymous, you're not going to enough meetings.

If you're looking for God, you'll never see God more at work than at an (__) A meeting.

In (__)A, it doesn't matter who is right–only who is left.

In (___) A we do it the old fashioned way, we earn our recovery.

In (___) A, it doesn't matter who is right; only who is left.

In (___) A, there are no losers—just slow winners.

In (___) A, there is a wrench for every nut.

In (___) A, we learn how to disagree without being disagreeable.

In (___) A, we surrender to win, not to whine.

In (___) A. there are no fatal decisions, as long as you don't pick up the first fix, pill, or drink.

In (___) Anonymous, it doesn't matter who is right; only who is left.

It is those who have relapsed the most who think (__) A does not work.

Let us live and give the (__)A.

Most (___) A people spend more time deciding where to have lunch than in choosing a sponsor.

Put (___) A first, everything you put second will be first class.

Some people are so successful in (___) A they turn out almost as good as they used to think they were when they were drinking and drugging.

The (___) A waltz: Steps 1, 2, 3

The best way to keep (___) A is to give it away.

The longer you're in (___) A the more you need (___) A. The more you need (___) A the more you want (___) A.

The steps are there to protect me from myself; the Traditions are there to protect (___) A from me.

There are no coincidences in (___) A.

There is no standing still in (___) A. You either forge ahead or slip.

Treatment is discovery and (___) A is recovery.

We came to (___) A to save our ass, and found out our soul was attached.

We didn't fly into (__) A on the wings of victory.

We have everyone in (___) A, from Yale to jail.

We see a miracle every night if we but attend an (___) A meeting.

What (__) A gives back to me could take me out again.

When God is holding your right hand and (__) A is holding your left, you have no hands with which to pick up a drink.

When newcomer meets newcomer in (__) Anonymous, it is worse than the 13th step-it's more like 26.

With (___) Anonymous you are part of the answer not part of the problem.

With the (___) A. rules of the road, you get to make U-turns.

You're living on borrowed time that you borrowed from (__) A.

Smile(s):

A sponsor is a push when stalled, a guide when you're lost, a smile when you're sad—and love.

All people smile in the same language.

Booze and Lose - or - Grin and Win

Forgetting how to smile is part of an alcoholic's memory loss.

Give your smile to the next person you meet.

Go the extra smile.

Smile like you mean it.

The way to break the ice is to crack it with a smile.

Sober: *Also see* Clean (Clean and Sober) *and* Sobriety

A sober alcoholic is like a turtle on a fence post: You know it had help.

Any thing you did drunk, you can do better sober.

Anyone can be a drunk. It takes an effort to be an alcoholic and a bigger effort to be a sober alcoholic.

Being sober doesn't *keep* you sober.

Better to have someone sober and hating you because you told them the truth, than have someone drunk and liking you because you told them a lie.

Call before you drink and we will help you stay sober. Call after you drink and you will help us stay sober.

Do it sober.

Getting sober is a process; relapsing is, too.

Going to a meeting doesn't make you sober any more than going to church makes you a minister.

Happy, Sober, and Me

If you are not grateful for your sobriety, you will not stay sober.

If you are sober, the miracle has happened. Stick around, the impossibilities take a little longer.

If you drink near beer, consider yourself near sober.

If you hang around those that drink, they'll get you drunk before you get them sober.

If you stay sober, you can always get another job.

If you take a drunken horse thief and sober him up, you have a sober horse thief.

If you want to stay sober, you will find a way. If not, you will find an excuse.

It is easier to stay sober than to get sober.

Make this a rule: Don't drink while you're sober.

Ride sober, live free.

Sober and Serving.

Sober is as sober does.

Stark Raving Sober.

Stay sober for yourself.

Staying sober is simple, but it's not easy.

The first-time sober is a gift; why waste it?

The highest you can go in AA is sober.

The longer you are sober, the narrower the path.

The most sober person today is the one who got up first this morning.

The paradox of recovery is a sober alcoholic.

The problems will still be there whether you're drunk or sober. Would you rather meet them drunk or sober?

The single most important thing to living life sober is a term called "showing up."

There are only three possible outcomes for alcoholics: Locked up, Covered up, or Sobered up!

Try to listen sober. Your ears work better that way.

Trying is what got you drunk; *doing* is what keeps you sober.

What's it going to take to stay sober? *Everything you have left.*

When the pain of staying sober becomes less than the pain of getting drunk, you'll stay sober.

When you are first getting sober, trust people, BUT build trust slowly and carefully.

www.alcoholicsanonymous.org: where sober people click.

You are only one drink away from a drunk.

You can think crazy as long as you act sober.

You don't get drunk watching another drink; you don't get sober watching another do the steps.

You get sober not with your head, but with you feet.

You never lose anything sober, you can get back by drinking.

Young, Sober, & Free

Your worst day sober is better than your best day drunk.

Sobriety: *Also see:* Clean (Clean and Sober) *and* Sober

AA does not teach us how to handle drinking, it teaches us how to handle sobriety.

Abstinence leads to sobriety. The program and 12 Steps lead to recovery.

Do Honest Sobriety

Don't fight drink, strengthen sobriety.

Double Digit Sobriety

If you are not grateful for your sobriety, you will not stay sober.

If you put sobriety first, everything you put second will be first class.

In sobriety, you are given permission to be ordinary.

It takes one month of sobriety for every year of drinking and using just to get our brains out of hock.

Law of Sobriety: You can't fall off the floor.

No matter how much sobriety you have, you can always improve yourself.

No matter how much sobriety you have, you will never rise above the level of human being.

One lie a day keeps sobriety away.

One thing about sobriety, if you don't drink, it lasts a lonnnnng time!

Our Higher Power gives us many gifts in sobriety. We just have to remember to unwrap them.

Put sobriety first to make it last.

Since it is One Day At A Time, then whoever awoke the earliest today has the most sobriety.

Sobriety doesn't open the gates of heaven to let us in, it opens the gates of hell to let us out.

Sobriety is a constant process of uncovering, discovering, and discarding.

Sobriety is a gift, the price of which is eternal vigilance.

Sobriety is a gift.

Sobriety is a grant, not a gift. A gift is something we get to keep forever. A grant is contingent on us doing something to keep it.

Sobriety is its own reward.

Sobriety is like peeling an onion; it comes off in layers and sometimes we cry.

Sobriety is like sex. If it doesn't feel good, you're not doing it right.

Sobriety is never an accident.

Sobriety is not a dress rehearsal

Sobriety is not for people who need it; it's for people who want it.

Sobriety is the only thing you earn and pay for at the same time.

Sobriety Priority

Sobriety ruins your drinking.

Sobriety, on loan from God.

Sobriety, then serenity.

The secret to long term sobriety: Don't drink; don't die.

The world's record of sobriety is 24 hours.

Three keys to sobriety: get a sobriety date and don't change it; get a sponsor; get a home group.

Try not to place conditions on your sobriety.

We know how to be dedicated to our disease. Dedication to sobriety seems less clear.

We're not against alcohol, we're for sobriety.

Whatever you put before your sobriety will be the first thing you lose.

When things are going great, sobriety is good. When things are going bad, sobriety is better.

Whoever gets up first in the morning has the most sobriety.

You can't be fired for on-the-job sobriety.

You're ready for sobriety when the alcohol doesn't work anymore.

Solution(s): *Also see* Answer(s)

A good scapegoat is nearly as welcome as a solution to the problem.

Alcohol is not the problem; alcoholism is

Anger is not a solution.
Don't force solutions.
If a solution isn't practical, it isn't spiritual.
If life was a problem to be avoided, drinking was the perfect solution.
If not this, then something better.
If you have to force the solution, then it's not the solution.
If you're not the problem, there is no solution.
It is not possible to have all your problems solved, but have you removed yourself from the solution?
Live in the solution!
Live in the solution, not the problem.
Make the solution so big, the problem does not exist.
Stay in the solution.
Suicide is a permanent solution to a temporary problem.
There are no chemical solutions to spiritual problems.
We have been seekers of external solutions to internal problems.
What you thought was the solution became the problem.
When we dwell on the problem, the problem gets bigger. When we dwell on the solution, the solution gets bigger.
When you can't find the solution to a problem, look for the soulution to the problem.
"Why" questions keep you in the problem while "How" questions keep you in the solution.
You are the problem, but you are also the solution.
You will never have a problem that is worse than the old solution you found for it.

Sorrow(s): *Also see* Grief
It isn't destructive to feel sorry for ourselves, it's destructive to stay stuck feeling sorry for ourselves.
Shared joy is double joy; shared sorrow is half sorrow.
Sorrow looks back. Worry looks around. Faith looks up.
The opposite of joy is not sorrow; the opposite of joy is cynicism.
We drank to drown our sorrows but our sorrows learned how to swim.

Sorry: *Also see* Apologize *and* Amends
It isn't destructive to feel sorry for ourselves it's destructive to stay stuck feeling sorry for ourselves.
The quickest way to end an argument is to say, "I'm sorry you feel that way. You may be right."
We believe in "Living" amends not "I'm sorry" amends.
You can not feel sorry for yourself and laugh at the same time. So take your levity seriously.

Soul(utions):
All of us leave footprints in the sands of time—some the impression of a great soul—others the mark of a heel.
Bring the shoes and the soul will follow.
Do not put the "sole purpose" of any fellowship above the "soul purpose."
If you gain the whole world but lose your soul, what have you gained?
It's time for an enema of the soul.
Walk on soles, not on souls.
We came to AA to save our ass, and found out our soul was attached .

When you can't find the solution to a problem, look for the soulution to the problem.

Speak(er-ing): *Also see* Talk(ing)
Actions speak louder than bumper stickers.
Actions speak louder than words.
Cursing is for conversational cripples.
Examine what is said, not who speaks.
God speaks through people, don't worry about which ones.
Hitting bottom happens when reality speaks to you clearly.
If anyone speaks badly of you, live so no one will believe it.
If you must talk about others speak as though they were standing next to you.
Share your experience, strength and hope, not just your garbage.
Speak when you are angry and you will make the best speech you will ever regret.
Suit up, Show up, Sit up, and Speak up!
You can speak your mind here. Nobody is paying attention anyway.

Speed:
Speed kills. Don't meth around.
Speed kills.

Spiritual(ality): *Also see* Spiritual Experience
Cleaning the house IS spiritual cleaning.
Confusion is a very high spiritual place to be.
Criticism and finding fault *are not* spiritual gifts.
Do not become so spiritual that you are of no earthly value.
God wants spiritual fruit, not religious nuts.
Growing Old is Natural... Growing Up is Spiritual...
How we treat others is a consequence of the depth of our own spirituality.
If a solution isn't practical, it isn't spiritual.
It's a physical, mental, and spiritual disease.
Let the spirit work in you, without you.
Most people hope to avoid hell; spiritual people have been there.
Our emotional circumstances often keep us from seeing our spiritual possibilities.
Our spiritual possibilities are unlimited when we willingly decide to live them.
Random acts of Spirituality
Recovery is a daily reprieve based upon the maintenance of your spiritual self.
Religion is for people who are afraid they'll go to hell. Spirituality is for people who have been there.
Religion is for those who want life after death. Spirituality is for those who want life BEFORE death!
Religion is man talking to man about God. Spirituality is God and Man talking.
Self-centeredness is a casualty of spiritual growth.
Spiritual bankruptcy takes the meaning out of everything else.
Spirituality is not leaving point A to go to point B; it's leaving point A.
The biggest obstacle to a spiritual life is lack of attention.
The more you have on the inside, the less you need on the outside.
The slogans are Band-aids; the steps are the salve; your Spiritual Source is your safety.
The Spirit within you is stronger than the spirits you pour in you.

The spiritual part of recovery is like the wet part of the ocean.
The ultimate defense against the first drink is a spiritual one.
There are no chemical solutions to spiritual problems.
We claim spiritual progress not spiritual perfection.
You may be a religious mutt, but you're a spiritual pure bred.
You must go within or you go without.
Your Higher Power gave you a kit of spiritual tools; it is up to you to use them to build a durable shelter.

Spiritual Awakening: *Also see* Spiritual Experience
A spiritual awakening does not change your world, it changes your perception of the world.
Don't close your eyes, it's time for your spiritual awakening.
Nobody ever found recovery as a result of an intellectual awakening.
Some people have to have material awakenings before they can have spiritual awakenings.
Sometimes before you can have a spiritual awakening, you have to have some rude awakenings.
We're not human beings sharing a spiritual experience…but spiritual beings sharing a human experience.
You can't have a spiritual awakening until you are in a spiritual place.
You woke up this morning clean and sober. That's your spiritual awakening.

Spiritual Experience: See *Spiritual Awakening*

Sponsor(s):
A recovering alcoholic without a sponsor is much like leaving Dracula in charge of the blood bank.
A self sponsored person is a good example of unskilled labor.
A signpost, like a peer, only warns you about the road ahead. But a map, like a sponsor can show you how to get where you want to go.
A sponsor is a push when stalled, a guide when you're lost, a smile when you're sad—and love.
A sponsor is someone who holds the light while you dig.
A sponsor's prayer: Whether I call them 'Baby' or 'Pigeon' or 'Squirrel' please don't let them become parrots.
As you sponsor others, remember this: If you are trying to recreate someone in your own image, then one of you will be redundant.
Be nice to newcomers; one day they may be your sponsor.
Being an alcoholic is like being trapped in a box, and the instructions for getting out of the box are on the outside of the box. You need someone to read them to you.
Call your sponsor before you pick up.
Call your sponsor before, not after, you take the first drink.
Your Big Book is your sponsor too.
Call Your Sponsor!
Don't place your sponsor on a pedestal. It is only from a high place that they can fall.
Don't put a question mark where your sponsor puts a period.
Don't rely on your sponsor to call you. It's your job to call him or her.
For Women: A male sponsor will pat your ass and a female will save it.
Get a sponsor; get a program; get into service; get a Higher Power in your life; get a life; get it

right. Wake up and smell the recovery.

Get out of yourself: be a sponsor.

If at first you don't succeed, do it like your sponsor told you.

If you hold on to your Sponsor with one hand and a Sponsee with the other, you can't pick up a drink !!

If you think you have a good idea you might want to get second opinion from your sponsor.

If you're happy, notify your face. If you're not, notify your sponsor.

It is better to have someone sober and hating you because you told them the truth, rather than have someone drunk and liking you because you told them a lie.

It takes less time to do something right, than to explain to your sponsor why you did it wrong.

Minor slips are unfinished drunks until you tell your group and sponsor.

Most program people spend more time deciding where to have lunch than in choosing a sponsor.

Nobody's perfect, not even your sponsor.

On the road to a slip, the first step is to get rid of your sponsor.

People who seek a sponsor without faults, will be without a sponsor.

People who sponsor themselves have fools for sponsors.

Put on your shoes and walk them through it.

Share with your sponsor the "take it to the grave" stuff.

Sobriety doesn't come with instruction books, that's why we have sponsors.

Spiritual and emotional growth does not depend so much upon success as it does upon\ failures and setbacks

Sponsor saying: Who's not doing it your way today?

Sponsors are lighthouses, not foghorns.

Sponsors carry the message—not the person.

Sponsors have bullshit filters in their ears, so they can translate what you say.

Sponsors: have one, use one, be one.

Sponsors: they won't let you, get you.

Sponsorship is great. You get to tell people what to do and if it works, you can try it!

Sponsorship—The art of helping an alcoholic grow up without putting them down.

Take the mess to your sponsor, take the message to the meeting.

Talk to your sponsor first.

Tell it to your sponsor, or you will be telling it to a bartender.

The list of "perfect" sponsors, is a blank sheet of paper on the bulletin-board.

There are some people who learn from the mistakes of others and then there are the rest of us.

They say you don't have to like your sponsor; they just have to have something you want—like a life.

Three keys to sobriety: get a sobriety date and don't change it; get a sponsor; get a home group.

When the newcomer is ready, the sponsor will appear.

You cannot improve if you only have yourself as a model.

You have to grow up for yourself no matter who your sponsor is.

You need newcomers to tell you where you came from; old-timers, to tell you where you could go, and a *sponsor* to tell you where you are at.

Your sponsor helped you up. Don't let them down.

Your sponsor is willing to make mistakes, if you are willing to learn from them.

Steps: *Also see* the section on Freudian Sips

Step 0. This shit has got to stop.

Step 1.
God Help me!
Honest sobriety is knowing a drug is a drug is a drug.
Just put Step One in front of the others.
Step One only works when you do the other 11.
Take the First Step, not the Thirst Step
The first step is the only step a person can work perfectly.
The journey begins with the first step.
The journey of a thousand miles begins with the first step.

Steps 1-3 (short forms):
New York Steps 1, 2, and 3: "I can't, He can, so let Him!
Step 1: You Messed Up. Step 2: It Can Be Fixed. Step 3: But Not By You.
Steps 1, 2 & 3: I can't, God can. I think I'll let Him.
Steps 1, 2 & 3: Uncover * Discover * Recover
The (__)A Waltz: Steps 1, 2, 3
Steps 1, 2 & 3: Just Accept, Don't Reject, and Don't Expect.
With the first three steps, you get the courage to work the rest. When you work the rest,
you get rid of the garbage so you can work the first three
Step One, Step Two, Step Down (regarding service work)

Step 2.
We can do what I can't.
Came. Came to. Came to believe.

Step 3:
Do what you can, let go of what you can't, and leave the results to a Higher Power.
Do your Third Step every morning and turn your will over to the care of the God of your
understanding. At night, take a Tenth Step to see how God's doing.
There is no "Amen" at the end of the 3rd step prayer, only after the 7th Step Prayer.
The emergency form of Step 3: "Skip it".
The Third Step is the Swiss army knife of the Steps: It helps you do everything.
When saying the Third Step Prayer, don't give God instructions, just report for duty.

Step 4:
A thorough 4th Step will ruin your ability to hold resentments.
Get to know a stranger, do a 4th Step today.
If you don't take a 4th, you'll soon pick up a 5th.
Nothing pushed down inside of us stays down for very long.
Put down the magnifying glass you use to look at others and look in the mirror.
The biggest challenge of doing the 4th Step is picking up the 600 pound pencil.
Garbage in, garbage out—dump yours out regularly
Uncover to Recover.

Step 4-5:

Through the 4th and 5th Steps we learn who we really are. Once we know who and what we are, we don't have to be what we were.

Steps 4-9:

Steps 4-9: The six-pack of steps.

Step 5:

It's time for an enema of the soul.

Take the fifth or drink a fifth.

Through the 4th and 5th Steps we learn who we really are. Once we know who and what we are, we don't have to be what we were.

Step 7:

There is no "Amen" at the end of the 3rd Step Prayer, only after the 7th Step prayer.

Step Sevenly

Step 8:

Try to live your life without adding to your 8th Step list.

Step 9: *Also see* Amend(s)

The wreckage of the past is environmentally safe and bio-degradable.

A step in time saves nine.

Step 10:

Do your Third Step every morning and turn your will over to the care of the God of your understanding. At night, take a Tenth Step to see how God is doing.

Step 11:

If you only pray when you need something fixed, you're turning God into a repairman.

Step 12:

A candle loses nothing by lighting another candle.

Be where you are supposed to be, do what you are supposed to do, when you are supposed to do it.

Practice these principles in all your affairs—or change your affairs.

Step Twelve: I am responsible to them—Not for them.

When you make a 12-Step call and you don't drink, it is successful.

Step 13:

Newcomer meets newcomer in AA is worse than the 13th Step-it's more like 26.

Step 1 plus Step 12 equals Step 13.

Step 13: My life is unmanageable, and I want to share it with you.

This is a 12-Step-program not 13.

Steps 1-12:

AA Two Step: 1, 12; 1, 12

Steps 1-3, the Surrender Steps; 4-9 the Action Steps; 10-12, the Maintenance Steps

There's safety in numbers: one through twelve.
The 12 Steps: 1 to 3: Clear up; 4 to 9: Clean up; 10 to 12: Group up.
The Steps: Give up. (Steps 1,2,3) Clean up. (4,5,6) Make up. (7,8,9) Keep up. (10,11,12).
The easier, softer way *is* 1 through 12.

Abstinence leads to sobriety. The program and 12 Steps lead to recovery.
After you work the 12 Steps, the 12 Steps begin to work you.
Don't make the only thing you do in moderation be the steps.
Don't wait to get better to do the steps; do the steps now to get better.
Experience the 12-steps; don't examine them.
If you do not find "the peace of mind" you keep hearing about in AA, try working the steps.
If you have never experienced the results of working the 12 Steps, no explanation is sufficient.
If you have experienced the results of working the 12 Steps, then no explanation is necessary.
It says: "Here are the steps we *took*," not *suggested*, not *understood*.
It's the twelve steps, not the twelve standstills.
Life is a dance if you take the steps.
No matter how many years you are from your last drink or drug, you are only 12 Steps away from the next.
Nothing is so bad that a drink or drug won't make it worse and nothing is so good that working your steps won't make it better.
Once you pick up a drink, the steps are totally bewildering.
One step at a time
Slow and sure.
Sometimes a half of step at a time looks mighty big.
Step over bodies if you have to.
Step up to the program.
Steps: They work, if you work them.
Take baby steps
Take one day and one step at a time. Don't ever look too far ahead.
The answer is in the Steps.
The first step adds years to your life, the rest add life to your years.
The most important word in the steps is the first one, "We..."
The most productive ups and downs are getting up for a meeting and down to the steps.
The slogans are Band-aids; the steps are the salve; your Spiritual Source is your healing.
The Steps are there to protect you from yourself; the Traditions are there to protect the program from you.
The Steps are your daily bread, not cake for special occasions.
The Steps keep us from suicide; the Traditions, from homicide.
The Twelve Steps are but suggestions, as is pulling the rip cord on a parachute.
The Twelve Steps are like wrenches in a toolbox – they'll fit any nut that walks in the door.
There's no elevator, you have to take the Steps.
These are not the Steps we discussed, or memorized, or analyzed. These are the steps we took.
They work if you work them and won't if you don't.
Two main fears about working the steps. The first fear is they will not work. The second fear is they will work.
Watch Your Steps
We take the steps, but it's funny where the steps take us.

What step are you on?

When all else fails, follow directions.

Where do you find recovery? Twelve steps past any lengths.

Work the Steps. You may still have living problems but you will no longer have problems living.

You can take the elevator going down, but you gotta take the steps back up.

You can work the steps to *get* out of trouble or you can work the steps to *stay* out of trouble.

You cannot work the steps too soon, because you do not know how soon it may be too late.

You don't get drunk watching another drink. You don't get serenity watching others do the steps.

You don't have to understand how the steps work for them to work.

You don't wait and get well enough to do the steps; you do the steps to get well.

Strength(s):

For every infirmity we suffer, God has given us a countering strength.

Going to any lengths are our strengths.

If there is someone weaker than you, be kind to them. If there is someone stronger than you, be kind to yourself.

Resistance is only a waste of strength.

Lengths Become Strengths

Strength in powerlessness.

Strength in surrender.

Stress: *Also see* Nervous

God does not hurry.

If you're too busy to pray, you're too busy.

You can be a human being-you don't have to be a human doing.

Struggle: *See* Resist(ance)

Stupid(ity):

The difference between stupidity and genius is that genius has its limits.

There are no stupid questions, only stupid answers.

Don't assume evil motives for what stupidity can explain.

Keep it simple stupid (KISS)

Egotism is the drug that soothes the pain of stupidity.

Success(full):

A rich person is one who knows she has enough.

Any failure will tell you—success is nothing but luck.

Contempt and success are both difficult to handle, but one is ultimately more enjoyable

Failure is a necessary pathway to success.

Failure is success if we learn from it.

Failure isn't fatal; success isn't permanent.

Follow success and you will be successful; follow failure and you will fail; stick with the winners and you will be a winner.

If at first you don't succeed, you're running about average.

If at first you don't succeed, redefine success.
If at first you don't succeed, destroy all evidence that you tried.
If at first you do succeed, try not to look astonished.
Many people believe in luck to explain the success of those they don't like.
Nothing succeeds like persistence.
Only in a dictionary will you find success before work
Some people are so successful in AA they turn out almost as good as they used to think they were when they were drinking.
Spiritual and emotional growth does not depend so much upon success, as it does upon failures and setbacks.
Success and failure share a common denominator; both are temporary!
Success is how high you bounce when you hit bottom.
Success is never fatal. Failure is never final.
Success is not getting what you want; it's knowing what you don't need.
Success is not what you have, but who you are.
Success means getting up just one more time than you fall.
Success means getting your "but" out of the way.
Successful living must be practiced daily.
The longer you've been in recovery, the more successful you've been in the past.
The road to success is always under construction.
The secret of success is to start from scratch and keep scratching.
The two hardest things in life to handle are success and failure.
There is no tragedy bad enough that a drink or drug won't make it worse, and there is no success good enough that a toast won't toast you.
Things work out best for those who make the best of the way things work out.
When you make a 12 Step call and you don't drink, it is successful.

Suggestions:
All our suggestions are free. The ones you don't take are the ones you end up paying for.
First Edition suggestion: Read the black parts.
For 'suggestion' you have two choices: Take it or leave it.
The Twelve Steps are but suggestions, as is pulling the rip cord on a parachute.
This is a program of suggestions.

Suicide:
If you commit suicide you're killing the wrong person.
If your thinking of committing suicide, wait five years; otherwise you will have killed the wrong person.
Suicide is a permanent solution to a temporary problem.
Suicide is such a long term decision. While living has so many more variables.
The steps keep us from suicide; the traditions, from homicide.

Support:
Not asking for support is a sign of weakness.
Support is s two way street, giving and getting.

Suffer(ing): *Also see* Misery
Alcoholics suffer from sick self-preoccupation.

Alcoholics suffer from terminal uniqueness.
For every infirmity we suffer, God has given us a countering strength.
If you suffer from low self-esteem, do estimable things.
Most of the catastrophes you suffer in life, never happen.
Pain is mandatory, suffering is optional.
Pain: It's either suffering or service.
The program fixes it so we don't have to suffer from insanity anymore. Now we can enjoy it!
Why are you suffering someone else's pain?

Surrender: *Also see* Let Go
97% surrender is a lot harder than 100% surrender.
Don't quit; Surrender.
Fight the urge to fight: replace it with surrender
Getting stuck means you are in between surrenders.
In AA, we surrender to win, not to whine.
Is this a surrender or a cease fire?
Strength in surrender.
Surrender Allows Change
Surrender is riding the bus in the direction it's going.
Surrender is victory. We win by giving up the fight.
Surrender means following the direction God's finger is pointing.
Surrender to win.
Surrender, don't quit.
The expression of surrender is to live your life in harmony with the universe.
The quality of your recovery is proportional to the quality of your surrender.
To the mind that is still, the world surrenders.
When you find yourself in a hole, stop digging.
When you're sick and tired of being sick and tired.

Sympathy: *Also see* Pity Pot
In a bar, we got sympathy--as long as our money lasted. In AA, we get understanding for nothing.
Sympathy falls between shit and syphilis in the dictionary.
When you find yourself in a hole, stop digging.

Talk(ing):
Doing is better than talking.
Eventually every alcoholic will have his last drink. Those of us in AA get to talk about ours.
If you must talk about others, speak as though they were standing next to you.
If you talk the talk, then walk the walk.
Most of the time we don't communicate; we just take turns talking.
One alcoholic talking to another one equals won.
People who say you can't talk about drugs in an AA meeting are usually on them.
Pray daily, God is easier to talk to than most people.
Religion is man talking to man about God. Spirituality is God and Man talking.
Talk does not cook rice.
Talk it out, don't act it out.
Talk or die.

Talking about the spiritual part of the program is like talking about the wet part of the ocean.
The opposite of listening is waiting to talk.
Walk like you Talk
Walk the Talk.
Watch how you talk to people you don't know; you may be talking to an angel.
When the mouth stumbles, it is worse than the foot.
When you talk, you can only say something you already know. When you listen—you may learn something somebody else knows.
Zip the lip.

Telephone:
Before you pick up, pick up the phone.
Call before you drink and we will help you stay sober. Call after you drink and you will help us stay sober.
To Postpone it: Phone it
One alcoholic talking to another one equals won.
Use the telephone.
Help is only a phone call away.
Make use of telephone therapy.
Pick up the telephone before you pick up a drink.
To Postpone it, Phone it

Temper: *Also see:* Anger(y)
If you lose your temper, you lose.
If you lose your temper, you've lost.
People who fly into a rage often make a bad landing.
Self-pity is just a temper tantrum with God.
Temper is what gets most of us in trouble. Pride is what keeps us there.
The longer we keep our temper the more it improves.
You can't get rid of a bad temper by losing it.

Temptation:
Don't worry about avoiding temptation; as you grow older, it will avoid you.
Lead us not into temptation. We can find it for ourselves.
You are less likely to fall into temptation if you don't walk along the edge.

Test:
Talking about the spiritual part of the program is like talking about the wet part of the ocean.
Yellow chip: Urine chip, by now your urine is clean and you can pass the piss test.

Thank (ful, you): *Also see* Gratitude (Grateful)
If you are having a difficult time being thankful, the problem may be your memory.
Keep it simple and remember to thank yourself.
Thank you for sharing my pain.
The shortest prayers are "Thank you" and "Help."
When we stop to think more, we stop to thank more.

Therapy: *Also see* Professional(s)
With the 12 Steps, you have break throughs, not break downs.
Make use of the telephone therapy.
Do not let the newcomer's inner child run our meetings. This is not play therapy.

Think(ing & thoughts):
Alcoholic thinking keeps us in rebellion and slavery.
All that we are is the result of what we have thought.
Although thoughts are things, they are not actions; although feelings are real, they are not facts.
Be careful of your thoughts; they may become words at any moment.
Be more concerned with what God thinks about you than what people think about you.
Because my mind thinks something doesn't necessarily make it so.
Before you pick up a drink, think it through.
Don't drink, don't think and go to meetings.
Don't get lost in thought. It's unfamiliar territory.
Don't waste time thinking about what thinking can't change.
Don't think and drive.
Don't believe everything you think.
Don't entertain the thought.
Drinking and thinking is as bad as drinking and driving.
Every good thought is a prayer.
Fear of expressing ourselves makes us prisoners of our thoughts.
Fill your head with positive thoughts and there won't be room for the negative.
FOCUS FIRST
Guilt is a sure sign your thinking is unnatural.
If you're thinking about going to a meeting, go to the meeting, and then think about it.
It's a lot easier to react than it is to think.
Remember, your best thinking got you here in the first place.
Right thought changes things.
Stink'n think'n : you don't have to put your head in a garbage can to know it stinks
Stinking thinking leads to stinking drinking which causes stinking problems.
Stinking thinking precedes drinking.
The three most dangerous words for an alcoholic: "I've been thinking…"
There is no trouble so bad that thinking about it won't make it worse.
Think God. Thank God.
Think the drink and the drug through.
Think, Think, Think.
Think, Think, Think. Not-Feel, Feel, Feel!
Thinking about what you'll say before you share, or what you should have said after you share means you missed the meeting.
Thinking of drinking?
We came here for our drinking and stay here for our thinking.
We can act ourselves into right thinking much earlier than we can think ourselves into right action.
What others think about you is never as important as what you think about them.
What people think of you is none of your business.
When we stop to think more, we stop to thank more.

Whether we think good things about ourselves or whether we think bad things about ourselves, mostly we are thinking about ourselves.

You are responsible for what you think of you. You are not responsible for what others think of you.

You can change any thought that hurts into a reality that hurts even more.

You cannot think your way into a better way of living, but you can live your way into a better way of thinking.

You cannot think your way into right actions. You have to act your way into right thinking.

You don't have a problem unless you think you do.

You have to think everything you believe, but you don't have to believe everything you think.

You're responsible for what you think of them, not responsible for what they think of you.

Your best thinking got you drunk.

Your best thinking got you here.

Time: *Also see* Now
Add life to your years and years to your life by not wasting time reliving other times.

Alcohol may shorten your life but you will see twice as much in half the time.

All of us leave footprints in the sands of time—some the impression of a great soul—others the mark of a heel.

Ask an alcoholic what time it is and he'll tell you how to build a clock.

Comedy is tragedy plus time.

Everything in God's time (and God doesn't wear a watch.)

Give time, time.

If you want to know God's will, spend time with Him.

It came to pass; it didn't come to stay.

It takes less time to do something right than to explain why you did it wrong.

It takes time to get your brains out of hock.

It's never too late.

Nothing is a waste of time if we use the experience wisely.

One Day at a Time.

One day takes time.

Right place, right time

Start meetings on time regardless of who is there or who is not there.

This too shall pass.

Time is natures way of keeping everything from happening at once.

Time is the ego's enemy, not love's.

Time takes time.

When God made time, He made plenty of it.

When you kill time, remember it has no resurrection.

When you're feeling overwhelmed, remember to take things one at a time—one day at a time.

Why waste time reliving the past when you can spend it worrying about the future?

You can have a week end in the middle of the week.

You're living on borrowed time, that you borrowed from your program of recovery.

Today: *Also see* Yesterday, Today & Tomorrow *and* Day

Tolerance:
Don't try to teach a pig to sing. First, pigs can't sing and secondly, it annoys the pig.

Tolerance: the ability to put up with those you'd like to put down.

Tomorrow: *See* Yesterday, Today & Tomorrow *and* Day

Tough Love: (Caring for Someone else)
The three C's: "I didn't cause it, I can't control it, and I can't cure it."

Tough Times:
A short version of the serenity prayer: Forget it!
Are you going to let bad times make you bitter or make you better?
Difficulties are God's errands.
God will never give you more than you can handle.
How you feel is rarely an indication of how you're doing.
If you drink at the bad news you got today, you'll never know you could get through it without drinking.
In the middle of difficulty lies opportunity.
It's a cinch by the inch; it's hard by the yard.
Keep coming back no matter what.
My worst day sober was better than my best day drunk.
Nothing is so bad that a drink won't make it worse.
Reached the end of your rope? Tie the knot and hang on.
That which doesn't kill you, serves to make you stronger.
We're not exempt from the shit in life because we are clean.
When the going gets tough, the tough get drinking.
When we dwell on the problem, the problem gets bigger. When we dwell on the solution, the solution gets bigger
When you resist difficulty, you antagonize it and it will bite you back.

Traditions:
The Steps are there to protect you from yourself; the Traditions are there to protect the program from you.
The Steps are to get us well. The Traditions are to get the group well. Since we are part of the group, we must also work the Traditions.
The Steps keep us from suicide; the Traditions, from homicide.

**Travel(ing*):* Also see *Journey* and *Path(s)*
Along the road well traveled, there are many pity potholes.
Even if you're on the right track, you'll get run over if you just sit there.
Happiness is not a place we arrive at, it is the way we travel.
If you do not know where you are going, then any road will take you there.
If you don't know which direction to take, you haven't acknowledged where you are.
It's not a matter of where you stand, but in what direction you're headed.
No speeding in the trudging zone.
Put one foot in front of the other.
Recovery is not a destination, but a road we travel.
The Road to Recovery is ALWAYS under Construction.
What is important is not where you are, but what direction you are facing.
When you come to the fork in the road—take it.

Where ever you go, there you are.

Treatment: *Also see* Rehab(ilitation)
A treatment center is where you go and pay $15,000 to find out that A.A. meetings are free.
Aftercare, the beginning of life.
Let nothing that others do to you alter your treatment of them.
Treatment is discovery and the program is recovery

Trigger(s): *Also see* Slip(s)
If you hang around a barber shop, eventually you're going to get clipped.
When someone's pushing your buttons, hit the "MUTE" on your remote.

Trouble(s): *Also see* Problem(s)
If everything is coming your way, you're in the wrong lane.
If you are having trouble believing in a power *greater* than yourself, just try believing in a power *other* than yourself.
If you don't remember what God did for you yesterday, you'll have trouble trusting Him for today.
It's easier to stay out of trouble than it is to get out of trouble.
Man is the only varmint who set his own trap, baits it, and then steps in it.
Our lives become so different once we learn to magnify our blessings the way we do our troubles.
The trouble with many of us is that in trying times we stop trying.
The trouble with most of us is that we would rather be ruined by praise than saved by criticism.
The trouble with staying home and isolating is you get a lot of bad advice.
There is no trouble so bad that thinking about it won't make it worse.
To get out , go through.
Use adversity.
What a different world this would be if people would magnify their blessings the way they do their troubles.
You can work the steps to *get* out of trouble or you can work the steps to *stay* out of trouble.
You many not have been in trouble every time you drank, but every time you got into trouble, we bet you were drinking.
You're in trouble when you get emotionally involved with yourself.
You're in trouble when you think you know something.

Trust:
As you learn to trust your Higher Power, you no longer need to carry a gun.
Detachment comes with the development of spiritual trust.
Faith is not belief without proof, but trust without reservation.
God had trust in me that I would have trust in Him.
Humans invented alcohol; God invented the ocean. Whom do you trust?
If you don't remember what God did for you yesterday, you'll have trouble trusting Him for today.
Never trust your tongue when your heart is bitter.
Thank God for what you have, TRUST GOD for what you need.
The only one you have to trust 100% is God.
The price of trust is truth.

There are really only two choices: Worry or trust God.
To be considered trustworthy, one must be trust-wordy.
Trust God.
TRUST HAPPENS
Trust in God, clean house, and work with others.

Truth:
And the truth shall set you free, but not till it's finished with you.
Beauty and truth are admired; pain is obeyed.
Believe those who are seeking the truth. Doubt those who have found it.
Better to have someone sober and hating you because you told them the truth, than have someone drunk and liking you because you told them lie.
Faith is not belief without proof it is trust without reservations.
Improve your memory; tell the truth.
Nothing ruins the truth like stretching it.
Prevent truth decay—read your Big Book.
The price of trust is truth.
The truth will set you free, but first it will piss you off.
There are no single truths, there are only simple truths.
True happiness comes to the person who seeks and finds how to help others.
Work the steps and join us. Don't worry about overstepping the truth and becoming a Spiritual Giant in our times.

Try(ing):
A winner is a loser who keeps on trying.
Don't try to be normal; try to be healthy
Formula for failure: trying to please everyone.
God gives us tasks to do knowing we are incapable of doing them perfectly but not incapable of trying.
Nothing beats failure like a try.
The best approach to any angle is the "try" angle.
The trouble with many of us is that in trying times, we stop trying.
Try again. You can't fall out of the gutter.
Trying is what got you drunk; doing is what keeps you sober.
Trying to pray *is* praying
We are not failing as long as we are trying.

Twent-Four/24-hour
It's a 24 hour program.
It's a twenty-four-hour reprieve.
The record for the longest sobriety is twenty-four hours.
There are very few decisions that cannot wait 24 hours.
With that, I'll take another 24.

Understand(ing):
Better to understand a little than to misunderstand a lot.
Confidence is the feeling you have before you understand the situation.
I hear, I forget. I see, I remember. I do, I understand.

If you don't understand the concept of a Higher Power, go down to the ocean and try to hold back the waves.

It says: "here are the steps we *took*," not *suggested*, not *understand*.

Life must be lived forwards, but it can only be understood backwards.

Nothing about life is to be feared; it is only to be understood.

We receive love and understanding from strangers and we make progress as we in turn give it to new strangers.

You don't have to understand how the steps work for them to work.

Unique(ness): *Also see* Difference(s)

Alcoholics suffer from terminal uniqueness.

What you think makes you unique and different are the things you have most in common with other alcoholics and addicts!

Unity:

Unity, Service & Recovery

United We Stand... Divided We Stagger.

Use(ing): *Also see* Pick-Up

Addiction is a lifestyle whereby we love things and use people. Recovery is a lifestyle whereby we love people and use things.

If you are done using, you can't work the program bad enough; if you're not done using, you can't work the program good enough.

If you want to quit USING; you are going to have to quit USING.

Victim(ize):

The difference between a victor and victim is ability. Response-ability.

The victims of alcoholism are those around us.

There are no victims, only volunteers.

Try not to be a persecutor, victim or enabler.

We are all victims of victims.

When you continually don't like the way people treat you, it is usually because you are cooperating with the treatments.

Vision(alize):

Envision yourself as God envisions you.

Every day is a day when we must carry the vision of God's will into all of our activities.

~*Alcoholic's Anonymous* p 85

Visualize it.

Yesterday is but a dream, tomorrow but a vision. Today well lived is a gift, that's why they call it the "Present."

Your vision will become clear only when you look into your heart. Who looks outside, dreams.

Walk: *Also see* Talk

Walk like you talk.

Walk on soles, not on souls.

Walk the walk, don't just talk the talk.

You are less likely to fall into temptation if you don't walk along the edge.

Wants and Needs:
(_____) Anonymous is not for people who need it, not for people for want it, but for people who do it.

A signpost, like a peer, only warns you about the road ahead. But a map, like a sponsor can show you how to get where you want to go.

Advice is the least heeded when most needed.

Alcoholics don't need chaos in their lives; they demand it.

All fear is about either not getting what you want or losing what you already have.

Decide what you want to be—pay the price and be what you want to be.

Experience is something you don't get until *after* you need it.

Experience is what you get when you don't get what you want.

Few of us realize that God is all we need until God is all we have.

First we work the program because we have to. Then we work the problem because we are willing to. Finally we work the program because we want to.

God looks beyond our faults to see our needs.

God wants for you what you would want for yourself, IF you had all the facts.

God wants saints who have been sinners.

Happiness is appreciating what you have, not getting what you want.

Happiness is wanting what you have, not having what you want.

Happiness isn't getting everything you want. It's wanting what you've already got.

If it's something you want, it's your will. If it's something that happens to you, it's God's will.

If the newcomer could see no joy in our existence they would not want it.

If you can't get what you want, learn to want what you get.

If you don't want what we have, we will cheerfully refund your misery.

If you make yourself available, you'll get what you need when you need it.

If you really want to stay sober, you will find a way. If not, you will find an excuse.

If you want to feel better, clean house. If you want to get better, find God.

If you want to get maximum attention make a *big* mistake.

If you want to know God's will, spend time with Him.

If you want to know what's in your heart, listen to your mouth.

If you want to make an easy job seem mighty hard, just keep putting it off.

If you want to put the world right—start with you.

If you want what we've got, you'll do what we've done.

In order to get what you want, you must do something you've never done.

On final judgment day, do you want what you deserve or do you want a forgiving God?

Our need is God's opportunity.

Sobriety is not for people who need it, it's for people who want it.

Sometimes the worst things in life happen after you get what you think you want.

Sometimes you have to stop looking to find what you need.

Success is not getting what you want; it's knowing what you don't need.

Thank God for what you have. TRUST GOD for what you need.

The more you have on the inside, the less you need on the outside.

The more you have, the more you want.

We fear the things we want the most.

When what one needs to do becomes what one wants to do, change becomes simple.

When you feel needy, get up and give.

When you're grateful for what you have, you don't need much.

Worry is a prayer for something you don't want.

You are exactly where God wants you to be.
You get what you need and inevitably find out it was what you wanted all the time.
You need all the help you can give.
You only *have* to go to meetings until you *want* to go to meetings.

We: *Also see* Us
Always remember we are being taken care of.
God only lends us people when we need them.
"I" is for illness. "We" is for wellness.
It isn't "me" and "you" anymore, it's "we" and "us."
It says in the Big Book: "*We* insist on being happy."
It says: "here are the steps we *took*," not *suggested*, not *understand*.
Our program takes the "M" in "Me" and "turns it over" to create "We." This is a "We" program.
Together, we can do it.
United We Stand... Divided We Stagger.
We all have the same last name, "Alcoholic!"
We are all special cases.
We didn't all arrive on the same ship, but we are all in the same boat.
We may not have it all together, BUT together we have it ALL!
We together can do what I alone cannot.

Weak(ness):
If there is someone weaker than you, be kind to them. If there is someone stronger than you, be kind to yourself.
Not asking for support is a sign of weakness.
Not being able to ask for help is a real sign of weakness.

Whine
Stop Global Whining
Winners Don't Whine and Whiners Don't Win.
Whiners don't win.

What:
If only—What if—As if—The three "realities" of the alcoholic.
Replace "What ifs" with "What is"
What? Me?

Why:
Chapter Five is called "How It Works," not "Why Me?"
Knowing "why" is the booby prize of life.
People who ask "Why?" keep others from getting things done. Those who ask "Why not?" get things done.
We don't care why you're here, it's why you stay.
Why me? Why not!
"Why" questions keep me in the problem while "How" questions keep me in the solution.

Will(power): *Also see* God's Will; Self-will; Willing(ness)
Don't be afraid to try something for fear you will fail; if you have not the will to try you have already failed.

Is your program powered by Will Power or Higher Power?
Telling a drunk to use willpower is like telling someone who took a laxative to "hold it."
The will to win is not nearly as important as the will to prepare to win.
Willpower tells me I must, but willingness tells me I can.
Willpower: our willingness to use a Higher Power.

Willing(ness): *Also see: HOW*
Always pray for willingness.
First we work the program because we have to. Then we work the program because we are willing to. Finally we work the program because we want to.
If faith without works is dead, then willingness without action is fantasy.
Our spiritual possibilities are unlimited when we willingly decide to live them.
Pain gives me willingness, my Higher Power gives me recovery.
The essence of all growth is a willingness to change for the better.
Willingness is the key to acceptance.
Willingness is the key.
Willpower tells me I must, but willingness tells me I can.
Willpower: our willingness to use a higher power.

Win(ners):
A Day Clean is a day won.
A winner is a loser who keeps on trying.
A winner makes commitments; a loser makes promises.
Booze and Lose - or - Grin and Win.
Conquest is not as important as connection.
Define yourself by what you do and how you do it, not by who wins.
Double Winner: a member of both AA and Alanon.
Follow success and you will be successful; follow failure and you will fail; stick with the winners and you will be a winner.
Having it our own way—isn't winning.
In AA, we surrender to win, not to whine.
In NA, there are no losers--just slow winners.
None of us came here on a winning streak
NOW turned around is WON.
Quitters never win and winners never quit.
Stick with the Winners!
Surrender is victory. We win by giving up the fight.
Surrender to win.
The will to win is not nearly as important as the will to prepare to win.
The Winners are stuck with me.
Whiners don't win.
Winners – people who tell you what they did and not people who tell you what they think you ought to do.
Winners do what they have to do and losers do what they want to do.
Winners Don't Whine and Whiners Don't Win.
Winning isn't everything but losing sucks.
You must be present to win.

Withdrawal: *See* Detox

Wisdom:
Wisdom is the ability to see the obvious.
The beginning of *wisdom* is a firm grasp of the obvious.
Slogans are wisdom written in shorthand.

Workaholic's Anonymous
TGIM: Thank God it's Monday

Work(ing): *Also see* Job
(__)A does not work in theory it only works in practice.
AA will work if you work it.
After you work the 12 Steps, the 12 Steps begin to work you.
An alcoholic is an individual who takes the most simple program and works on it until he has eventually reduced it to its most complicated form.
Better to be a worker among workers than a headstone among headstones.
First we work the program because we have to. Then we work the problem because we are willing to. Finally we work the program because we want to.
God does not work well under supervision.
How does it work? It works just fine.
If faith without works is dead, then willingness without action is fantasy.
If hanging around CDA doesn't work, try hanging inside CDA.
If you come here and are done using, you can't work the program bad enough; if you're not done using, you can't work the program good enough.
If you have never experienced the results of working the 12 Steps, no explanation is sufficient.
If you have experienced the results of working the 12 Steps, then no explanation is necessary.
If you're not independently wealthy, work for a living. If you are not independently healthy, work the steps for a living.
If your life worked so well, what are you doing here now?
It is those who have slipped the most who think AA does not work.
It works if you work it, so work it 'cause you're worth it.
It works if you work It.
Just because you're not getting what you pray for, doesn't mean prayers don't work.
Keep coming back, it works!
Keep coming back, it works…don't go away; it works even better!
Many of us fail to recognize "opportunity" because most of the time it is disguised as hard work.
No Where to *Now Here*. It works.
Only in a dictionary will you find success before work
Our program will work for people who believe in God. Our program will work for people who don't believe in God. Our program will not work for people who believe they are God.
Practice love and service at work and at home and not just in meetings.
Pray as if it's all up to God, work as if it's all up to you.
The best way to get your prayers answered is to get up off your knees and go to work.
The harder you work, the luckier you get.
The program didn't work for me, until I worked the program.
The program does not work in principle. It only works in practice.

The shortest sentence in the Big Book is, 'It works.'"
The shortest sentence in the First Edition, "It works!"
The slogans work much better for me when I decorate my life with them rather than decorating the walls with them.
There's God's will and there's your will and there's a space in between. If you do the work, eventually the space will disappear and it will be God's will.
Things work out best for those who make the best of the way things work out.
Trust in God, clean house, and work with others.
We only need to work this program thoroughly one time: NOW.
Work the program, not the problem.
Work the steps and join us.
Work towards matching your will to your Higher Power's and not your Higher Power's will to yours.
You can work the Steps to *get* out of trouble or you can work the Steps to *stay* out of trouble.
You cannot work the steps too soon, because you do not know how soon it may be too late.
You cannot work the steps too soon, because you do not know how soon it may be too late.
You don't have to understand how the Steps work for them to work.
You have to work a full program in a half way house.

Working with Others: *Also see* Steps:12 *and* Service *and* Sponsor(s)
A good exercise for the heart is to bend down and help another up.
Carry the message, don't carry the drunk; however, if necessary, carry the drunk to the message.
Carry the message, not the drunk.
Carry the message, not the junkie.
Don't point a finger; point the whole hand (reach out).
Get it, give it, grow in it
Give a damn; be a channel.
If you're not working with others, then others will be working with you.
Pass it on.
Pick them up, as long as they don't pick up.
Plant seeds, reap recovery.
Reach Out
Say what you mean, mean what you say, and don't say it mean.
The healthy person finds happiness in helping others. Thus, for him unselfishness is selfish.
The only thing we take from this world when we leave is what we gave away.
The only time we should look down on anyone is when we are reaching over to help them up.
To the desolate alcoholic, the act of kindness can be the difference between getting "better" or getting "bitter."
What would my Higher Power do?
When working with others, if they're not ready to learn, we can't say anything right. And if they're ready to learn, we can't say anything wrong.
When you work with a drunk, the drunk you're working with is you.
You are not obligated to pay it back when people help you, you are obligated to pay it forward.
You have to give it away to keep it.
Your job is to carry the message, not deliver the drunk.

Worry:
Don't worry about finding your feelings; they will find you.
Don't worry about tomorrow, your Higher Power is already there.
Don't hurry. Don't worry. Don't compare.
God speaks through people, don't worry about which ones.
Guilt is concerned with the past. Worry is concerned about the future. Contentment enjoys the present.
If you pray, don't worry. If you worry don't pray.
If you're going to worry, why pray?
Instead of worrying about what you can't do, think about what your Higher Power can do.
It's not the "yets" we have to worry about, it's the "again's."
Most things we worry about never happen.
Prayer changes things. Worry changes nothing.
Some worry about the wreckage of the past, some dwell in the wreckage of the future.
Sorrow looks back. Worry looks around. Faith looks up.
There are really only two choices: Worry or trust God.
There are two days a week you should never worry about-yesterday and tomorrow.
Today is the tomorrow you worried about yesterday.
Today, take care of yourself. Tomorrow you can worry about them.
When you're filled with regrets of yesterday and worries about tomorrow, you've lost today in which to be grateful.
Why waste time reliving the past when you can spend it worrying about the future?
Worry – God knows all about you.
Worry about tomorrow saps today of its strength.
Worry doesn't prevent disaster; it prevents joy.
Worry gives a small thing a big shadow.
Worry has produced strong results for some of us…almost everything we worried about has not come to pass.
Worry is a prayer for something you don't want.
Worry is an ironic form of hope.
Worry is as useless as a handle on a snowball.
Worry is interest on fear.
Worry is like a rocking horse, it keeps you moving but never gets you anywhere.
Worry is like sitting in a rocking chair; you can do it all day long and get nowhere.
Worry is the interest paid on trouble before it comes due.
Worry is the rehearsal for failure.
Worry slows recovery.
Yesterday is gone; forget it. Tomorrow never comes; don't worry. Today is here; get busy.
You can't change yesterday, but you can ruin today by worrying about tomorrow.
You never have to worry about low self-esteem when you do esteeming things.

Worse(t):
(___) Anonymous will be judged by the worst behavior of its' members.
Denial: My worst day as a resistor far surpasses my best day as a captive.
Don't be a W.C.S. person. That's Worst Case scenario.
Even when the situation seems to be at its worst, give it two more weeks.
If you resist it, it gets worse; if you accept it, it gets better.
It gets worse, so you have to get better.

Measure others by their best moments, not their worst.
My worst day sober is better than my best day high.
Sometimes the worst things in life happen after you get what you think you want.
The worst abuse excuse: it's not that bad *yet.*
The worst day sober is better than the best day drunk.
When you feel your worst, try your best.

Wrong:
Do not condemn the judgment of another because it differs from your own. You may both be wrong.
Even if you do the right thing for the wrong reason, it's still the wrong thing to do.
For an alcoholic something's wrong when nothing is.
If something is right, it can be done. If it is wrong it can be done without.
If you are in the wrong place, the right place is empty.
If you are right, you don't need to be angry. If you are wrong, you can't afford to be angry.
If your thinking of committing suicide, wait five years; otherwise you will have killed the wrong person.
It takes less time to do something right than to explain why you did it wrong.
No decision (right or wrong) is complete until it is fully accepted.
People in recovery can be very opinionated and often wrong, but never in doubt.
The is an easy answer to your problem that is neat, plausible, and wrong.
There is no right way to do the wrong thing.
There's room for more than one opinion and none of them has to be wrong.
To be wronged is nothing unless you insist on remembering it.
To err is human but you need to admit it.
When nothing in your world seems to measure up, there is something wrong with the yardstick.
When things go wrong don't go with them.
When you are wrong, step forward; when you are right, step back.
When you know you are wrong, admit it. When you know you are right, shut your mouth.
You have the right to be wrong.
You may not always know what is right but you sure know what is wrong.

WWW:
www.AlcoholicsAnonymous.org - where sober people click.
www.CDAweb.org - where clean and sober people click.
www.NA.org - where clean people click.

Yesterday, Today & Tomorrow: *Also see* Day
Be you today.
Do not be anxious about tomorrow, for tomorrow will be anxious for itself.
Don't worry about tomorrow, your Higher Power is already there.
Every day is perfect. The problem is, you don't know until tomorrow.
Everything can go wrong today and you are still ok.
Everything that is happening is God's plan for you today.
God won't give you more today than you can handle, but don't be piling on yesterday and tomorrow.
If you aren't happy today, what are you waiting for?

If you don't remember what God did for you yesterday, you'll have trouble trusting Him for today.

If you drink at the bad news you got today, you'll never know you could get through it without drinking.

If you have one eye on yesterday and one eye on tomorrow, you'll be cockeyed today!

If you keep one foot in yesterday and one foot in tomorrow, you're just pissing all over today.

If you treat people badly today, you get to reap the benefits tomorrow.

If you're *that* angry, the thing to do is to write it down and look at it tomorrow.

It's not what you were—it's what you are today.

Junk for today...

Just for today...

Live for today. Yesterday's history. Tomorrow's a mystery.

Love like there is no tomorrow.

Never put off till tomorrow what you can forget about forever.

Remember yesterday, dream of tomorrow, but live for today.

Resentment is when you didn't get your way yesterday. 'Anger' is when you don't get your way today. 'Fear' is that you won't get your way tomorrow.

Sponsor saying: Who's not doing it your way today?

The person with the most sobriety today is the one who got up first this morning.

There are two days a week you should never worry about: yesterday and tomorrow..

Today is a gift; that's why it's called the 'present.'

Today is a very important day–it's the only day you have.

Today is the first day of the rest of your life.

Today is the tomorrow you worried about yesterday.

Today, we have a choice.

Tomorrow is today's mystery as today becomes tomorrow's history.

Try to remember what the fight was about yesterday.

Was today really necessary?

We only drank on days beginning with "T"-Tuesdays, Thursdays, Today, Tomorrow...

When you think of yesterday without regret and tomorrow without fear, you are on the road to recovery.

Why put off today, what you can put off tomorrow?

Worry about tomorrow saps today of its strength.

Yesterday is but a dream, tomorrow but a vision. Today well lived is a gift, that's why they call it the "Present."

Yesterday is history, tomorrow is a mystery, but today is a gift—that's why they call it the present.

Yesterday is like a canceled check already spent. Tomorrow is a promissory note you do not have yet. Today is cash. Spend it wisely.

Yesterday's home run may not be enough to win the game today.

You can't change yesterday, but you can ruin today by worrying about tomorrow.

You're only a wrist away from a drink today.

Young People:

Young people don't get sober, they get caught.

Young, Sober, & Free

You're only young once. You can be immature forever.

Zero:
Swallow your pride—zero calories.
Zero in on recovery.
Zero-tolerance

Zone:
No speeding in the "trudging" zone.
When your comfort zone is no longer comfortable, comfort yourself knowing that you are about to grow.
Zone in.

Walk Softly

I used to resent "they." Now I believe I am one.

SECTION TWO: *I HEARD IT THROUGH THE GROUPVINE*

These are the sometimes profound, sometimes helpful and often funny thoughts we have overheard in meetings and during conventions. We know who said some of the adages, and it will be noted. Often we don't know who said them and so there is no credit given. If it was you, thanks!

The thoughts listed here usually don't qualify as sayings, proverbs, or slogans because of their personal nature, but just as often the distinctions are arbitrary. We felt these ideas on recovery were worth repeating even if they don't qualify as slogans. Send us what you think is worth repeating so it can make the next edition! The Groupvine section includes:

> **About Al-Anon and Co-dependent Stuff**
> **About Character (Defects and Otherwise)**
> **About Drinking and Drugging**
> **About Meetings**
> **About Relationships**
> **About Slips**
> **About Spirituality**
> **About Sponsors**
> **About Working the Program**
> **About Working with Others**

About Al-Anon and co-dependent stuff

A normal person is just someone you don't know very well. ~Jean Houston
Any chance I had of being the victim I took, because it was a lot easier to blame you than to look at my own life
As long as you don't change anything, I'm flexible.
Boundaries of convenience are not boundaries.
Detachment is the bridge to success. ~Barbara B.
Detachment: Loving concern minus interference. ~Peg L.
Enabling: If things get any worse, I'll have to ask you to stop helping me.
Everyone is entitled to my opinion.
Forget it. Drop the subject. There is no reason to be bitter just because you are right.
I belong in the university of "what's the matter you." ~Al M
I didn't cause it!!! I can't cure it!!! I can't control it!!! So I guess I'll turn it over.
I gave the best 20 years of my life to my family and its taken them 20 years to recover from it. ~Blanche D. Alanon Speaker
I had so many skeletons in the closet, I had to build a walk-in. ~Shelly M.
I was a *victim* of my biggest character defect: self-pity.
I'm not a plus – I'm not a minus – I'm an equal. ~A.B.C. Bob
I'm not co-dependent, am I? ~ Dick Friesen
If I take responsibility for myself who will take care of everyone else?
If you want to get something done, just tell an alcoholic he can't do it!
I'm an alcoholic, al-anon, enabler, and acoa. I'm multitasking. ~Mary S, Tulsa, OK

I'm diagonally parked in a parallel universe.

In Al-anon, my drug of choice is anxiety.

Insanity is the same person asking the question, answering the question & acting on it. ~Tim C.

My spouse had a drinking problem. It was me.

No one cares how much you know until they know how much you care. ~Dick B., Kihei, HI

Outside of desperately needing you, I'm not co-dependent. ~ Dick Friesen

Put as much energy into letting go as you have into trying to control. You'll get much better results. ~Melody Beattie

…justifying of self is blaming someone else. ~Edgar Cayce

Responsibility: I didn't want it. It was thrust upon me by birth.

The trouble with my perfection is if I wasn't the best I was automatically the worst.

What has your attention has your life. ~Cheri W

What other people think of you is none of your damn business. ~Joe, & Mary Esther, FL

When "Easy" does it, sometimes it is only half done.

Worrying: The answer to all my worries was as close as the next prayer.

About Character (Defects and Otherwise)

Conscience is that sixth sense that comes to my aid when I'm doing wrong and about to get caught.

Don't confuse me with facts, my mind's already made up!

Efficiency is doing things right. Effectiveness is doing the right thing. ~Zig Ziglar

Every once in awhile reality intrudes on my fantasies.

Excuses are simply my lack of faith in me.

Help my words stay sweet and tender, for I may have to eat them tomorrow.

I always know the right thing to say-after the right time to say it has passed.

I always see two points of view. One that is wrong—one that is mine.

I always wanted to be somebody, but I should have been more specific.

I am a seeker of external solutions to internal problems.

I can go from grateful to hateful in a second.

I choose to see my coffee cup as half full rather than half empty.

I don't get even; I get odder.

I don't have to get emotional about my feelings

I don't need your attitude – I have one of my own.

I don't have a solution but I admire the problem.

I have done no wrong, still I am sorry.

I have learned that when amends are made to me – I say 'thank you' but I don't have to go back for seconds.

I just got lost in thought. It was unfamiliar territory.

I just want revenge. Is that so wrong?

I know I'm alcoholic 'cause I have a low tolerance for reality. ~Anonymous

I laid my body parts on the altar of this disease to have surgeries to get medication. ~Grace, Las Vegas

I like to count my disasters every single day.

I may be wrong but I'm never in doubt.

I may look busy but I'm just confused.

I may not know what right is but now I know what is wrong.

I may not walk the way I talk, but thank God I don't walk the way I think.

I never forget what I forgave and forgot.

I never met an obligation or resentment I couldn't run from.

I often obsessively pursue feeling good, no matter how bad it makes

I only have a problem with intimacy when you get too close.

I only have one character defect left ... and it's just that I think about myself damn near all the time.

I only have two active brain cells left... and today they aren't speaking to each other. ~Anonymous

I prefer not to be confused with complexity starting from the bottom is pretty simple.

I still take people's inventories. I just don't announce them at the group level.

I tried controlled unmanageability... it didn't work.

I tried to contain myself, but I escaped.

I used to have a handle on life... but it broke off.

I used to resent "they." Now I believe I am one.

I was looking over my college transcripts and realized that there were semesters that my grade point average was lower than my blood alcohol content! Jane H. of Capistrano Beach (CA) for today's AWSI:

I used to resent people who said they came from dysfunctional families because they had an excuse for ending up here. ~Dick R. MD

I used to think I was a social butterfly, but I found out I was just a social fly.

I want instant results and I think I can make that happen.

I was a scream in search of a mouth.

I was a *victim* of my biggest character defect: self-pity.

I was taking a walk one day enjoying God's gifts when out of nowhere my head mugged me.

I worry all the time about being obsessive compulsive.

I'd climb a tree to tell a lie when I could have just as easily stayed on the ground and told the truth.

I'm a loner who needs people.

I'm making progress. I used to get pissed off when other people were sober and I was drunk.

I'm really a very persuasive person; I can convince myself of anything.

I'm still crazy as hell but if I don't drink maybe nobody will notice.

I'm uncomfortable with perfect. I don't trust people who don't have mental breakdowns on a regular basis.

I've stopped drinking and using, but not pissing people off.

If I am not happy with me—other people suffer.

If I could drink normally, I'd drink every night.

If I woke up today feeling like I did every day when I was acting out, I'd take myself to the emergency room.

If I would listen more, I would talk less!!!

If I'm not the problem there is no solution.

If it weren't for a small deficit in my humility, I'd be perfect.

If life was fair we would all be dead. ~Tim B., Shippensburg, PA

If my brain didn't need me for transportation, it would have killed me a long time ago!

If there is one thing I can really depend on, it's my ego.

If you don't like what people are saying about you, maybe you should stop doing things they are talking about. ~Dave P., Costa Mesa, CA

If you have reached a dead end, could it be you are sitting on it?

If you say "don't" – I want to

If you're a drunk and a horsethief and you stop drinking...you're a sober horsethief. The steps help us learn how to stop stealing horses. ~Quay H.

I'm having an eviction party in my head---no renters allowed!

I'm not much, but I'm all I think about.

I'm really a very persuasive person; I can convince myself of anything.

Insanity: doing the same thing over and over again and expecting different results. ~Albert Einstein

It took me a long time to realize that when I hate somebody it doesn't hurt them. Only me.

It's a sure bet my enemies aren't spending every waking hour obsessing on how much they hate me.

It's easy to see the difference between ourselves and assholes..., unless, at the moment, we're the asshole.

It's hard work taking everyone else's inventory. Worst of all, they seldom seem grateful!

It's all right to sit on your pity pot now and again. Just be sure to flush when you are done.

It's hard waking up with someone you don't like when you are sleeping alone. ~ Brad

I've been beating up on myself so much I feel like hitting myself

Lack of honesty always brings fear. If I always tell the truth I never have to remember what I said.

Longing for the right answer has kept me from discovering the answers that are already there.

Man is the only varmint who set his own trap, baits it, and then steps in it.

me feel.

Mind? Mind? What Mind? I find it hard to think about what I'm thinking about. Especially when I can't remember what it was I was thinking. Surely this will get better.

My default setting is "Fear."

My disease had so much control over my life that it not only made me do things I did not want to do, but would not let me do the things that I wanted to do.

My experience has been that my character defects and shortcomings do not go away, they go into remission. ~overheard in Broken Elevator Group

My family put the "fun" in dysfunctional.

My old outlook used to be "Look out!"

My opinions may have changed, but not the fact that I am right.

My sense of reality has calluses. Insanity is normal for me.

My two favorite subjects: Me and more. ~Tony

Negativity is my disease asking me to come out and play.

No matter how good things get, my capacity to make myself unhappy is always equal to it.

No matter where you go, there you are. ~Buckaroo Banzai

Normal people don't put bail money in their monthly budget. ~ Bud, Provo, UT

Opportunity is missed by most people because it is dressed in overalls and looks like work. ~Thomas A. Edison

Outside of desperately needing you, I'm not co-dependent. ~Dick, Arizona

Part of my ego—is into being better and smarter than others—and it ain't easy.

People in recovery are creatures that, told "thou shalt not", have no choice but to do it.

Realize that you are the problem and that wherever you go, you take you with you

Relative to the geographic cure: "What I needed was a change in attitude, not a change in latitude!" ~ Rick B., Watsintown, PA

Revenge is so disturbing to the alcoholic's "peace of mind" it bars his chances for "Contented Sobriety."

Seemingly bad days are usually days when I don't get my own way.

Self will imprisoned me far more than bars ever did.

Sometimes I have too much willingness. I ooze willingness. I sit there all day trying to turn sloth into meditation. ~Lyle, west Virginia

Sometimes I wish I could be someone else. Then I realize the only thing I haven't tried, is being myself.

Sometimes when I'm angry I have the right to be angry, but that doesn't give me the right to be cruel.

Sometimes, I think my mind honestly believes it can kill me and get away with it.

The happiest moments in my life are those when I'm not thinking about myself

The longer I'm sober, the drunker I was.

The most influential person who will talk to you all day is you, so you should be very careful about what you say to you! ~Zig Ziglar

The program fixes it so we don't have to suffer from insanity anymore. Now we can enjoy it!

The time is always right to do what is right. ~Martin Luther King, Jr.

The trouble with my perfection is if I wasn't the best I was automatically the worst.

Things aren't necessary going wrong just because they're not going my way.

We push denial out the door and it sneaks back in the window. ~Greg, Australia

We were not that good at being bad. ~Patti W.

What you do today doesn't go into your past, it goes into your future to confront you. ~Stan S.

When all else fails, I still have my guilt to fall back on.

When I came to AA I wanted to die. Death wasn't the problem. Waiting for it was.

When I came to AA I was a walking middle finger. ~ Carla, Long Beach, CA

When I look into a mirror, I take a good look, because this is the guy that got me here.

When I was trying to figure out what I wanted to be when I grew up, alcoholic wasn't anywhere on the list.

When I'm in my head, I start to believe my own press releases.

When I'm not in the crisis I love, I love the crisis I'm in.

When my only reason for doing something is "because I have the right!" it usually turns out wrong.

When the pain of where I am is worse than the discomfort of where I am going, then I'll move.

When things go wrong, don't go with them. Elvis Presley

Who can I blame for my problems? Give me just a minute...I'll find someone.

With my self-image I had little going for me, plus some less.

Worry does not empty tomorrow of its sorrow, it empties today of its strength. ~Corrie Ten Boom

Yea, I have an allergy to alcohol. Every time I drink, I break out into handcuffs. ~Wirt

You don't have to be sick to want to get well. But if you don't want

About Drinking and Drugging

Addiction is thinking every year that this year will be different, then finding out it's exactly the same.

Alcohol allows you to use it until it uses you. ~ Frank N

Alcohol did not make me look like a man it made me feel the way men looked.

Alcohol may shorten your life, but you will see twice as much in half the time.

Alcoholism comes to a person; a person doesn't go looking for it. ~ Sister Maurice

An alcoholic can be counted on to have an opinion on just about everyone and everything at all times.

An alcoholic reading about the evils of drink, will give up reading.

An alcoholic was someone I didn't like because he drank as much as I did.

Anyone can be a drunk. It takes an effort to be an alcoholic, even a bigger effort to be a sober alcoholic.

As an addict, I'd rather talk than listen.

Before I came into NA, I was dead, but I did not know enough to lay

Before I came to Alcoholics Anonymous I was just killing time until I died.

Before I got to AA, I was dying for a drink.

Blackout Boogie. Here's how it's done: Every few beats careen wildly in a direction. It doesn't matter which direction, because you will eventually crash into a table loaded with drinks. No need to apologize! If they could afford to buy those, they can surely afford to buy others.
~Luke Schmaltz

But enough about me; what do *you* think of me?

Did you ever listen to a practicing alcoholic try to explain why he/she was right. Here we have logic which makes no sense.

down.

Drink up and be somebody. ~ Denver Joe from Wino wisdom

Drinking didn't drown my problems, it irrigated them.

Every time I draw a sober breath I'm like a fish out of water.

Everybody I drank with was an alcoholic, *except* me.

For me, my worst day sober is not better than my best day drinking. But my worst day sober is better than my last day drunk.

Funny...I ruined my health by drinking to other's!

Give drugs an inch, and they will become your ruler. ~Charles M., Norfolk

Having a tremendous capacity for alcohol may make us proud, but it is like telling someone who has tuberculosis that they cough very well.

I am only stoned on the days that end in y.

I didn't get into trouble every time I drank, but every time I got into trouble I was drinking.

I don't have a drinking problem....I just can't drink tequila.

I don't know if I was born an alcoholic but when I took the drink the alcoholic was borne.

I don't remember if I had blackouts.

I failed my urine test.

I got the monkey off my back but the circus is still in town.

I had alcoholic amnesia. I forgot everything but my enemies.

I hated getting drunk, it interfered with my drinking.

I like to keep a bottle of stimulant handy in case I see a snake, which I also keep handy. ~WC Fields

I must have been drunk when I promised to stop drinking.

I need just enough to tide me over and then I need MORE.

I planned on dying young when I was drinking. Trouble is, alcohol wouldn't let me die and wouldn't let me go. ~Jean C.

I said "no" to drugs, but they wouldn't listen.

I suffered from acute automobile poisoning. I don't remember 3 parked cars hitting me. ~Joe, Provo, UT

"I think, therefore I am" by the great philosopher Descartes or "I drink, therefore I am" by the great philosopher Bacardis. Shelly M

I used to drink in those classy bars, the kind that had a sign, "Do not put serving spoon in your mouth.

I used to quit drinking a thousand times a day and it was always forever.

I used to think I was a social butterfly, but I found out I was just a social bar fly.

I was a problem drinker; every time I drank, I had a problem.

I was an alcoholic when I entered the bar, and I was just a drunk when I came out.

I was hit by so many bottoms I felt like a public toilet seat.

I was the type of person who would eat and drink everything you had in your medicine cabinet.

I'm an addict. I believe I was born with it and I don't think it has anything to do with my toilet training, inner child, or mother. ~ Shelly M.

If USING is interfering with your work, you're probably a heavy USER. If work is interfering with your USING, you're probably an ADDICT.

If we have a rat in the cellar, we have a choice: go down there and feed it or starve it.

It's all a matter of perception. To me, being "a periodic" meant that periodically I QUIT drinking! ~Penny P from the As We See it, email group

If you know the brand name of toilets, you are either an alcoholic or a plumber. ~Jumping Joe, Salt Lake City

If you think the program is too simple, go out and drink some more. By the time you get back you'll be simple enough for the program.

Is alcohol the cause of my problems or the result?

It wasn't my job that caused me to drink, it was the unwinding from my job.

Japanese proverb: "First the man takes a drink, then the drink takes a drink, then the drink takes the man."

Just because I'm an alcoholic doesn't mean I have to act like I'm drunk.

Most alcoholics would rather die than learn about themselves. In fact they do.

My brain said more, but my body said *enough!*

My disease had so much control over my life that it not only made me do things I did not want to do, but would not let me do the things that I wanted to do.

My drug of choice was actually a drug of No Choice.

My drug of choice was more.

My drug of choice was whatever you had.

One of the reasons I don't drink, I want to know when I'm having a good time.

Part of my ego—is into being better and smarter than others—and it ain't easy.

Regarding bad things happening to good people: First of all, things aren't that bad and you're not as good as you think you are.

Seen it all, done it all, can't remember most of it.

The bottom started falling out faster than I could lower my standards.

The difference between a problem drinker and an Alcoholic is that: When the alcohol is taken away from the problem drinker, the problem goes away. When the alcohol is taken away from the Alcoholic, the problem begins. ~ Gus R., Santa Monica, CA

The insanity of this disease is that I kept getting drunk. Then I'd be drunk and insane.

The longer I'm sober, the drunker I was.

The split toilet seat was invented by an alcoholic...when he used it he stopped cracking himself in the head. ~ Allen H.

The trouble with being a drunk is that you can never sure how many beers you had last night.

When I'm in my head, I start to believe my own press releases.

There's one thing that I've never been addicted to and that's work.

This is a discussion of alcoholism. Ism drinking or ism not?

Today I wouldn't take a drink for a million dollars but some day I might take one for nothing.

We only drank on days beginning with "T"-Tuesdays, Thursdays, Today, Tomorrow...

We're here because we're not all there, because if we were all there we wouldn't be here. ~ Father Marti When you drink You have lost The right To be right. ~ Ken, Long Island, NY

When I drank, blacking out was my profession.

When I used mind-affecting chemicals, I got tore up from the floor up.

When I'm high, I'm ten foot tall and bullet proof.

While the fallen can reach their goal in Twelve Steps, it takes many more very large steps and any number of blind leaps to attain true alcoholism. ~ Chad J. Kiser

You know you're an alcoholic when you misplace a decade. ~Paul Williams, singer, songwriter

About Meetings

Someone asked when I would stop going to those AA meetings and I told him, "Oh, about four or five days before my next drink." ~Nick, Murrey, Utah

A gal reported she had just finished one financial amend was almost immediately presented with another one from her past that she had been avoiding. An old-timer leaned over and said, "When the debtor is ready, the creditor will appear." ~ Stanley M.

As an alcoholic, I'd rather talk than listen.

Fellowship: I might be weird, but so are you!

The banana that leaves the bunch is the one that gets peeled. ~ Sister Maurice

I am not so concerned with who is here for their first thirty days, I want to know who is here for their last 30 days. Dick R. MD

I came here for my drugging and stayed here for the hugging.

I get something out of every meeting...even if it's mad. ~ Tom S., San Clemente, CA

I go to the meetings for all sorts of reasons, but I don't know what they are, so I keep going to meetings.

I had a vision problem—I couldn't see going to meetings.

I like hugs. No one hugs a drunk—drunk.

I never realized how crowded the center of the universe was until I went to these 12 Step meetings.

I'd rather be in a meeting by mistake than out drunk by mistake.

I'm grateful to be here. I'm grateful to be anywhere.

If you're looking to have an image in NA, look around at the meetings

In response to the tees that read: *I'm not an alcoholic, I'm a drunk. Alcoholics go to meetings.* I'd like to see a tee that reads: *I'm an alcoholic. I go to meetings. When I was a drunk, I went to jail.* ~Penny Pennington

Maybe some of the people who go to meetings are well-adjusted, rationale, mature adults – probably the Alateens.

Meetings take the bastard out of me. ~Jack

Meetings are free.

Shared by fiftyish A.A.: I saw this was a teen meeting, and I figured I was emotionally ready.

The idea that alcoholics, drug addicts, sex addicts, overeaters, smokers, etc, etc, should all just go to NA Meetings because a disease, is a disease, is a disease...was started by a treatment center that only had one van.

The longer we are in the program, the worse our stories get.

The topic is "living in the now?" I used to live in the now when I was drinking—as in "let's go get drunk right now."

The morning after my first meeting I woke up and heard the birds singing and knew it was the birds.

The reason I keep going to meetings is because the Basic Text has no pictures in it.

The voices in my head often shout to me as I'm about to start sharing at a meeting. "Dramatize it! Dramatize it!"

They tell us that even if our ass falls off we should put it in a bag and take it to a meeting. There's a reason for that because there's a good chance your brain is in the bag too. ~Jumpin' Joe, Salt Lake City

What you are speaks so loudly that I can't hear a word you are saying.

When I came into the program, I was sued, screwed, and pursued.

When I start to listen it's amazing what important things others have to say.

When I talk, I can only say something I already know. When I listen, I may learn something somebody else knows.

You can speak your mind here. Nobody is paying attention anyway.

About Relationships

My basic problem is that I flee from those who want me and I pursue the rejecters.

There are two sides to the argument, mine and shithead's.

I was willing to get to know God I just had no desire to get acquainted with his whole damn family.

The most important relationship is between God and me.

I take care of my heart. I do not run up hill and I don't run down people.

When you can't have what you want, it's time to start wanting what you have. ~Kathleen A. Sutton

Hug often. Hug well. ~ Kathleen Keating, *The Hug Therapy Book*

How can I miss you if you won't go away?

The definition of addiction..."anything that takes the place of my relationship with my higher power."

When I change myself, you get better.

The perfect relationship is when the rock in his head fits the hole in mine.

What you think of me is not my business

The perfect relationship is when the rock in his head fits the hole in mine.

No matter how good a friend someone is, they're going to hurt you every once in a while and you must forgive them for that.

What you think of me is not my business.

There are two sides to the argument, mine and shithead's.

No person with whom we are enamored of will be able to give us the full love we seek. Only mindless morons and pets do that.

When I change myself, you get better.

When I think about how hard it is to change myself, I should know how hard it will be to change you.

It's not old behavior if I'm still doing it.

Before recovery—I used people and loved things. Since recovery—I love people and use things.

One flake is OK but 2 flakes is a storm! Ronnie R.

My program teaches me that I will have peace of mind in the exact proportion of the peace of mind I bring into the lives of others.

About Slips

All slips are serious—some are fatal. Minor slips are unfinished drunks unless they are confessed to the group to yourself, and to your sponsor.

I heard that there is actually a new pill that can make a normal drinker out of an alcoholic! Your supposed to take one a day. Shoot, give me 10 or 11 of those suckers!!!

I know nobody can make me drink, but there are some people who really make me thirsty.

I thought I wanted to commit suicide, but all I needed was a hamburger.

I'd never trade my worst day sober for my best day drunk.

If I had spent as much time trying to get sober as I spent trying to make people think I was trying to get sober—I would have more sober time.

Even if you're on the right track, you'll get run over if you just sit there. ~ Will Rogers

If they invented a little purple pill that would cure my alcoholism, I'd probably overdose on those purple pills. ~ Ed V. at the Homestead AA Room, Homestead Florida

On relapse: "I never did anything in moderation...except maybe the steps."

Re: O'Doul's-non-alcoholic beer is for non-alcoholics. ~ Don, Chicago

Relapse is NOT a part of recovery. ~ Shelly M

Someone who had thirty years of sobriety had a slip. Asked what happened, the person replied, "I started counting the years and stopped counting the days."

Sometimes I get rebellious. Sometimes I get bored. But I just don't pick up.

The one I always have to watch is me; I always got myself drunk.

About Spirituality

A Higher Power is someone who makes everything turn out the way it is supposed to, whatever *that* is.

At first we thought the 'God thing' was a crutch. Turns out to be stilts. ~ Sent in to the AA Grapevine.

Before I came to AA, God and I had an agreement. He would take care of gravity I would take care of everything else.

Before spiritual awakening...work steps, make coffee, carry the message. After spiritual awakening...keep working steps, keep making coffee, keep carrying the message. ~Zen for the 12 Steps

Coincidences are God's way of remaining anonymous. ~Doris Lessing

Coincidences are spiritual puns. ~G.K. Chesterton

Do you believe in the existence of God, or in the existence of God *in your life*?

Don't Expect God to use you as a "Lighthouse" somewhere else, if he can't use you as a "Candle" just where you are!

Don't drive faster than your guardian angel can fly. ~ Randy B.

Every morning I get up and pray to God to reset my negative to positive.

Fear knocked on the door, faith answered and there was no one there. ~Jimmy B, Philadelphia

God doesn't do anything *to* us, but always *through* us. ~ Emmett Fox in his essay "Be Still."

God gave me a mouth that closes and ears that don't. That should tell me something.

God gives us problems—not to test our faith but to strengthen our faith. God knows the strength of my faith I'm the one who needs reminding.

God is a Presence, not a person. ~ Helene S. Sandy, UT

God loves you and I am trying.

God says "no" a lot but all He is really saying is wait – there is something better for you down the road.

Going to a meeting doesn't make me sober any more than going to church makes me a minister.

Higher Power is not against me because of my addiction. Higher Power is for me and against my addiction.

I am a realist. I count on miracles.

I don't understand this God stuff. I don't understand electricity either, but I won't sit in the dark until I figure it out. ~ Mosses Yoder

I had a protection order against God. ~Ray, Provo, UT

I hate these porcelain push prayers. ~ Roland, Heber, UT

I have a deep and abiding faith that comes and goes.

I know God will not give me anything I can't handle. I just wish that He didn't trust me so much. ~ Mother Teresa

I know that God knows what's best for me because I am living a life I never wanted any part of, I never would have wanted to know and I'm happier than I've ever been.

I love the word ego because it keeps me right sized, if my ego is leading the way I am easing God out. ~Beth K.

I love you, God loves you, and there's nothing you can do about it.

I show genuine willingness to God through good actions and not good acting.

When I got to the rooms of Alcoholics Anonymous it wasn't about whether or not I believed IN God, it was what I believed ABOUT God that caused me problems with the steps. ~Leslie C. for today's AWSI

I wanted to be famous and God made me anonymous.

I was taking a walk one day enjoying God's gifts when out of nowhere my head mugged me. ~ Marty W.

I was willing to get to know God. I just had no desire to get acquainted with his whole damn family.

I went to 8 years of Catholic school. I majored in guilt and minored in shame.

I'm making progress. I used to get pissed off when other people were sober and I was drunk.

If God drives you out, booze drives you back in.

If I could drink normally I would get drunk every night.

If you have a problem believing in God, go to an AA meeting and you'll see miracle, after miracle, after miracle. Seeing is believing.

If you're looking for God, you'll never see God more at work than at an AA meeting.

In a relationship there is me and her and God; I have my plans for us; God has his. Guess who will win?

It's not God's will that makes you miserable. It's your *resistance* to HP's will that causes the damage.

Lead us not into temptation. I can find it myself.

Look for your Higher Power everywhere, because that's where your Higher Power is.

Me looking for a Higher Power is like a fish looking for water.

My emotional circumstances often keep me from seeing my spiritual possibilities.

Prayer isn't talking to God. Prayer is 'reporting for duty!'

My experience has been that when I pray, it's best if I listen too! ~Penny P.

My first drink made me feel like everyone else. My second drink made me superior to everyone else. My third drink made me feel like God.

My Higher Power gave me a kit of spiritual tools; it is up to me to use them to build a durable shelter.

My Higher Power LOVES to extend itself.

My program is based on the Father, the Son, and the Holy Co-incidence. ~Billy, Murray, UT

My sobriety depends on who God is, not who I am. ~Duane M.

My spiritual awakening occurred when there was a flash of light with a cop behind it.

No person with whom we are enamored of will be able to give us the full love we seek. Only mindless morons and pets do that.

Nothing ever goes wrong in my life, whether I know it or not.

Okay, God, you can have my pride, anger, greed, gluttony, envy, and sloth, but I think I'll just hold on to lust for a while.

ON PROPHECY: "The meek shall inherit the earth -- they are too weak to refuse."

Pain gives me willingness; my Higher Power gives me recovery.

Prayer is talking to God; meditation is listening to God; medication is listening to your doctor (who is not God).

Removing my life and will from God is not as easy as I thought.

Someone said that the Higher Power is an imaginary friend for an adult. If that is true, then a spiritual awakening is when that imaginary friend gets real. ~Kim, Salt Lake

Sometimes I get to a point where God says, "One of us is going to change—Guess which one it is going to be."

Thank GOD I don't need a higher power.

Thank you, God, for the beautiful day I'm going to have if I can just get rid of my fucking attitude.

The answer to all my worries was as close as the next prayer.

The church basements where we meet are prayer-conditioned.

The difference between faith and trust: The guy at the circus going across the high wire in a wheelbarrow has faith he will get across. Trust is getting in the wheelbarrow.

The only way I could get through the fear of taking an inventory of "my business" was to go into partnership with God.

There are some days when I say: "What program?" "God who?"

There is God's will and there is your will and there is a space in between. If you do the work, eventually the space will disappear and it will be God's will.

They told me that giving was living, and living was loving, and loving was God.

I don't say the prayer to remind God of who I am, I say the prayer to remind ME of who God is!

Toughest problem in arithmetic is to learn to COUNT YOUR BLESSINGS. ~Ken, Long Island

We are all crazy, but thank God were not all crazy on the same day! ~Anonymous

We don't know God on a first name basis because then we wouldn't have to have any faith. ~Somebody's Sponsor

What we pray for may not be for our ultimate good. "No" can be an answer to a prayer as well as "Yes".

When I am nervous, it is God shaking the truth out of me.

When I turned my life over to God, I took it out of the hands of an idiot.

When I'm traveling down life's highway I start off in 1st gear, shift to 2nd gear and then to higher power.

Whenever I ask my sponsor advice about something, she always says, "I don't give advice. Get quiet and ask God. Get on your knees and just talk it over with God.

Work the steps and join us. Don't worry about overstepping the truth and becoming a Spiritual Giant in our times.

You don't want me using my spiritual tools on you. ~Suzanne, Las Vegas, NV
You grow to heaven, you don't go to heaven. ~Edgar Cayce
You're on a faith walk. ~Sharon H.

About Sponsors

A rudder will not guide a boat until the boat is moving. ~Oxford Group Pamphlet
After returning home from a business meeting I found myself with a huge resentment for a
fellow at the meeting that was really bugging me. I immediately called my sponsor to
"complain". My Sponsor stopped me mid scream and said, "do you have a mirror?" Of course,
I said "Yes, in the bathroom." My sponsor then instructed me to hang up the phone, go into the
bathroom, turn on the light, look in the mirror and you will find the S.O.B that is bugging you.
~Overheard in a meeting
Being an alcoholic is like being trapped in a box, and the instructions for getting out of the box
are on the outside of the box. You need someone to read them to you!
Do you have trouble hearing? No, I have trouble listening!!!
Early on when I was so troubled and sad, my sponsor would say to me "I dare you to be happy
today." ~Pat M.
Every year my sponsor sends me a get well card.
For years I tried to explain why I drank. Now that I'm sober in AA I don't need to explain why I
don't drink except when I'm trying to help someone.
Get a sponsor; get a program; get into service; get a Higher Power in your life; get a life; get it
right. Wake up and smell the recovery.
Guidance show us which is the right side—not which side is right. ~Oxford Group Pamphlet
I have a list of "perfect" sponsors, it's the blank sheet of paper on the bulletin-board.
I kinda feel like I did when I first started AA. my ego is really tied up in being an "Old-timer".
I suffered from alcoholism in sobriety when the "ism" stood for, "I Sponsor Myself". ~ Wirt
If I don't reach out, I turn from an alcoholic to an assoholic.
If you want to whine, call your friends. When you are ready to hear the solution, call your
sponsor! ~Patty E.
More light comes in through two windows than one. ~Oxford Group Pamphlet
My sponsees challenge me to be a better person. Some with their questions. Some with their
actions. ~Cathy B.
My sponsor gave me permission to add these five words "Or else I'm gonna die" to the end of
each step which made them a lot easier to work.
My sponsor is a member of the CIA: Catholic Irish Alcoholic.
My sponsor says I'm trying. Very trying.
My sponsor says that I cannot get ahead until I learn to be here.
My sponsor taught me that I am not the con man. I am the mark.
My sponsor tells me I'm making progress. Before I used to think suicide. Now I'm thinking
homicide.
My sponsor told me they don't lock you up for being crazy, only for acting crazy.
Overheard from Sponsee to Sponsor: "Don't you know who I think I am?"
Please do not feel personally, irrevocably, totally responsible for everything. That's my job.
Sponsors are like Ford; they have a better idea. ~Lori, Orem, UT
The truth will set you free! But first it will hurt like hell. ~Matt, MI
They say you don't have to like your sponsor; they just have to have something you want—like
a life.

When I asked my sponsor, early in recovery, "How do I 'let go?'" She said, "The same way you take your hand off a hot stove." ~Vicki from AWSI

When I work with a drunk, the drunk I'm working on is me.

When your sponsor tells you to get your head out of your ass, stick around until you hear a pop.

About Working the Program & Recovery

A pencil, paper and a Big Book can straighten out a whole nest of mind snakes.

AA is the same wherever you go, how we abuse it is different. ~Roy L.

Alcoholics Anonymous is not my whole life but it keeps my life whole!!!

Alcoholism operates on many levels. Recovery operates on many levels. Let's hope they are the same levels.

All my life I wanted to be someone; now I wish I had been more specific.

As I clear my brain and being I can accept my life—I think!

Be sober, be watchful. ~1 Peter 5, 8

Before I came to AA God and I had an agreement He would take care of gravity I would take care of everything else.

Before I came to Alcoholics Anonymous I thought being called an alcoholic was an insult.

Before I came to Chemically Dependent Anonymous, I was just killing time until I died.

Before I came to the program I had no choice. I had to use. Now I have a choice.

Being normal is being able to stop at a red light. ~Mike

Conscience is that sixth sense that comes to my aid when I'm doing wrong and about to get caught.

Don't bother me – I'm living happily ever after.

Drill your soul in right principles, that when the time comes, it may be guided by them. To wait until the emergency is to be too late. ~Marcus Aurelius (Emperor of Rome)

Even if it turns out I'm not an alcoholic it's the best dam mistake I ever made.

Everything I need is provided, and everything I want I have to work for.

Fellowship: If 2 million plus recovering alcoholics are wrong, I'm screwed.

For me, my worst day sober is not better than my best day drinking. But my worst day sober is better than my last day drunk.

Forgiveness is very important. It's not the people that I'm busy hating that are suffering – it's usually the people around me who take the punishment.

Gossip, rumors, backbiting, loose tongues, and verbal altercations: Sometimes AA meetings are like the corner bar, without the alcohol.

He who laughs, lasts. ~Mary Pettibone Poole

How does it work? It works just fine

"How it works," works for me.

How lucky it is for us there is no quick cure for alcoholism. Otherwise we would not have time to learn what we need to learn.

Humility is a perpetual quietness of heart. ~From Dr. Bob's desk plaque

I am a seeker of external solutions to internal problems.

I am an addict because of what drugs did for me. I am an NA member because of what drugs did to me.

I am an alcoholic because of what alcohol did for me. I am an AA member because of what alcohol did to me.

I am an alcoholic. I'm also an addict. I'm addicted to Alcoholics Anonymous.

I am not one of those people who has memorized the Big Book – I figure that's OK because it's all written down for me to look up.

I am willing to make the mistakes if someone else is willing to learn from them.

I came to the program to save my ass and found it was attached to my soul.

I can see clearly now, the brain is gone.

I don't walk around being pissed off because I don't have enough. I walk around knowing I have more than I deserve. ~Rob B., CDA Conference

I don't work the program to get my life back; I work the program to get my life forward.

I don't have a solution, but I admire the problem.

I had a better impression of myself before I worked the steps and got to know who I really am." Tim B. from As We See It (online)

I had to learn how to float in this program because I'm a sinker.

I had two fears about working the steps. The first fear is they would not work for me. The second fear is they would work for me.

I have not walked on water but after working the steps I've walked on air.

I haven't found it necessary to take a drink or a substitute pill today. ~Jim M., MD

I knew I was getting a handle on sobriety, when I started having illusions of adequacy. ~Sherry H.

I never got drunk watching another drink. I never got serenity watching others do the steps. This is a program of action.

I prefer not to be confused with complexity; starting from the bottom is pretty simple.

I thought I deserved to win the lottery because I stopped drinking.

I thought I was a thinker with a drinking problem. It turns out I was a drinker with a thinking problem! ~Anonymous

I thought when I stopped drinking that my life was going to be one long dental appointment.

I was like a chocolate Easter Bunny. I looked pretty on the outside but I was hollow on the inside. If anyone presses too hard in one spot, I would collapse. What happens in AA is we fill up the bunny. ~Lyle

I wasn't an alcoholic until I stopped drinking.

I'm feeling better than I think I am.

I'm getting more and more like my grandma, and I'm kinda happy about it.

I'm making progress. I used to get pissed off when other people were sober and I was drunk.

I'm not afraid I would take a drink and die I'm afraid I would take a drink and live.

I'm so grateful to be where my feet are today. ~Carol, Las Vegas, NV

I'm sober today because I don't want to get sober again. ~Ken, Long Island, NY

I'm still acting the way I want to be, so that one day I will be the way I act.

I'm still crazy as hell but if I don't drink, maybe nobody will notice.

If I take one step at a time, (in order) pretty soon I find I'm walking the walk. Talking the talk is not so important.

If I don't reach out, I turn from an alcoholic to an assoholic.

If I had known that I was going to live this long, I would have taken better care of myself.

If I learn from my mistakes I'm getting a fantastic education.

If I take one step at a time, (in order) pretty soon I find I'm walking the walk. Talking the talk is not so important.

If I were as hard on my friends as I am on myself, they would probably never speak to me again.

If it looks like a Duck and it Quacks like a Duck it's probably a Duck.

If it wasn't for A.A., I'd be myself! ~Earl A.

If the sun comes up and goes down, and I don't get drunk in the middle, it has been a good day.

If you keep fighting yourself and keep losing, you are the winner!

If you want to know your past - look into your present conditions. If you want to know your future - look into your present actions. ~George Carlin

If you're going to be successful in this program, you've got to learn to become a verb.

Important things are simple. It's the simple things that are hard. ~Don Marshall

In AA the years go by quickly. I seem to have problems with the days.

In recovery my drug of choice is anxiety.

In the beginning, it wasn't the parts of the book that I DIDN'T relate to that worried me... it was the parts of the book that I COULD relate to that worried me.

It was not my best *thinking* that got me drunk, it was my best *drinking*. My best thinking got me here.

It's a million dollar program and you only get a nickel at a time.

It's not the fear of the other life that keeps me from drinking. I don't want to lose the new one I've found.

It's not changes that people resist, it's letting go. ~William Bridges

Just as I am not independently wealthy and need to work to stay solvent, I am not independently healthy and I need to work (my steps) to stay sober. ~Shelly M.

Let one vulture live, and he'll pick your bones. ~Lynne, Cuba, KS

"Life" is what happens while we were making other plans. ~John Lennon

My Dad taught me to build sand castles, out of mortar. ~Shelly M

My home group members are not perfect and neither am I, so we suit each other perfectly.

No seniority in AA - One drink and back to the vomit. ~Campsie Mick, Sydney Australia

Nothing is so bad that a drink or drug won't make it worse and nothing is so good that working my steps won't make it better.

One of the freedoms AA has given me to be a regular person in a whole world instead of being an insignificant person lost in my own little world.

One of the freedoms CDA has given me to be a regular person in a whole world instead of being an insignificant person lost in my own little world.

Our goal. Not to have something, but to be something. Not to get something, but to give something. Not to rule, but to serve.

Our program won't keep you from going to hell nor is it a ticket to heaven. But it will keep you clean and sober long enough for you to make up your mind which way you want to go.

Recovery is just one damn thing after another. Of course, living in my disease was too. I just didn't notice it then.

Relief Lies in Two Four Letter Words that Begin with *F*: Steps Four and Five. ~ P 29, *Young, Sober, & Free* Today I get to be a willing participant in my life. ~Tasha, Orem, Utah

Remember this, the choices you make in life, make you. ~John Wooden

Self-mastery is a continuous program—a journey . . .Men do not suddenly become righteous any more than a tiny acorn suddenly becomes an oak. ~S. Kimball

Shared by fiftyish A.A.: I saw this was a teen meeting, and I figured I was emotionally ready.

Since I came into CDA, I find I still have living problems but I no longer have problems living.

Sober is being comfortable with myself out of control. When I am in control, I am not sober.

Some people are so successful in A.A. they turn out almost as good as they used to think they were when they were drinking.

Some people dream of worthy accomplishments, while others stay awake and do them. ~Anonymous

Some people say that the 12 Steps brainwash us. Thank God, because that's how I got clean!
Some people say we can look at step-3 as; I came—I came to—I came to believe. My God—
that's a years work right there.

Sometimes I get rebellious, sometimes I get bored but I just don't get drunk.

Sometimes recovering people must do twice as much as others to be thought of as half as
good—luckily this is not difficult.

Take a no BS approach to working your program.

The 10th step is not to get you out of trouble but to keep you out of trouble. ~Glenn C., College
Park, MD Don't knock anything in this program. It could be the rock you perish on. ~Broken Hill
Jack, Australia

The barometer of where I am in my life is not what I have, but what I can give.

The best thing about the future is that it comes only one day at a time. ~ *Abraham Lincoln*

The best way we know of to treat PMS (Poor Me Syndrome) is get rid of the words "It ain't fair"
and "Why me?"

The first step adds years to my life, the rest add life to my years.

The longer I'm in AA the more I need AA. The more I need AA the more I want AA.

The only way I could get through the fear of taking an inventory of "my business" was to go
into partnership with God.

The program has taught me to think faster than my mouth.

The world has not singled me out for pain; the world has singled me out for progress.

There are enough drunks in the world; they certainly won't miss me.

There are no "musts" in AA but a whole lot of "you damn well betters." ~Old Timer

There's a difference between "I cannot drink for the rest of my life" and "I can *not* drink for the
rest of my life."

There's a lot in recovery you have to walk through and there's a lot you have to walk around.
~Helene S.

They say you can lead a horse to water and you can't make it drink. I say you can ride the hell
out of it in the desert and lead it to water and it will drink! ~Bill B., Glen Dale, MD

They told me this too shall pass—and it did. Kinda like a kidney stone.

This is a ' JUST FOR TODAY' program. If you are clean and sober

Though no one can go back and make a brand new start, anyone can start from now and
make a brand new ending. ~Carl Bard

Today I am leading a life. When drinking, I was a life being led.

Today, my one day.

Today, you are tied for first place in NA.

Trying is what got me drunk; doing is what keeps me sober.

We can remain recovered as long as we remain recovering. We are not drink proof.

We cannot become what we need to be by remaining what we are."
~Max DePree

We cannot do everything at once, but we can do something at once. ~Calvin Coolidge

Welcome to recovery – the largest group of people in the world to go from adolescence to
senility without passing through maturity.

When deeds speak, words are nothing. ~African Proverb

When I accept myself, I change. When I accept others as they are, they change. ~Ken, Long
Island, NY

When I am restless, irritable, and discontent, I'm wishing, wanting, or worrying. ~Billie M.

When I came to AA I wanted to die. Death wasn't the problem. Waiting for it was.

When I can laugh at my disease I know that I'm recovering.

When I change the way I look at things, the things I look at change! ~Debbie A.-- AWSI.

When I get a chip on my shoulder, I remember the chip in my pocket. ~Brent, Oklahoma City

When I pray for strength, my Spiritual Source sends me burdens so that I can build strength.

When I was told this was a selfish program I knew I could do it well.

When I was using, I was a "childish adult." When I started to recover, I became an adult trying to develop my child like qualities. ~Camille, Denver

When I'm down, I take a Step and then the Step takes me.

When my comfort zone is no longer comfortable, I comfort myself knowing that I am about to grow.

When my thinking is confused, I'm confused about my thinking.

When one door closes another opens, but we often look so long and so regretfully upon the closed door that we do not see the one which has opened for us. ~Alexander Graham Bell

When using, life is like a roller coaster: up and down, up and down. In recovery, life is still like a roller coaster: up and down, up and down—only now you get to ride in the car, you are not tied to the tracks. ~Bill B., Bowie MD

When we first came into the program we had two choices: to use or not to use. By the time we had thirty days clean and sober, most of us had narrowed our choices down to eight!

Without expectations, everything means something. ~Pat M.

Write down three "proofs" a day--proof that recovery is working in your life. When you're down, you'll have a million points of reference to realize how much good there is all around you.

You can get off the elevator anytime, but if you get back on it's only going down. ~Aaron, Derry, NH

You don't have to use even if your ass falls off, and if your ass does fall off we'll teach you a new way to sit. ~Rachael

You have one chance to live each day, so go for it. ~Cheri W.

About Working with Others

Being an alcoholic is like being trapped in a box, and the instructions for getting out of the box are on the outside of the box. You need someone to read them to you (and you must listen!)

Do we stop loving a newcomer after they learn to love themselves? Of course not, but then they're not a newcomer any more.

For years I tried to explain why I drank. Now that I'm sober in AA I don't need to explain why I don't drink except when I'm trying to help someone.

I have often regretted my speech, never my silence.

I Love you. That is my business and it is true whether you love me or not. You can add to my life, but you can't take away from it. If you love me, that's an additional plus. ~Chuck C., Los Angeles

If you could only solve your own problems as well as you think you can solve everyone else's.

If you want to drink, that's your business. If you want to stop drinking, that's our business. ~Ralph R, 1944, Forth Worth, Texas

Only some of us learn by other people's mistakes. The rest of us have to be the other people. ~Carol, Chicago, IL

People didn't recruit me for this program, alcohol did; and it did a good job.

Qualifications for me to help you, 1) you have to need it, 2) you have to want it, 3) you have to ask for it, 4) you have to ask me.

The fellowship is full of willing people. Five percent are willing to do the work and ninety-five percent are willing to let them.

The happiest moments in my life are those when I'm not thinking about myself.

The way you lead a horse to water determines whether or not he will drink. ~Bill B., CDA Conference

The world ain't gonna kiss my butt just because I'm getting sober

These guys offered me *steps*. I needed a *ladder* to get out of hell.

When you find my life empty, put program into it.

Wow, you're really on a pink cloud. Don't worry, hon., this too shall pass.

You can lead a horse to water but you can't make him drink. But you sure as hell can make him thirsty. ~ Father Joe Martin

You can't do it for me, but I can't do it for myself.

You people in A.A. taught me to give up what I couldn't afford to keep, to keep what I couldn't afford to lose. ~Pete H.

Your family won't always be there for you. It may seem funny, but people you aren't related to can take care of you and love you and teach you to trust people again. Families aren't biological.

We're
Human
Y'idiot

Section Three: *Acronymity is the foundation of all our oral traditions*

This section contains:

ACRONYM ANECDOTES
ALPHABET ACRONYMS
STANDARD ACRONYMS

ACRONYM ANECDOTES

A T T I T U D E: 1+20+20+9+20+21+4+5=100%

GOD, *as you understand him*:
> **For the Atheist**: Good Orderly Direction
> **For the Religious**: Get Out Devil
> **For the Fellowship**: Group Of Drunks
> **For working the 12 steps**: Grow Or Die
> **For the newcomer**: Grace Over Disease
> **For our daily reprieve**: Grant One Day

Which "isms" affect you?
> **Alcoholism:** I, Self, and Me with an Incredibly Short Memory.
> **Recidivism:** I Sponsor Myself.
> **Narcissism:** InSide Me.
> **Pessimism:** I Sabotage Myself.
> **Optimism:** Incredibly Spiritual Moments.

ALPHABET ACRONYMS

THREE 'As': AWARENESS
ACCEPTANCE
ACTION.

THREE 'As': AFFECTION
ATTENTION
APPRECIATION

FOUR 'As': ACCEPTANCE:
APPROVAL
APPRECIATION
APPLAUSE

FIVE 'Bs': That buzz around and tempt us.
BARS
BOOZE

165

       BROADS
       BELLY
       BOREDOM

THREE 'Ds': DEATH
            DIS-EASE (Physical and Emotional)
            DIS-APPOINTMENT

THREE 'Ls': One of these usually brings us to recovery
            Liver
            Lover
            Lawyer

THREE 'Ps': PERFECTIONISM (leads to)
            PROCRASTINATION (leads to)
            PARALYSIS

THREE 'Rs' OF SOBRIETY:
       REMEMBER
       RENEW
       REJOICE

SEVEN 'T's: Take Time To Think The Thing Through

Knowing God to a "T": Think God. Thank God. Trust God.

STANDARD ACRONYMS

AA: Absolute Abstinence
AA: Acknowledge Acceptance
AA: Adventurers Anonymous
AA: Altered Attitudes
AA: Altruistic Action
AA: Attitude Adjustment
AA: Alive Again
AA: Avoid Anger

ABC: Acceptance, Belief, Change
ABC: Ashtrays, Broom, Chairs
ABC: Ashtrays, Broom, Coffee

ACT: Assertive, Calm, Tactful

ACTION: Any Change Toward Improving One's Nature
ACTION: Any Change To Improve Our Nature.
ACTION: Always Careful To Investigate Others Needs

ADDICT: Anybody Doing Drugs In Compulsive Trouble

AIDS: Active In Dangerous Sex
AIDS: Addicts Injecting Dirty Syringes

ALCOHOLICS: A Life Centered On Helping Others Live In Complete Sobriety

ANGER: Any No Good Energy Rising

ALE: Alibis, Lies, Excuses

ANONYMOUS: Actions Not Our Names Yield Maintenance Of Unity and Service

ASAP: Always Say A Prayer

ASK: Ass-Saving Kit

BAR: Become Alcoholic Ruin
BAR: Beware Alcohol, Run

BIBLE: Basic Instructions Before Leaving Earth

BIG BOOK: Believing in God Beats Our Old Knowledge
BIG BOOK: Believe In God, Because Others Obviously Know

BS: Belief System
BS "But" Syndrome

BUD: Building Up To A Drink

BUT: Bottoms Up Twice
BUT: Being Unconvinced Totally

BYOBB: Bring Your Own Big Book

CA: Caring Attitude
CA: Come Always
CA: Complete Adjustment

CAN'T: Carry A Negative Thought

CARE: Comforting And Reassuring Each Other

CDA: Can Discuss Anything
CDA: Can Do Anything
CDA: Can-Do Attitude
CDA: Connecting Diverse Alliances
CDA: Connecting Drugs to Alcohol

CHANGE: Choosing Honesty Allows New Growth Eventually

CLEAN: Completely Leaving Every Addiction Now!

CRAP: Carrying Resentments Against People

DAMM: Drunks Against Mad Mothers
DAM: Mothers Against Dyslexia

DEAD: Drinking Ends All Dreams
DEAD: Drugging Ends All Dreams

DENIAL: Don't Even Notice I Am Lying
DENIAL: Does Everybody Notice I'm Always Lying?

DETACH: Don't Even Think About Changing Him (Her)
DETACH: Don't Even Try And Change Him (Her).

DID: Do It Differently

DUES: Desperately Using Everything But Sobriety

EGO: Easing God Out
EGO: Edging God Out

EGG: Experience, Growth, Gain

EVA: End Verbal Abuse

FAILURE: Fearful, Arrogant, Insecure, Lonely, Uncertain, Resentful, Empty
FAILURE: Fearful, Angry, Insecure, Lonely, Unsure, Resentful, Empty

FAITH: Fabulous Adventure In Trusting Him
FAITH: Fantastic Adventure In Trusting Higher Power
FAITH: Fear Ain't In This House
FAITH: Fear And Insecurity Trust Him
FAITH: Finding Answers In The Heart
FAITH: Finding Answers In The Higher Power
FAITH: For All Is Through Him.
FAITH: For An Instant Trust Him

FAMILY: Fellowship And Meetings, I Love You.

FEAR: Fuck Everything And Run
FEAR: Face Everything And Recover
FEAR: False Evidence Appearing Real.
FEAR: False Expectations Appearing Real
FEAR: Forget Everything And Run.
FEAR: Forgetting Everything's All Right.
FEAR: Fornicate With Everything And Run.

FEAR: Frantic Efforts to Appear Recovered
FEAR: Future Events Appearing Real
FEAR: Failure Expected And Received
FEAR: False Expectations Actually Realized

FINE: Feeling Insecure Neurotic = Emotional
FINE: Freaked out, Insecure, Neurotic and Emotional
FINE: Frustrated, Insecure, Neurotic and Emotional
FINE: Fucked up, Insecure, Neurotic and Emotional
FINE: Fearful, Insecure, Negative, Egotistical

FGO's: Fucking Growth Opportunities

FOG: Fear Of God
FOG: Fear, Obligation, Guilt

FUBAR: Fucked Up Beyond All Recognition

GIFT: God Is Forever There
GIFTS: Getting It From The Steps

GMC: God Made Coincidences

GOD: Get Out Devil
GOD: Go On Dreaming
GOD: Great OutDoors
GOD: Group Of Druggies
GOD: Group Of Drunks.
GOD: Giver Of Desires
GOD: Give Over Decisions
GOD: Good Orderly Direction

GUILT: God Understands I Lack Trust

HALO: Helping A Loved One

HALT: Horny, Arrogant, Lazy, and Tragic
HALT: Happy, Appreciative, Lovable, Teachable.
HALT: Have A Laugh Today
HALT: Hungry, Angry, Lonely, Tired

HALTS: Hungry, Angry, Lonely, Tired and Serious

HALTS FEAR: Hope, Acceptance, Love and Tolerance Stops Forgetting Everything's All Right

HELP: Hope, Encouragement, Love, Patience
HELP: His Ever Loving Presence

HEART: Healing, Enjoying and Recovery Together

HIT: Hang In There

HOPE: Hang On, Peace Exists.
HOPE: Hang Onto Power Everyday
HOPE: Happy Our Program Exists
HOPE: Hearing Other Peoples' Experiences
HOPE: Helping Open People's Eyes

HOW: Hang Onto Winners
HOW: Honest Open Willing
HOW: Honest, Open-minded and Willing
HOW: Honesty, Open-mindedness, and Willingness.

HP: Higher Power
HP: Higher Powered
HP: Hired Power
HP: Holy Presence.

INTIMACY: In-to-me-I-see

ISM: I Sabotage Myself
ISM: Inability to See Myself
ISM: Incredibly Short Memory
ISM: Incredible Spiritual Moment.
ISM: I, Self, Me
ISMS: From I, Self, and Me

KISS: Keep It Simple and Serene
KISS: Keep It Simple and Sober
KISS: Keep It Simple Smarty
KISS: Keep It Simple Stupid
KISS: Keep It Simple Sweetheart
KISS: Keep It Simple, Surrender
KISS: Keep It Super Simple

LET GO: Leave Everything To GOD Okay?

LOVE: Living Our Values Everyday.
LOVE: Living Our Victories Everyday
LOVE: Letting go Of Virtually Everything

MADD: Mothers Against Drunk Drivers

MMM: Meetings, Meditation, and Masturbation

NA: Nazi Atmosphere

NA: Nazi Attitude
NA: Never Alone
NA: Nice Attitude
NA: No Addiction
NA: No Anger

NEW: Nothing Else Worked

NOW: No Other Way

NUTS: Not Using The Steps

OA: Only Answer
OA: Our Answer

ODOP: One Disease, One Program

OUR: Open Up in Recovery
OUR: Openly Using Recovery

PACE: Positive Attitude Changes Everything

PAID: Pitiful And Incomprehensible Demoralization

PEACE: Practice Empathy And Compassion Everywhere

PCing: Pink Clouding

PHD: Poor Helpless Drunk

PMS: Physical, Mental, & Spiritual
PMS: Piss, Moan, & Snivel
PMS: Poor Me Syndrome
PMS: Pour More Scotch
PMS: Pre-Meeting Syndrome

PRIDE: Personal Recovery Involves Defeating Ego

PROGRAM: People Relying on God Relaying a Message

PUSH: Pray Until Something Happens
PUSH: Pick Up Sponsor Help

RAGE: Raving Angry Gut-level Ego

RELATIONSHIP: Real Exciting Love Affair Turns Into Outrageous Nightmare, Sobriety Hangs In Peril

RELAPSE: Recovery Exits Life And Program Seems Empty
RELAPSE: Reliving Every Low And Pitiful Scene Exactly

RID: Restless, Irritable and Discontented

SASTO: Some Are Sicker Than Others
SAWTO: Some Are Weller Than Others

SIT: Stay In Today.

SLIP: Sobriety Loses It's Priority
SLIP: Sobriety Lost It's Priority
SLIP: So Long, I'm Perfect
SLIP: Something Lousy I Planned
SLIP: Stupid Little Idiotic Plan.

SOB: Sober Old Bag
SOB: Sober Old Bastard
SOB: Sober Old Biker
SOB: Sober Old Bitch

SOBER: Son Of a Bitch, Everything's Real
SOBER: Staying Off Booze Enjoying Recovery
SOBER: Simply Observe Bill's Exemplary Recovery
SOBER: Simply Observe Bill's Experience in Recovery

SOLUTIONS: Saving Our Lives Using The Inventory Of Needed Steps

SOS: Secular Organization for Sobriety
SOS: Save Our Selves

SPONSOR: Sober Person Offering Newcomers Suggestions On Recovery
SPONSOR: Sane Person Offering Newcomers Suggestions On Recovery

SRO: Standing Room Only

STAR: Start Talking About Recovery

STEP: Solutions To Every Problem

STEPS: Solution To Every Problem Sober
STEPS: Solutions To Every Problem in Sobriety

STOP: Sicker Than Other People
STOP: Start Turning Over Problems
STOP: Simplify The OPtions

TEAM: Together Everyone Achieves More.

TGIF: Thank God I'm Forgiven.

TGIM: Thank God It's Monday (for the workaholic)

THINK: The Happiness I Never Knew

TIME: Things I Must Earn
TIME: This I Must Earn
TIME: This Is My Education

THINK: Thoughtful, Honest, Intelligence, Necessary, Kind

TRUST: Try Relying Upon Step Three

UFO: Unidentified Fear Object

WHY: We're Human Y'idiot
WHY: We're Humans Yearning
WHY: What Happened Yesterday?

WILLING: When I Live Life, I Need God

WISDOM: When Into Self Discover Our Motives
WISDOM: Words In Steps Do Open Minds.

WOW: Willingness Over Willpower

WWBBD: What would Bill and Bob do?

YANA: You Are Not Alone

YET: You'll End There
YET: You're Eligible Too

Half gallons availed us nothing…

SECTION FOUR: *FREUDIAN SIPS...*

(Uh, Slips, I mean)

Ok, we've all heard about Freudian Slips. These "slips" are not related to the "relapse," but they do tell us something about what we're thinking of our recovery. It's a slip of the tongue (pun intended) of a person trying to work our program--and they come from the lips of the newcomer as well as the old-timer. The most amusing Freudian Slips heard in the rooms are usually when a member inadvertently misquotes our Basic Texts, Twelve Steps, and Twelve Traditions.

In this chapter we have four segments to amuse you:

MISQUOTED SLOGANS
BIG BOOK BITES
HELLO, MY NAME IS......
WATCH YOUR STEPS & TRIPDITIONS

MISQUOTED SLOGANS

One lay at a time.
Oozie does it.
Sleasy does it.
Thirst things first.
Worst things first.
Prepare for the thirst
The Power of Positive Drinking

BIG BOOK BITES

Dyslexic Sponsor
A newcomer asks her sponsor what the Big Book has to say about sex. The sponsor mixes up the page number and instead of saying page 69, she tells the newcomer page 96, where she reads:
Do not be discouraged if your prospect does not respond to you. Search out another alcoholic and try again. You are sure to find someone desperate enough to accept your offer.
We find it a waste of time chasing a man who cannot or will not work with you.

Chapter Five of Alcoholic's Anonymous:
Quote: Rarely have we seen a person fail who has thoroughly followed our path. Misquote: Thoroughly have we seen a person fail who has rarely followed our path.
Misquote: Rarely have we seen a person thoroughly follow our path

Quote: They are naturally incapable of grasping and developing a manner of living which demands rigorous honesty.
Misquote: They are naturally incapable of grasping and developing a manner of liver which demands rigorous honesty.

Quote: At some of these we balked.
Misquote: At some of these we barked.

Quote: We stood at the turning point.
Misquote: We stood at the churning point.

Quote: Half measures availed us nothing
Misquote: Half gallons availed us nothing.

Quote: What an order, I can't go through with it.
Misquote: What? An order?? I can't go through with it!!!

Quote: Do not be discouraged.
Misquote: Do not be encouraged.

Quote: That we are alcoholic and could not manage our own lives.
Misquote: That we are alcoholic and could not damage our own wives.

Quote: That probably no human power could have relieved our alcoholism.
Misquote: That probably no human power could have believed our alcoholism.

Quote: God could and would if he were sought.
Misquote: God could and would if he were fought.
Misquote: God could and would if he were bought.

Quote: Here are the steps we took, which are suggested as a program of recovery.
Misquote: Here are the steps we took, which are suggested as a program of discovery.

Chapter Six of Alcoholics Anonymous:
Quote: ...we will be amazed before we are halfway through.
Misquote: ...take a drink and be amazed before you are halfway through.

Quote: We will comprehend the word serenity and we will know peace.
Misquote: We will comprehend the word cemetery and we will know peace.

Quote: That feeling of uselessness and self-pity will disappear.
Misquote: That feeling of usefulness and self-pity will disappear.

Quote: We will lose interest in selfish things...
Misquote: We will lose interest in elfish things...

Quote: Our whole attitude and outlook upon life will change.
Misquote: Our whole gratitude and outlook upon life will change.

Quote: Fear of people and economic insecurity will leave us.
Misquote: Fear of people and economic inferiority will leave us.

176

Quote: We will intuitively now how to handle situations that used to baffle us.
Misquote: We will intuitively know how to baffle situations that used to handle us.

Quote: As we go through the day, we pause when agitated
Misquote: As we go through the day, we use paws when agitated

Chapter Eight of Alcoholic's Anonymous
Quote: You think he ought to know the subject better, as everyone should have a clear understanding of the risk he takes if he drinks too much.
Misquote: You think he ought to know the subject better, as everyone should have a clear misunderstanding of the risk he takes if he drinks too much.

Chapter Nine of Alcoholics Anonymous:
Quote: We absolutely insist on enjoying life.
Misquote: We absolutely resist enjoying life.

HELLO, MY NAME IS......

Following the collapse of a member's chair at a meeting: Hi, my name is _____, and I'm powerless over gravity.......

Hi, my name is _____. Sorry I'm late for the meeting—I had to work. I am self-supporting through my own contributions.

Hello, My name is_____. I'm an alcoholic and my problem is me.

Hello my name is _____and my hair is chemically dependent.

My name is _____, and I'm an alcoholic. The topic is humility? I'll pass.......

Hi, my name is _____ and I'm a recovering thinker.

WATCH YOUR STEPS & TRIPDITIONS

Step Won, True and See
Step Won, Step True, Step Thee
Take the First Step, not the Thirst Step

Step 1: We were powerless over alcohol and our wives had become unmanageable.
We admitted we were powerless over alcohol - that our loves had become unmanageable.
We admitted we were powerless over alcohol - that our lives had become unmentionable.

Step 2: Came to believe that a power greater than ourselves could restore us to vanity

Step 3: Turned our bills and our wife over to God as we understood Him.

Turned our will and our loves over to God as we understood Him.
Turned our will and our lives over to the care of God as we misunderstood him.

Step 4: Take a searching and fearless moral sinventory

Step 8: Made a list of all persons we had armed...
Made a list of all persons we had charmed...
Made a list of all the people we have harmed and asked God
to remove them. (The dry drunk's Eight Step)

Step 9: Made direct amends to such people wherever possible, except when to do so would
injure ourselves.
Made direct revenge to such people wherever possible...

Step 10: Continued to take personal sinventory
Continued to take personal inventory and when we were wrong probably admitted it.

Step 11: Sought through prayer and medication...

Step 12: Practice the principles without having affairs...

Tradition 1: Personal property depends on AA unity.

Tradition 2: Our breeders are but trusted servants. (for SA)
Our eaters are but trusted servants. (for OA)
Our leaders are but twisted servants.
Our readers are but trusted servants.

Tradition 3: The only requirement for membership is a desire to stop thinking.
The only requirement for AA membership is a desire to stop stinking.

Tradition 4: I am self-supporting through my own contributions.

Tradition 11. Our relationship policy should be based on attraction rather than promotion.

Tradition 12: Animosity is the spiritual foundation of all our traditions.
Anonymity is the spiritual foundation of all our tripditions.

Did they really mean to say *that*? Have you heard a good Freudian Slip lately? If so, send it to
Shelly@day-by-day.org. for inclusion in the next edition of *Walk softly and Carry a Big Book:*
official and unofficial sloganeering from the 12-Step programs. If you are the first to send in an
original that we don't already have, we'll send you a free copy of the next edition. Be sure to
put "Freudian Slip" in the subject bar.

Walk Softly

Pray and wait for the answer. If you don't get an answer, that's the answer.

SECTION FIVE: *HIGHER POWERED PAGES*

(Religious and Spiritual)

ABOUT PRAYER
ABOUT THE SERENITY PRAYER
PRAYERS WE LIKE IN RECOVERY
STEP PRAYERS

ABOUT PRAYER

All Prayer
For all prayer is answered. Don't tell God how to answer it. ~Edgar Cayce

Busy
If you're too busy to pray, you're too busy.

How to End your Prayers
End your prayers with a Thank You, Thank You, Thank You!!! The first thank you is for what it was like. The second thank you is for what happened. And the third thank you is for what it is like now.

How to Pray
Trying to pray *is* praying.

I sought
I sought my self, my self I could not see....I sought my GOD and he eluded me....I sought my fellows and found all three.

Meaning of Prayer
If your prayers don't mean anything to you, they mean even less to God.

Prayer and Action
Pray as if everything depends on God; work as if everything depends on you.

Prayer Answered
Pray and wait for the answer. If you don't get an answer, that's the answer.

What is Prayer?
When you pray, you are talking to God, when you meditate, you are listening to God. Prayers are us calling God. Intuition is God answering. Every good thought is a prayer.

Why Pray?
Pray daily, God is easier to talk to than most people. Prayer. It helps!

ABOUT THE SERENITY PRAYER

Serenity Prayer, Common Version used in 12 Step Groups

God, Grant me the SERENITY
to accept the things I can not change,
the COURAGE to change the things I can,
and the WISDOM to know the difference.

According to many sources there are hints of the wording of the Serenity Prayer throughout history. The concepts – but not the wording – have been traced back to Boethius (480-524 AD) author of the book, Consolations of Philosophy. *(from http://stpaulsparish.org)*

The General's Prayer Version
1957, Anita R., found a card from England in a New York Bookstore with a prayer called "The General's Prayer" attributed to the fourteenth century. *(from August/September 1992 BOX-459)*

Almighty God, our Heavenly Father,
give us Serenity to accept what cannot be changed,
Courage to change what should be changed,
and Wisdom to know the one from the other;
through Jesus Christ, our Lord.

Oetinger Version
A German University professor, Dr. Theodore Wilhelm, under the pseudonym Friedrich Oetinger (a real 18th century priest), included this version in one of his books leading many to believe that the Priest Oetinger was the original author: *(from August/September 1992 BOX-459)*

God, give me the detachment to accept those things I cannot alter;
the courage to alter those things I can alter;
and the wisdom to distinguish the one thing from the other.

Niebuhr Version
1932, Dr. Rienhold Niebuhr of the Union Theological Seminary, in New York City wrote what we call the Serenity Prayer, as the ending to a longer prayer. In 1934, Dr. Howard Robbins used, with permission, this short version and published it in a compilation called, *Dr. Robbins Book of Prayers. (AA Grapevine, January 1950)*

"Mrs. Reinhold Niebuhr told an interviewer that her husband was definitely the prayer's author, that she had seen the piece of paper on which he had written it, and that her husband-now that there were numerous variations of wording -"used and preferred" the following form" *(August/September 1992 BOX-459)*

God, give us grace to accept with serenity
the things that cannot be changed,

Courage to change the things which should be changed,
and the wisdom to distinguish the one from the other.

AA's Originally Printed Version
In 1939, an obituary came to the attention of an early AA member, Jack, who had read it in the New York Times, which read: *(from http://open-mind.org/Serenity.htm)*

Mother, God grant me the serenity to accept things I cannot change,
courage to change things I can,
and wisdom to know the difference. Goodbye.

Jack brought this obituary to the AA office and the simple prayer reflected the fledglings organization's values so deeply that they printed up 500 wallet-sized cards. Passing them out, the 'Serenity Prayer' quickly became an integral part of meetings and group spirituality. *(from AA Grapevine, January 1950)*

God give me the Serenity
To accept things that cannot be changed,
Give me Courage to change things that must be changed,
And Wisdom to distinguish one from another.

Kates Version
On page 67 of the out-of-print booklet, "Between Dawn & Dark," by Frederick Ward Kates which was published by the Upper Room in 1957, reads: *(from http://open-mind.org/Serenity.htm)*

Almighty God, our heavenly father, give us serenity
to accept what cannot be changed,
courage to change what should be changed,
and wisdom to know the one from the other. Amen   *Fourteenth Century*

Codependents' Version
(from www.coda.org)

God, Grant me the Serenity
To accept the things I cannot change;
Courage to change the things I can;
and Wisdom to know it is me.

Layman's Version
(from the Daily Reprieve)

God, Grant me the Serenity,
To accept the things
I have already done.
Courage to face the things
That I may do next.
Wisdom to keep
My big mouth shut. Amen.

Long Version of the Serenity Prayer

God grant me the Serenity
To accept the things I cannot change;
Courage to change the things I can;
And Wisdom to know the difference.
Living one day at a time;
Enjoying one moment at a time;
Accepting hardships as the pathway to peace;
Taking, as Jesus did, this sinful world as it is,
Not as I would have it:
Trusting that You will make all things right
If I surrender to Your Will;
So I will be reasonably happy in this life
And supremely happy with You forever in the next. Amen

Long version of the Prayer from *Noel D. from Ireland at AAHistory.com*

God take and receive my liberty,
my memory, my understanding and will,
All that I am and have, He has given me

God grant me the serenity
to accept the things I cannot change,
Courage to change the things I can,
And wisdom to know the difference

Living one day at a time
Enjoying one moment at a time
Accepting hardships as the pathway to peace
Taking, as He did, this sinful world as it is,
Not as I would have it

Trusting that He will make all things right
If I surrender to his will
That I may be reasonably happy in this life
and supremely happy in the next. AMEN

Short Versions

Short version of the Serenity Prayer . "Screw it".

Short version of the Serenity Prayer: "Lighten up."

Silly Version

God grant me the senility to accept the people I can not stand...

A Woman's Version

Dear Lord, I pray for:
Wisdom, To understand a man.
Love, To forgive him and
Patience, For his moods.
Because, Lord, if I pray for Strength
I'll just beat him to death.

PRAYERS WE LIKE IN RECOVERY

Asking Prayer

I asked God for strength, that I, by myself, might achieve. I was made weak, that I must do together what I can not do alone.

I asked for health, that I might do greater things. I was given infirmity, that I might do better things.

I asked for riches, that I might be happy. I was given poverty that I might be wise.

I asked for power, that I might have the praise of men. I was given powerlessness, that I might feel the need of God.

I asked for all things, that I might enjoy life. I was given Life, that I might enjoy all things.

I got nothing that I asked for, but everything that I hoped for. Almost despite myself, my unspoken prayers were answered. I am among all people, am most richly blessed.

Burdens

Pray not for a lighter burden but for a stronger back.

The CDA Third Step Prayer

I will to will your will.

The Comfort Prayer

Lord, grant that I may seek rather to comfort than to be comforted – to understand, than to be understood – to love , than to be loved. *12 Steps and 12 Traditions* P 99

The "Dear God" Prayers

Dear God, Don't let me get in your way today.

Dear God, Fill my mouth with worthwhile stuff, and nudge me when I've said enough.

Dear God, fill my mouth with worthwhile stuff, and nudge me when I've said enough.

Dear God, Grant me patience--now!

Dear God, I'm not what I want to be. I'm not what I'm going to be, but thank you God, I'm not what I used to be.

Dear God, Make what I should be change me, whatever the cost.

Dear God, Please remind me that nothing is going to happen to me that you and I can't handle together.

Dear God, Protect me from your followers.

Dear God, Teach me how to give without remembering and to take without forgetting.

Dear God, Teach me to laugh again, at myself.

Dear God, Teach us to laugh again but, God don't ever let us forget that we cried.

Dear God, Thank you for all you have given me, for all you have taken away from me, and for all you have left me.

Dear God, Why is it that when I get on the right road, it's all up hill?

The "Dear Child" Prayers

Dear Child, I am handling all your problems today. Don't worry and *don't* help. Love, God

Dear Child, I have a lot for you to do today. You don't have to thank me now...

Dear Child, I'm working on all your issues and I'll help if only you'll stay out of my way! Love God

Dear Child, Please do not feel personally, irrevocably, totally responsible for everything. That's my job. Love, God.

Dear Child, Relax. I am in charge. Love, God

Taped to a bathroom mirror: Dear Child, Good morning; this is God; I will *not* be needing your help today.

God's Grace

There but for the grace of God, go I.

Humility Prayer

Lord, I am far too much influenced by what people think of me. which means that I am always pretending to be either richer or smarter or nicer than I really am.

Please prevent me from trying to attract attention. Don't let me gloat over praise on the one hand or be discouraged by criticism on the other. Nor let me waste time weaving imaginary situations in which the most heroic, charming witty person present is myself.

Show me how to be humble of heart like you.

The Lords's Prayer

Our Father who art in heaven, Hallowed be Thy name.
Thy kingdom come, they will be done, on earth as it is in heaven.
Give us this day, our daily bread
And forgive us our sins as we forgive those who sin against us.
Lead us not into temptation, but deliver us from evil,
For Thine is the kingdom, and the power, and the glory, forever. Amen.

Oldtimer's Prayer

The old timers used to say that the world's most difficult prayer was "Oh Lord, be as good to me today, as I was to my fellowman, yesterday."

The Only One Prayer

I am only one. But, Lord, I am one. I cannot do everything but, I can do something. What I can do, I ought to do and what I ought to do, by the grace of God, I will do.

Prayer for Today

I bless this day and give thanks for my life.
(repeat 3 times)
I forgive completely all people who have hurt me.
(repeat 3 times)

I ask all people I have hurt to please forgive me.
(repeat 3 times)
I apologize to myself for my wrongs to myself and others.
(repeat 3 times)
I apologize for all my hurts and wrongs to all life forms.
(repeat 3 times)
With this release comes freedom, peace, power and continually renewing life.
from a Hawaiian Shaman who wishes to remain anonymous, From Ruth fiscals web
pages---http://www.spirithaven.com/inspirat.htm

Prayer for Today

Please make me an instrument of Thy peace.
Where there is hatred, let me sow love;
Where there is injury, pardon;
Where there is doubt, faith;
Where there is despair, hope;
Where there is darkness, light,
And where there is sadness, joy.

Prayer of St. Francis

Lord, make me an instrument of they Peace—
Where there is hatred, I may bring Love;
Where there is wrong, I may bring the Spirit of forgiveness;
Where there is error, I may bring truth;
Where there is doubt, I may bring faith;
Where there is despair, I may bring hope;
Where there are shadows, I may bring light;
Where there is sadness, I may bring joy;
Lord, grant that I may seek rather to comfort than to be comforted;
To understand, than to be understood;
To love than to be loved.
For it is by self-forgetting that one finds;
It is by forgiving that one is forgiven;
It is by dying that one awakens to Eternal life.

SANSKRIT PROVERB (PRAYER)

Look to this day
This very life of life
In its brief course lie all
The realities and verities of existence
The bliss of growth
The splendor of action
the glory of power--
For yesterday is but a dream
And tomorrow is only a vision
But today, well lived
Makes every yesterday a dream of happiness
and every tomorrow a vision of hope.

Look well, therefore to this day

The Set Aside Prayer
God please set aside everything I think I know about myself, recovery, You, and the Twelve Steps; that I might have an open mind.

Shortest prayers
The shortest prayers are "Thank you" and "Help."

Solution Prayer
When I find myself worrying, I say this prayer: "I believe in one Mind and one Power and the Power I serve also serves me. I trust that the solution to this situation is in the best interests of all concerned." Robea from Al-anon

Strength Prayer
I seek strength not to be superior to my brothers, but to be able to fight my greatest enemy, myself. ~Traditional Native American Prayer

Take Time
Take time to think, it is the source of power.
Take time to read, it is the foundation of wisdom.
Take time to play, it is the secret of staying young.
Take time to be quiet, it is the opportunity to see God.
Take time to be aware, it is the opportunity to help others.
Take time, to love and be loved, it is God's greatest gift.
Take time to laugh, it is the music of the soul.
Take time to be friendly, it is the road to happiness.
Take time to dream, it is what the future is made of.
Take time to pray, it is the greatest power on earth.
There is a time for everything...
                                        Eccl. 3:1

The Willingness Prayer
I pray for the willingness to be willing to be willing to let go absolutely. *Meeting Wisdom,* P 97

Word Prayer
Help my words stay sweet and tender, for I may have to eat them tomorrow.

STEP PRAYERS

Step 1, short form
Dear God, HELP!

Steps 1-3, short form
I can't, God can, I think I'll let Him.

12 Steps, short form

Trust God, Clean House, Serve Others. ~Dr. Bob

Third Step Prayer

- God, I offer myself to thee to do with me and to build with me as thou wilt. Relieve me of the bondage of self, that I ay better do they will. Take away my difficulties, that victory over them may bear witness to those I would help of they power, they love, and they way of life. May I do they will always. ~Alcoholics Anonymous
- I will to will your will. ~Chemically Dependent Anonymous
- Take my will and my life. Guide me in my recovery. Show me how to live. ~Narcotics Anonymous

Seventh Step Prayer

- My Creator, I am now willing that You should have all of me—good and bad—I pray that You remove every single defect of character which stands in the way of usefulness to you and my fellows. Grant me strength, as I go out from here to do Your bidding. ~Alcoholics Anonymous
- I will to will your will. Help me to grow in trusting your path for me. Take away any obstacles that I have placed in the way; I release them now. I accept the challenges ahead as opportunities and gifts. Let my gratitude show itself in service to you."
  ~Chemically Dependent Anonymous